Corrupt Illinois

CORRUPT ILLINOIS

Patronage, Cronyism, and Criminality

Thomas J. Gradel
and Dick Simpson

Foreword by Jim Edgar

University of Illinois Press
Urbana, Chicago, and Springfield

Library of Congress Control Number: 2014033691
ISBN: 978-0-252-07855-2 (paperback)
ISBN: 978-0-252-09703-4 (e-book)

publication supported by
Figure Foundation

make no promises but one:
serve just, just promise.

Contents

Foreword by Jim Edgar   ix

Preface   xi

1. Corrupt Illinois   1

2. Machine Politics and Stolen Elections   17

3. The Sorry State of Illinois   37

4. Aldermanic Corruption   53

5. Chicago City Haul   71

6. Crook County   93

7. Suburban Scandals   117

8. Police Abuse and Corruption   131

9. Jailbird Judges and Crooked Courts   151

10. Congressional Corruption   167

11. Ending the Culture of Corruption   193

Acknowledgments   209

Appendix I. Highlights in Illinois'
History of Corruption, 1833 to 2014   211

Appendix II. Illinois Governors, 1961–2014   217

Appendix III. Chicago Mayors, 1955–2014   220

Appendix IV. U.S. Attorneys for the Northern District of Illinois, 1964–2014   222

Notes   225

Index   261

Foreword

I HAVE KNOWN MANY GOOD MEN AND WOMEN in politics and government over my career. They have served the public interest well.

However, as Tom Gradel and Dick Simpson conclusively prove in *Corrupt Illinois,* there is a dark side to our political history as well. Corruption has too often flourished. More than two thousand people in government in Illinois have been convicted on corruption charges in federal court over the last few decades. It is shameful that the Chicago metropolitan region is the most corrupt in the nation and that the state of Illinois is the third most corrupt state.

We have made some progress in adopting more restrictive laws and regulations to curb some of the worst abuses, but the authors show us how much more we need to do.

Corrupt Illinois is the most comprehensive account of corruption in our state ever published. It proposes cures, which will take decades to implement fully, but which deserve our attention now. We can only move forward by understanding our past and the culture of corruption that has too often pervaded our state.

Public service is an honorable profession when ethics guide it. The great accomplishments of the past cannot be allowed to have corruption overshadow them. There are real costs of corruption in tax dollars and in loss of faith in government.

Corrupt Illinois is a clarion call to action. It illustrates the many patterns that corruption has taken and its root causes in machine politics and an individualistic political culture that has allowed corruption to flourish. But in the twenty-first century we can take a different road and create a better future.

Jim Edgar
Former Illinois Governor

Preface

SINCE THE LATE 1960S, as one public-corruption exposé after another dominated the front pages of daily newspapers and led the evening TV news, we expected heads to roll; corrupt practices to be eliminated; and those responsible to be voted out of office. But substantial reforms didn't happen. The most recent scandal was soon forgotten. Then after a year, another government unit was investigated, different bureaucrats were indicted, and a few additional politicians were convicted and sent to jail. Like Bill Murray's day in the movie *Groundhog Day,* it keeps happening, again and again. But we not only observed chronic corruption, we also experienced firsthand the impact of machine politics as we struggled with others to pass laws to reform politics.

Our experiences have led us to question why corruption scandals keep happening, why the general public seems so resigned to corruption, and why effective correction measures are so rarely taken. Although the general public hears about specific instances of corruption, it is not aware of its extent, its underlying causes, or its cost to our daily lives. Thus we have set out to document the severity of corruption, which we had planned to publish in an *Encyclopedia of Illinois Corruption.* That was not entirely practical because there were so many public crooks to catalog—more than two thousand since 1976. Court records, inspectors general's reports, biographies, and, most of all, thousands of juicy news reports were not easy to locate and systematize. But with the help of an ever-changing team of student researchers, we achieved part of our goal by creating a substantial database now available on the Internet at http://www.uic.edu/depts/pols/ChicagoPolitics/chicagopolitics.htm.

However, simple lists of corrupt officials do not stir souls and will not motivate the public to demand significant reforms. So we began to analyze the assembled stories of corruption in all its myriad forms. We wanted to know what caused sometimes good and honest men and women to fall prey to so many schemes. As we looked at the database and at the stories of public betrayal, we began to discover distinct patterns. How governors and high-state officials steal is different from the patterns of aldermanic, suburban, or police corruption, for example. Moreover, the patterns of corruption in the nineteenth century have evolved considerably by the twenty-first century.

In this volume, we present a case study of corruption of a single state from its beginnings as a territory two hundred years ago. Our hope is that by providing these examples we will also expose the root causes. We further provide, based upon this study and the studies of others around the world, a plan of action to create a positive political culture and to curb the culture of corruption that has been our inheritance.

Our basic conclusions are inescapable. Illinois is among the most corrupt states and Chicago is undoubtedly the most corrupt city in our nation. There is a severe cost to this corruption at many levels. We can no longer afford to sustain these moral, political, and monetary costs. Change is both possible and desirable. It is our hope that our book can contribute to that end.

Corrupt Illinois

Following his arrest by the FBI for extortion and trying to sell a vacant U.S. Senate seat, Governor Rod Blagojevich was impeached and removed from office. In 2011, he was convicted of wire fraud, bribery, attempted extortion, and conspiracy. *Photo courtesy of Sun-Times Media.*

CHAPTER 1

Corrupt Illinois

PUBLIC CORRUPTION HAS BESMIRCHED Illinois politics for a century and a half. Even before Governor Rod Blagojevich tried to sell the vacant U.S. Senate seat to the highest bidder, the people of the state were exposed to outrageous corruption scandals. There was, for instance, Paul Powell, a downstater, former secretary of state, and old-style politician. He died leaving hundreds of thousands of dollars from cash bribes hoarded in shoeboxes in his closet. There were the thirteen judges nabbed in Operation Greylord who were convicted for fixing court cases.

Four of the last nine governors of Illinois went to jail—Otto Kerner, Dan Walker, George Ryan, and Rod Blagojevich. They were preceded by other governors such as Joel Matteson, Len Small, and William Stratton, who were indicted or found culpable in civil or legislative hearings but were not convicted in criminal courts and were not sent to jail.

Kerner was the first governor to be convicted of bribery, conspiracy, and income-tax evasion in a case involving racetrack stock improperly acquired while in office. Dan Walker was convicted after leaving office for bank fraud at a savings-and-loan bank he acquired.

The case of George Ryan, a pharmacist and former chairman of the Kankakee County Board, involved felonies by high-ranking officials as well as bribery committed by frontline clerks and inspectors. He was convicted of eighteen counts of corruption for leading a scheme in which bribes were paid to his campaign funds as both secretary of state and governor. Secretary of state employees sold truck-driver licenses in return for bribes that were partially given to the Ryan campaigns. This led to fatal accidents by unqualified truck drivers.

The last governor (still in prison) is Rod Blagojevich, who has become the face of Illinois corruption. Even before he was convicted, he was impeached by the Illinois legislature and thrown out of office. Similar to former Governor Ryan, he was convicted on multiple counts. He had established a corrupt network of businessmen, political appointees, and politicians. He shook down businessmen and institutional leaders for bribes. He appointed corrupt individuals to various boards and commissions to shake down hospitals, racetracks, road builders, and government contractors. He is most remembered for trying to sell off Barack Obama's U.S. Senate seat after Obama was elected president in 2008.

But it is not only governors who are corrupt. Corruption pervades every part of the state—not every town and government office, but too many. Among the convicted congressmen, perhaps the most colorful was the swaggering Dan Rostenkowski, Mayor Richard J. Daley's man in Washington.

Among state officials, the most well-known was the "good old boy" Paul Powell. Secretary of State Powell grew up in Vienna, Illinois, in downstate Johnson County. He was first elected to the state legislature, where he rose through the ranks to be elected speaker by a downstate coalition of legislators. From there he ascended to the secretary of state position, where, like later Secretary of State George Ryan, he would use that post to enrich himself. Although Powell never earned more than thirty thousand dollars a year, his estate was worth $4.6 million, including racetrack stocks like those Governor Kerner took as bribes. The most memorable aspect was the eight hundred thousand dollars found in shoeboxes in his hotel room in Springfield.

To round out a more modern corruption montage, there is the strange tale of Rita Crundwell, the comptroller and treasurer of downstate Dixon, Illinois. Dixon is most famous as the home of former President Ronald Reagan. Crundwell's story illustrates that corruption is not necessarily limited to high state officials or denizens of big-city Chicago. She managed to steal an amazing fifty-three million dollars to fund a very high lifestyle over a number of years. She persisted even in recession years, when the town had to make severe cutbacks in public services. She accomplished this by the simple expedient of opening a fake checking account and transferring city funds to that account. For her crimes, she received a twenty-year prison sentence, and her horses and jewelry were auctioned off to reimburse part of the stolen funds. The media, particularly television, prominently displayed pictures of her swimming pool, home, horses, and jewelry, which average citizens in Dixon could not afford.

Corrupt politics in Illinois have always been colorful. At the beginning of the twentieth century, Chicago aldermen were paid a stipend of less than two hundred dollars a year. Yet the *Chicago Record,* a newspaper of the time, revealed: "In a fruitful year the average crooked alderman has made $15,000 to $20,000"—big money in those years.[1]

Most Chicago aldermen were on the take. In the famous "Council of the Gray Wolves," which lasted from 1871 to 1931, the journalist and crusader William Stead wrote that no more than ten of the seventy aldermen in the council "have not sold their votes or received any consideration for voting away the patrimony of the people."[2] As the leading Democratic paper, the *Chicago Herald,* put it, aldermen in "nine cases out of ten [are] a bummer and a disreputable who can be bought and sold as hogs are bought and sold at the stockyards."[3]

Things were no better in the state legislature. In the second decade of the twentieth century, forty state lawmakers accepted bribes to elect William J. Lorimer to the U.S. Senate. He was later thrown out of the Senate. The scandal contributed to the passage of a U.S. constitutional amendment in 1912 establishing the direct election of senators by the people rather than by the state legislatures. In the following century, Illinois residents seemed resigned to government corruption.

Times may be changing, however. Since Governor Rod Blagojevich's indictment and conviction, a groundswell of public support for ending corruption has developed. A 2009 Joyce Foundation public-opinion poll showed that more than 60 percent of Illinois residents list corruption as one of their top concerns, even higher than the economy or jobs. More than 70 percent of Illinoisans favor a number of specific reforms. Yet such reforms get enacted only after long, drawn-out battles, if at all, because of the pervasive culture of corruption.

Separately, an Illinois Ethics Commission and a Chicago Ethics Reform Task Force have met and issued reform recommendations, and some of these have become state law or city ordinances. But corruption persists. Taming corruption in Illinois will take changing the culture of corruption in addition to the passage of ethics and campaign-finance regulations.

The Most Corrupt City in
One of the Most Corrupt States

Public or political corruption occurs whenever public officials use their insider information or their official position for public gain. In some cases, infractions may seem minor, but cover-ups or the failure of officials to take corrective action only increase corruption and underline Illinois' culture of corruption. A lot of corrupt deals in this state occur with a "wink and a nod," overlooking the corruption that is hidden underneath.

Whether specific misdeeds by government officials can successfully be prosecuted changes over time. Generally speaking, the laws become stricter, and investigators and prosecutors improve their methods. But despite changes in law and prosecution, using a public position for private gain has always been wrong and is usually illegal. Yet, such corruption has reigned in Illinois for over 150 years.

Chicagoans, like bragging Texans, tend to revel in being the biggest or first at anything. It is part of our inferiority complex about being the "Second City." For many years, but more intently since the colorful Blagojevich trials, we have been known as the most corrupt city in the United States. Based upon the corruption convictions in U.S. federal courts, Chicagoans can legitimately boast that we are the most corrupt metropolitan region in America.[4] Nonetheless, it is shameful to be first in corruption.

The corruption-conviction statistics by which we measure these crimes are from the Federal Judicial District of Northern Illinois, which means that Chicago's corruption data covers the suburbs, not just the evil city. In chapter 7, we report on the shocking extent of suburban corruption, which includes far more than the usual notorious suburban towns like Cicero and Rosemont.[5]

Much like its largest city, Illinois is also corrupt. It is the third most corrupt of the fifty states. Illinois' main competitors for the most-corrupt title are other havens of machine politics like Louisiana, New Jersey, and Florida.[6] And you have to go a long way to be worse than Louisiana, with their rich corruption-gumbo legacy of the infamous Long family. Louisiana's crooked governors like Edwin Edwards and its racist gubernatorial candidate, the tax cheat David Duke, closely rival Illinois' convicted governors. Whether or not Illinois is more crooked or has more colorful rogues than our erstwhile rivals, by anyone's account we are one of the most corrupt states in the nation.

Our title of most corrupt doesn't only rest with statistics. Here, as they used to say on the TV program *Dragnet,* are "Just the facts, ma'am." Of the last nine

Table 1.1 Federal Public Corruption Convictions by Judicial District 1976–2012

Rank for Convictions	District (Major cities)	Total				
		2010–12	2000–2009	1990–99	1976–89	1976–2012
1	**Illinois-Northern (Chicago)**	**112**	**367**	**610**	**508**	**1597**
2	California-Central (Los Angeles)	95	383	595	268	1341
3	New York-Southern (Manhattan)	57	242	398	550	1247
4	District of Columbia	127	342	393	239	1101
5	Florida-Southern (Miami)	62	404	437	108	1011
6	New Jersey (Newark)	102	410	264	202	978
7	Ohio-Northern (Cleveland)	109	333	314	173	929
8	Pennsylvania-Eastern (Philadelphia)	76	252	246	291	865
9	Virginia-Eastern (Richmond)	105	303	213	189	810
10	New York-Eastern (Brooklyn)	35	204	237	308	784
11	Texas-Southern (Houston)	86	267	205	116	674
12	Florida-Middle (Orlando)	62	230	179	159	629
13	Louisiana-Eastern (New Orleans)	84	230	173	117	604
14	Massachusetts (Boston)	59	187	159	193	598
15	California-Eastern (Sacramento, Fresno)	36	200	203	156	595

Illinois governors, four have been convicted of corruption—getting bargain-priced racetrack stock, manipulating savings-and-loan banks, covering up the selling of driver's licenses to unqualified drivers, shaking down contractors for campaign contributions, and trying to sell a U.S. Senate seat.

Chicago's city hall is a famous political-corruption scene as well. Thirty-three Chicago aldermen and former aldermen have been convicted and gone to jail since 1973. Two others died before they could be tried. Since 1928 there have been only fifty aldermen serving in the council at any one time. Fewer

Table 1.2 Federal Public Corruption Convictions Per Capita for Top Thirteen States with the Most Convictions 1976–2012*

Rank for Convictions Per Capita	State	Convictions 1976–2012	Population 2010	Convictions Per 10,000 Population
1	District of Columbia	1,101	601,723	18.30
2	Louisiana	1,031	4,533,372	2.27
3	**Illinois**	**1,913**	**12,830,632**	**1.49**
4	Tennessee	899	6,364,105	1.42
5	New York	2,631	19,378,102	1.23
6	Pennsylvania	1,597	12,702,379	1.26
7	Ohio	1,454	11,536,504	1.26
8	Virginia	942	8,001,024	1.18
9	New Jersey	978	8,791,894	1.11
10	Florida	1,865	18,801,310	.99
11	Georgia	899	9,687,653	.93
12	Texas	1,742	25,245,561	.69
13	California	2,498	37,253,956	.67

NOTE: This table was constructed using the top thirteen states with the most number of convictions. The cutoff point was 899 convictions. The population for each state, according to the 2010 census, was divided by 10,000. This figure was divided into the total number of convictions to derive a "per 10,000" conviction rate. Using the top thirteen states with the most convictions helps avoid skew from states with much smaller populations. If a conviction rate of all fifty states were calculated this way, the top ten would be (in order): District of Columbia (18.30), Louisiana (2.27), South Dakota (2.00), Mississippi (1.99), Alaska (1.94), North Dakota (1.81), Kentucky (1.50), Illinois (1.49), New Mexico (1.49), Montana (1.33).

than two hundred men and women have served in the Chicago city council since the 1970s, so the federal crime rate in the council chamber is higher than in the most dangerous ghetto in the city. In chapter 4 we detail the aldermanic corruption, and in chapter 5 we cover the rank-and-file corruption of City Hall bureaucrats.

In other chapters, we detail many aspects of corruption throughout the state. Altogether, 1,913 individuals were convicted of corruption in federal court between 1976 and 2012; of those, 1,597 convictions were in the greater Chicago metropolitan region. But there is plenty of corruption spread throughout the state at all levels, from small suburban town halls and county criminal courts to the halls of the legislature and state government in Springfield. We do not have a few "rotten apples"; we have a rotten-apple barrel and a pervasive culture of corruption.

In our studies, we often refer to officials convicted of corruption. But for each of them, there are many other public officials who did the same thing but didn't get caught or didn't go to trial in federal court. There are only three U.S. Attorneys in Illinois, and they have to focus on all federal crimes, not just political corruption. State's attorneys and attorneys general for the most part don't prosecute corruption. Therefore, much of it goes undetected. Inspectors general at the state, county, and city levels have shown conclusively in their reports that corruption in government is more pervasive than just the cases of those convicted would indicate.

Corruption is committed not only by those who break the law. Conflicts of interest are rampant even when they aren't illegal. It may be legal to give your brother-in-law a government job, but it is still a conflict of interest because you are not objectively determining who is the best qualified for that position. It may be legal to be a public official and have government contractors hire your law firm because they want to influence your decision on future government contracts, but it is a direct conflict of interest. These types of conflict of interest—when an official's economic interest rather than the public interest is served—occur much more frequently than outright crimes.

Nonetheless, the governor's mansion, Chicago city-council chambers, the state legislature, and quiet suburban city halls house more criminals and have a worse crime rate than most bad neighborhoods or towns. And we have elected and reelected officials in Illinois even after we knew they were corrupt. We reelected Dan Rostenkowski to Congress after his conflicts of interest were well known, and we reelected Rod Blagojevich as governor after the indictment of many of his cronies for corruption schemes.

Theories of Corruption

To understand corruption, its causes and possible cures, we can learn from other studies. Rasma Karklins in her work on corruption in former Soviet countries created a general typology of corruption with three classifications:

1. Everyday interactions between officials and citizens (such as bribery for licenses, permits, zoning changes, and to pass inspections).
2. Interactions within public institutions (such as patronage, nepotism, and favoritism).
3. Influence over political institutions (such as personal fiefdoms, clout, secret power networks, and misuse of power).[7]

We have all three types of corruption in Illinois, and each reinforces the other. In addition, Karklins found that many people in corrupt societies participate in and accept a low level of corruption because, they say, "everyone else does it" or, as in her book title, "the system made me do it."

We accept Karklins's typology of corruption, but we are left with the question of why this corruption is committed. Robert Klitgaard, in his book *Controlling Corruption,* argues that "[i]llicit behavior flourishes when agents have monopoly power over clients, when agents have great discretion, and when accountability of agents to the principal is weak." He offers this stylized formula: Corruption = Monopoly + Discretion - Accountability.[8] Thus, we begin our study of corruption in Illinois with the understanding that the use of public office for private gain occurs more frequently when there is a monopoly of power, great discretion in the hands of elected and appointed officials, and a lack of accountability. In Chicago and Illinois, this occurs at many levels, including everyday interactions between officials and the public, interactions within public institutions, and control over our governmental institutions.

Transparency International, which rates the corruption level of over 170 countries, has developed a model that they call the National Integrity System.[9] As Transparency understands it, a society's integrity is built upon a foundation of values and public awareness that evolves in politics, the economy, and culture. If the public values supporting honest government are strong and public awareness of possible corruption is high, various institutions, such as the three branches of government, the media, anticorruption agencies, and civil society, will create the rule of law, sustainable development, and a good quality of life. When these institutions work well, there will be less corruption and more integrity. Unfortunately, in Illinois the public values that support honest government are too weak, and therefore our institutions and laws are unable to prevent corruption.

There have been few quantitative studies to test the various hypotheses about corruption. One recent study of corruption in the United States is by Dartmouth Professor Emeritus Richard Winters. He used thirty-five years of the Justice Department's public-integrity data on corruption convictions in all fifty states. He finds that corruption, including corruption in Illinois, is predicted by the number of corruptible governmental bodies (and Illinois has by far the most units of government of any state in the union); the level of demographic population diversity; the size of the state; the number of college graduates; the level of civic involvement or civic culture; the level of civic distrust; and the existence of traditional (or machine) party organizations.[10] Civic distrust, in his study, is measured by national surveys asking respondents: "Generally speaking, would you say that most people can be trusted, or that you can't be too careful in dealing with people?" As expected, states with a high level of political-corruption convictions tend to have a higher level of civic distrust.

In this model, there are many things that cannot be controlled or changed. Illinois will continue to be a large state with its state capital many miles away from the Chicago metropolitan region, where most citizens and their media watchdogs reside. When the state capital is so removed from media scrutiny and public contact, politicians are freer to engage in corrupt acts.

Illinois also will continue to have population diversity, which in Winters's analysis means that officials will perceive acts of malfeasance as largely affecting a population that is unlike themselves.[11] As a city and state, we want to attract as many college graduates as possible, but we have somewhat limited ability to keep our college and university graduates with our state's current poor economy. Better-educated people help control corruption because they generally pay more attention to politics and government and are more likely to hold politicians accountable. To the degree that size, distance from the state capital, population diversity, and number of college graduates affect the level of public corruption, we have limited control over those contributing factors.

If we could eliminate some of the many separate units of government and several thousand government officials, it would leave fewer unmonitored officials to commit corruption. There are more than 540 governments with the power to tax in Cook County, 1,200 in the Chicago metropolitan region, and more than seven thousand in Illinois. Examples of governments that could be merged or eliminated include the four Mosquito Abatement Districts in Cook County, township governments that duplicate town governments, and school districts that govern only a single school. But efforts to merge or eliminate such units of government have mostly failed. When Evanston recently tried to merge its town and township government (since both have the same boundaries and the same governing board), it required passage of a separate state law to make that possible. While there have been a few small government mergers, the number of separate governments in Illinois is not decreasing, and that leaves open opportunities for unaccountable government officials to engage in various corruption schemes.

Contributing factors that we can affect are the civic or political culture, the level of civic distrust, and the existence of machine or traditional political-party organizations. We hope to show in this book that these factors matter, and that making smart changes has the promise of greatly reducing the level of corruption.

Our Culture of Corruption

Beyond corruption of an individual or Illinois' numerous scandals, there is a broader culture and history of corruption. Political culture involves the expectations of both citizens and public officials as to proper behavior. A good political culture is one in which citizens obey the laws, and public officials enforce them fairly and uniformly. A reformed political culture is one in which both citizens and officials abhor corruption and expect good government without bribes, patronage, nepotism, or any of the other common forms of corruption. Negative and positive political cultures are built by actions over time, from the time of original settlement to the current day.

The political scientist Daniel J. Elazar was the leading scholar of political culture as it shaped politics and government in midwestern states like Illinois.[12] He concluded that settlers of Illinois brought with them three different strains of political culture: *traditionalistic,* which believed that government should be limited to securing the existing social order; *moralistic,* which believed that government should promote the public good and public service; and *individualistic,* which sees politics as a marketplace where individuals and groups can promote themselves socially and economically, including by profiting from government activities.[13]

While elements of the traditionalist and moralistic reform-minded political culture are present in Illinois, the dominant political culture, especially in Chicago, is individualist. As Elazar puts it, "Politics in Illinois came early to be centered on personal influence, patronage, distribution of federal and later state benefits, and the availability of economic gain to those who were professionally committed to politics as their 'business.'"[14] The late, well-known acerbic newspaper columnist Mike Royko captured it best when he wrote that Chicago's official slogan should be "Where's mine?" We have yet to change this dominant culture.

Following Elazar, Jim Nowlan and his coauthors describe the individualistic political culture of Illinois this way: "[G]overnment and politics compose a marketplace in which participants exchange credits and debits as they pursue their goals. . . . [Illinois citizens] consider government not as an instrument for doing good but, rather, as a necessary evil."[15] The individualistic political culture may have begun with the original settlers of Illinois, but over nearly two hundred years it has been reinforced by the corrupt actions of elected officials, bureaucrats, businesspeople, and citizens.

For corruption to be rooted out in our state, government must be seen as an instrument for doing good, not a marketplace in which government goods, services, jobs, and contracts are given out as payoffs and patronage.

The former U.S. Attorney Patrick Fitzgerald has written about an additional aspect of our history and culture of corruption:

> Undoubtedly the most harmful consequence of endemic public corruption in a community is the apathy that it engenders—the culture of acceptance. Over many years of seeing corruption in almost every facet of government, many residents of a community begin to simply accept corruption as the immutable status quo. They come to assume government is broken and ineffective and destined to function corruptly. The consequences of this culture of acceptance in a community are many. Some residents simply disengage from the political process and no longer trust their government to function well or in their interest. Other residents may come to believe they must engage in corruption in order to gain government benefits themselves. Still others will begin to look the other way when they witness corrupt transactions. And honest folks are discouraged from entering politics or suffer from the skepticism engendered by others' misdeeds.[16]

He goes on to argue that vigorous investigation and prosecution of corruption can diminish Illinois' culture of acceptance of corruption. It is clear, however, that prosecution alone is not a sufficient cure.

Our book is animated by the theory that Illinois' corrupt political culture has been rooted in the individualist political culture from the early days of its founding, but it has been nurtured by the political machines and machine-like politics throughout the state. In the next chapter we will further define political machines, show how they have evolved over time, and how they perpetuate the culture of corruption.

History of Illinois' Culture of Corruption

Corruption in all its forms has a long history in Illinois. Each corrupt act has had the effect of reinforcing the culture of corruption that some of the original "individualistic" settlers brought with them. The first stolen elections were in 1833, when the town of Chicago was incorporated. The settlers voted to elect five trustees when they met at a hotel tavern. At the first town meeting, they decided by a vote of 12–1 to incorporate, but later research showed that two of the voters didn't meet residency requirements. Later in 1833, they voted 28–1 to elect a slate of trustees. But there were fewer than twenty-nine citizens living in Chicago at the time.[17] The ballot box was stuffed when the city was born. Other stolen elections were to follow.

There were problems in downstate Illinois at the time as well. In 1841, Governor Duncan had legal troubles, and Governor Matteson left office in 1856 owing the state a quarter of a million dollars for selling false script.

The first public-corruption prosecution in Chicago occurred in 1869, when fourteen Chicago aldermen and Cook County commissioners were tried for rigging a contract with the city and county government to paint city hall.[18] This period was characterized by other examples of corruption, including a city-council "ring" of aldermen on the take. They were known as McCauley's Nineteen, and they could be bribed as a group either to pass or defeat legislation. Later, at the turn of the twentieth century, politicians like "Hinky Dink" Kenna, "Bathhouse" John Couglin, and Johnny "Da Pow" Powers formed similar rings of crooked aldermen in the city council.

The courthouse, which also served as city hall and the county building, was a wooden structure in 1869. A contract was given to a private contractor to have it painted. The contractor, in turn, paid bribes to the aldermen and commissioners to get the profitable $128,500 contract. The contractor used a whitewash of chalk and water instead of paint, so after it rained it became obvious to all that the job was a scam. As a result of a criminal trial, four of the fourteen accused officials were convicted and given jail terms. Many of the others were defeated in the 1871 election, when reformers briefly came to power at city hall.

There have been occasional elections of reformers who fought for government reforms from time to time, but never with long enough control over the government to eliminate political corruption, or to change Illinois' underlying corrupt political culture.

This "culture of corruption" over the last century and a half exists largely because there are institutions that promote and support it. The chief institutions are the Democratic and Republican political party machines in the city, suburbs, and downstate. And business and labor unions were tolerant of this corruption. Indeed, they often contributed to it through bribes or campaign donations.

Various investigations by the FBI and prosecutions by the U.S. Attorney have provided a road map of city and state patterns of corruption. The Hired Truck investigation of crooked contracts in the 1990s (in which unneeded trucks were hired from private companies) led to the trial of Mayor Daley's patronage chief Robert Sorich. The prosecutors in that case described a flourishing political-party machine where it was possible to get a patronage job as long as the candidates had the right political or labor-union connections. Then the politically connected insiders gave out crooked contracts such as the trucking contracts.

Machine politics and corruption extend far beyond Chicago, as illustrated by successful prosecutions in investigations like Operation Safe Roads into the office of the Republican secretary of state and, later, Governor George Ryan, in which driver's licenses were sold for bribes. Lack of a strong reform movement and notoriously weak campaign-finance laws in Illinois perpetuated the politics of personal favors throughout the state.

A small sample of notable corruption cases in Illinois illustrates the scope of the problem:

- Operation Safebet, an FBI investigation that targeted political corruption and organized crime's control of illegal gambling and prostitution throughout the Chicago metropolitan area, resulted in the conviction of more than seventy-five individuals.
- Operation Gambat, a federal investigation into Chicago's First Ward's connections with organized crime, resulted in twenty-four individuals convicted or pleading guilty. Among the convicted were the First Ward alderman, a city-corporation counsel, the assistant majority leader in the Illinois Senate, and a judge convicted for fixing a murder case.
- Operation Greylord, a federal probe into the Cook County court system, brought convictions and guilty pleas from eighty-seven court personnel and attorneys, including thirteen judges.
- Cicero Town President Betty Loren-Maltese was convicted in 2002 of a scam that swindled the suburb out of twelve million dollars in insurance funds. Before his death, her husband, Cicero assessor Frank Maltese, had been convicted of serving as a bookmaker and warning the mob of police raids.
- Operation Board Games, which was centered on Governor Rod Blagojevich, ended up convicting fifteen people of rigging state contracts and shaking down campaign contributors, especially through the appointment of corrupt individuals to state boards and commissions.

To end the continuing corruption detailed in these investigations and others we describe in later chapters requires a comprehensive, long-term anticorruption strategy. It will be necessary to create a new political culture in which public corruption is no longer tolerated. We must evolve from machine politics to a more advanced form of democracy.

We must eliminate corruption at different levels, as Rasma Karklins's typology indicates. We must pass, and enforce, laws that limit the authority of public officials as to their discretion and monopoly of power if we are to hold them accountable, as Robert Klitgaard has suggested. We must build up the public values to support the institutions necessary for integrity in government, as Transparency International has advocated. Most of all, we must eliminate the political machines and machine-like political organizations that perpetuate corruption.

There are human costs of corruption. At least six deaths were caused by truck drivers who got their licenses by bribes during George Ryan's term as secretary of state. There were also deaths caused by fires and porch collapses because Chicago building inspectors were bribed.

The financial cost of corruption to taxpayers is estimated to be at least five hundred million dollars a year. There are costs of nepotism, patronage, and ghost payrollers. We pay employees who do not work. Inflated crooked contracts bilk the government and the taxpayers. There are all the costs of investigating and prosecuting corrupt officials. The greatest cost of all is the loss of citizens' faith in government.

We can change Illinois' political culture, but it will not be easy. We don't have to remain the most corrupt city in one of the most corrupt states in the union. Other cities in the world, like Hong Kong and Sydney, have changed from corrupt to clean. We can too. Nations do move up on Transparency International's index as they become less corrupt. In the same way, Chicago and Illinois can move from being the most corrupt to less corrupt over time if we have the political will to do so.

We know how to end corruption; we know how to clear our city's and state's besmirched names. But as Mayor Richard J. Daley taunted reformers in the 1970s, you just ain't got the votes. At least, not yet. Unless Chicagoans and Illinoisans decide to give a damn, we never will. But if a few—a determined few—really care, we can overcome our addiction to corruption and leave the hall of shame.

Richard J. Daley was Chicago's mayor and chairman of the Cook County Democratic party from 1955 until 1976. These dual roles allowed him to thoroughly dominate the Democratic machine. He controlled patronage, appointed public officials, and slated all of the party's candidates. He professed that he had no knowledge of the rampant corruption right under his nose. *Photo courtesy of Sun-Times Media.*

CHAPTER 2

Machine Politics and Stolen Elections

JIM NOWLAN AND HIS COAUTHORS in their book on Illinois politics repeat the story told by the former congressman and judge Abner Mikva to the University of Illinois at Chicago professor Milton Rakove about his experience as a college student. He was trying to volunteer to work in elections for the Democratic party, so he went to see his local Chicago Democratic ward committeeman. "I came in and said I wanted to help. Dead silence. 'Who sent you?' the committeeman said. I said, 'Nobody.' He said, 'We don't want nobody nobody sent.' Then he said, 'We ain't got no jobs.' I said, 'I don't want a job.' He said, 'We don't want nobody that don't want a job.'"[1]

This story illustrates several aspects of political machines. They are built on loyalty and around patronage precinct workers to deliver the votes necessary to get party candidates elected. The winning candidates then control the government and distribute the spoils of patronage jobs and city contracts and hand out city services as political favors to voters who vote for the party slate of candidates.

Chicago and Illinois have had a history of machine politics since at least 1871. Machine politics has been based first and foremost on winning elections. To win elections, it has often been necessary to use illicit means, such as paying voters or stealing votes. There are many stories of vote stealing in Illinois elections.

In 1972, the *Chicago Tribune* did a series on vote rigging in Chicago's skid-row area. It demonstrates one of the ways machine precinct captains stole elections. Reporter Bill Recktenwald dressed as a bum of the area, with a several-day-old beard. In his skid-row hotel lobby, he witnessed: "[P]recinct workers arrived at the hotel to sign up new voters. 'It didn't take long to see that something was wrong, because no one was there in front of the desk when they were registering people.' When [Recktenwald] checked the registration rolls, he saw that he had been among those involuntarily signed up to vote [under the fictitious name with which he had registered at the hotel]. 'James Joyce became a registered voter at the McCoy Hotel.'"[2]

In that same election, Recktenwald witnessed a precinct captain using the voting machine *seventy times* to fraudulently record votes that purportedly were cast by registered voters. In fact, those voters did not come to the polls and did not vote themselves. While vote-stealing techniques have changed since the methods witnessed by Recktenwald, election fraud has remained throughout Illinois' history.

In the twenty-first century we have touch-screen and Scantron ballot voting, and most precinct captains (other than those who engage in voter-registration fraud and ghost voting for missing residents) haven't learned to scam the system yet. The most common form of massive vote fraud now is rigging absentee voting in precincts, especially at nursing homes, where the elderly are easily manipulated by unscrupulous precinct captains who mark the seniors' absentee ballots for them. While election fraud may have lessened in Illinois in recent years, there continue to be election-fraud cases. Vote stealing provides a bedrock for the other forms of corruption we recount in our book.

Richard Winters, in his study of corruption, found that machine or traditional political parties were statistically a predictor of the difference in corruption convictions among states.[3] In our book we define such political machines as political organizations whose goal is to win elections and control of the government by means of patronage jobs for precinct workers, favors and government services for party voters, and contracts and licenses for businesses who contribute money to campaigns. Figure 2.1 shows how machine politics worked under the legendary party boss Richard J. Daley from 1955 to 1976. It worked much the same way in suburban DuPage County or in downstate Vienna under party bosses like Paul Powell.

Several aspects of this political system are critical. First of all, it depended upon winning elections so the spoils of government can be distributed. Second, it was an economic reward system. Although it provided symbolic recognition to ethnic groups as a reward for party support, it did not depend upon ideology or psychological rewards as reform political organizations do.

Figure 2.1 Richard J. Daley Machine.

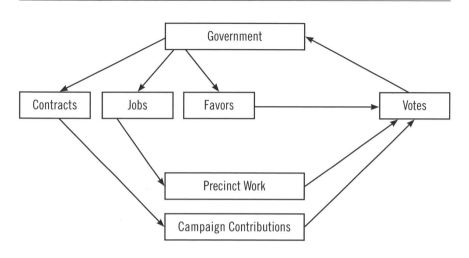

Source: Created by Dick Simpson, based on course lectures by Milton Rakove.

If you worked your precinct, you got a job at city hall or with other governments. If you voted for the machine, you got more government services delivered as favors than your neighbors. If as a businessman you gave money to fund campaigns, you got crooked contracts on which you made a handsome profit. So machine politics was primarily an economic exchange system—a perpetual-motion machine that didn't depend on ideals or personalities, although party leaders could be charismatic and inspire loyal supporters.

Milton Rakove, in his classic book on machine politics, *Don't Make No Waves, Don't Back No Losers,* describes machine politics this way:

> The machine believes with Machiavelli that men in politics are greedy, emotional, and passionate, and are not governed by reason, morality, or concern for their fellow man. It believes that men can be co-opted, bought, persuaded, or frightened into subservience to or cooperation with the machine. Every man has his price, according to the machine. . . . The Chicago Democratic machine is dedicated primarily to gaining and retaining office. . . . Its primary demands on its members are loyalty and political efficiency. In return, it carries out its obligations by providing its members with jobs, contracts, and its own "social security" system.[4]

A successful political machine stays in power for a long time. While it may occasionally lose an election, it projects an aura of invincibility. It is able to use the powers of incumbency and control of the electoral machinery to stay in power. New York's Tammany Hall party boss George Washington Plunkitt declared that reformers were only "morning glories" who had a brief bloom, but a political machine is like a giant oak that lasts a long time.[5]

It is the central thesis of our book that the individualistic culture of much of Illinois is translated into the institution of political-party machines. Control of the many governments throughout the state by political machines inevitably leads to a corrupt political culture in which corruption and the use of public office for private gain becomes accepted and pervasive.

If it is publicly accepted that it is all right to trade government jobs for precinct work, votes for favors, and campaign contributions for inflated government contracts, how is a party worker to distinguish "honest graft"[6] from taking a bribe for a zoning change or fixing a parking ticket? Machine politics always begets corruption—or, in the telling phrase from Rasma Karklins, the system makes them do it![7]

The First Political Machines

James Merriner wrote in his book about Illinois corruption, "The advent of Chicago's first crooked politician . . . is undocumented and open to interpretation. Perhaps some members of the town's first elected board of five trustees in 1833 were corrupt. That is, they were land speculators who did not operate entirely aboveboard."[8] Generally speaking, however, the era from 1833 until the Civil War in 1861 was one of booster government and relatively corruption-free. During the Civil War, government became partisan, as "civic wars" between Democrats and Republicans broke out in local and state government.[9]

After the Civil War, the political system changed once more. The first corruption court case in Chicago occurred in 1869, and corruption and machine politics soon spread throughout the state. In that year, fourteen aldermen, county commissioners, and former aldermen were indicted for accepting bribes to rig a $128,500 contract to paint city hall. Four of the public officials were convicted, and a number lost their positions in the next elections.

The city council of this time was controlled by McCauley's Nineteen, named after Alderman James McCauley, who headed a "ring" of corrupt aldermen. The *Tribune* characterized the McCauley Nineteen "as dishonest and corrupt as any that has ever disgraced any municipal government."[10] As a result, Roswell Mason, a civil engineer, was elected on a reform Peoples' Ticket in November

1869, and many of the crooked aldermen were defeated. More were ousted in the 1871 election, "but not enough to prevent thirteen Republicans and eight Democrats from organizing a new ring [of crooked aldermen]."[11]

In this post–Civil War era, Michael Cassius McDonald ascended. He was a gambler, saloon keeper, and the first party boss in Chicago. McDonald had been a successful card shark on trains and in New Orleans before permanently settling in Chicago in 1861. He avoided the Civil War draft and rose in the underworld "as the principal supplier of dice, cards, and political patronage."[12] McDonald soon owned a bar inside the Richard House Hotel, before opening his infamous Store tavern and gambling den at the corner of Clark and Monroe.

After the Chicago Fire of 1871, McDonald "was the first to detect the common bonds of interest of the criminal element and politicians and introduce one group to the other. The *Chicago News* gave McDonald credit 'for electing aldermen who lorded it in the city council and county commissioners who stole everything in sight, and for providing contracts for public works that had thievery written between the lines.'"[13] The alliance between crooked businessmen and politicians was simple. The houses of prostitution provided bribes and campaign contributions for ward committeemen and aldermen. The saloons, taverns, and bars went further and provided free lunch and beer to patrons who would climb onto horse-drawn wagons that went from polling place to polling place allowing saloon patrons to vote multiple times for favored politicians. This helped corrupt aldermen and ward committeemen to win their elections. Along the way, the political boss Mike McDonald and his successors obtained the power to prevent the police from raiding these fine business establishments.

After he became the biggest political boss of the city, McDonald was able to use his political clout as he "assigned locations for houses of prostitution, granted licenses for gambling, and distributed money from criminals to police officials, court employees and judges."[14] Among many long con schemes, which were crooked deals that would continue over years, McDonald supplied building stones to city construction crews who were replacing the old courthouse and city hall. It had burned down in the Chicago Fire of 1871. The resulting city hall building would be destroyed in turn and rebuilt in 1905 because of cheap materials and shoddy deals. In the interim years, McDonald and his allies made a fortune building and repairing city hall.

Mike McDonald's greatest period of political influence came with the election of Carter Harrison as mayor in 1879. As Richard Lindberg records:

McDonald reached the apex of his political power under . . . [Mayor] Harrison. In the fall of 1879, Mike took over as chairman of assessments for the Democratic Central Committee—responsible for fee collection and revenues levied against the myriad of ward clubs scattered across the city. In August, the First Ward organization [which would later be run by the rogue aldermen "Bathhouse" John Coughlin and "Hinky Dink" Kenna], with the blessing of the mayor, formally sanctioned Mike's behind-the-scenes contribution to the party by anointing him precinct committeeman. . . . McDonald deserved credit for the restoration of the Democratic Party and the success of his political cohorts in the recent election.[15]

McDonald would remain active throughout the nineteenth century to inaugurate what would also be called the "Era of the Gray Wolves." The end of the nineteenth and the early twentieth century was a time of political bosses in Chicago wards with their own little fiefdoms in the Democratic and Republican parties. Aldermen then gathered into "rings" to take bribes and distribute the spoils in the Chicago city council. In short, political parties and their graft, boodle, nepotism, and patronage jobs were decentralized into mini-machines from 1871 to 1931.

This changed again with Anton Cermak and later Democratic party machines of the twentieth century. Then new party bosses centralized power into a single party, often with a single strong leader like Richard J. Daley, who ruled Chicago as mayor and party boss from 1955 to 1976.

The rest of the state was organized into political fiefdoms by county as well. In some, good government was the dominant form of politics, but many suburban and downstate counties were run by political machines. Reformers, or "Goo Goos" (good government types), did arise to challenge various political parties locally or even statewide.[16] In Chicago, there were reform mayors like Edward Dunne and William Devers. Dunne would go on to become a reform governor like John Peter Altgeld. Each held office for a time, but in the long run political machines prevailed in Illinois.

Stolen Elections

Over the years, many elections in Chicago and in Illinois were stolen. The key for machine politics was continuing to win elections. Winning elections was critical to controlling government and its jobs, contracts, and policies. It is likely that the very first elections in Chicago in 1833 were rigged, as more votes were counted than there were voters. And that tradition of election fraud has continued to the present day.

The most famous "stolen" election was the presidential election of 1960, when the kingmaker Richard J. Daley is said to have stolen the election for John F. Kennedy. Even more importantly, from a local-politics standpoint, he was able to defeat Ben Adamowski, the Republican candidate for state's attorney, and elect instead Democrat Daniel Ward, who would protect machine politicians from prosecution.

Kennedy won the state by 8,858 votes out of 4,657,394 cast, and Dan Ward beat Adamowski by 25,000 votes. Adamowski "charged that Daley had stolen 100,000 Democratic votes in 10 machine-dominated Chicago wards and had become 'the most powerful political boss in America through a rigged election contest.'"[17]

Democrats and Republicans differed in their interpretation of the election. Based upon a canvass of less than one-third of Chicago precincts and only one kind of voting irregularity, Republicans erased more than half of the margin of victory for Kennedy and Ward. But Daley, probably correctly, countered in his testimony at the Illinois Election Board hearing that the same kinds of vote fraud were committed in Grundy and DuPage Counties by the Republicans.[18] Votes were stolen in the 1960 election by Democrats in Chicago and Republicans in the suburbs. Apparently, Democrats were just better at stealing votes.

Election fraud during the Council of the Gray Wolves period from 1871 to 1931 is well documented. To give one example of the scope of the election fraud in this period, in 1935, "more than one hundred election officials were sentenced to jail for fraud."[19]

The various techniques for stealing elections in the later twentieth century were also well known. Up until the last decades of the century, most polling places used paper ballots. With such a system, it was relatively easy to steal votes. If a voter died or moved before the election, the precinct captain, with the help of the election judges that he appointed, would simply vote in their stead. He would just fill out the paper ballot and put it in the ballot box.

Chicago Alderman Ed Burke is fond of telling the story of an elderly woman who lived all her life in a small Indiana town. She goes to her lawyer to draw up her will and specifies that when she dies, she is to be buried in Chicago. Her lawyer asks why on earth she would do this, since she had always lived in this small Indiana town. Well, she explained, "I want to continue to vote Democratic after I die." Certainly there are many documented election-fraud cases in which the dead vote, or like in Bill Recktenwald's *Tribune* exposé, fraudulent, nonexistent voters like James Joyce do.

In some of the paper-ballot precincts, the precinct captain would simply steal a single paper ballot when the polls opened. He would then stand outside campaigning. When one of his voters came up, the captain would give the voter the ballot he had already marked for the favored candidates. The voter would take the marked ballot with him into the polling place and obtain a new blank ballot. Once the voter drew the curtain to vote in secret, he would substitute the marked ballot for the blank one and place the marked one in the ballot box. When he left the polling place, he would give the new blank ballot to the precinct captain as proof he had cast the premarked ballot. In return, the precinct captain would either give him money—a five-dollar bill in the later years—or send him to the local tavern around the corner where he could get beer or liquor for doing his civic duty the Democratic machine way. The captain would then mark the blank ballot for the next voter. This technique was known as the paper-ballot chain. And without poll watchers for opposing candidates or honest election judges, it was unbeatable.

In a special election in 1969, Dick Simpson was helping coordinate the campaign of John Stevens, an African American social worker who was a reform aldermanic candidate in Committeeman George Dunne's Forty-second Ward. The machine candidate he was running against was Raymond Fried, a white machine precinct captain whose turn had come. However, Fried had cancer and made no campaign appearances. The black Cabrini-Green public-housing highrises were on the west side of the ward where Stevens served as a social worker. John Stevens, in addition to being black, articulate, and committed to social justice, was the logical candidate for the Cabrini-Green voters, since he knew their problems. He had worked with these voters for a long time. In each of the four paper-ballot precincts in the ward he lost the election by votes like 400–12 or 397–15. Voters in the rest of the ward used the new mechanical voting machines, which were difficult to scam when they were first introduced. The use of the chain ballot caused Stevens to lose the election in the ward by 742 votes. The paper-ballot voting was rigged in those precincts but Stevens' supporters couldn't prove it to reverse the election outcome. An irony of the election was that Fried died ten months later, and the machine insider Burton Natarus was appointed to replace him in the city council.

Patronage

Patronage is another base of machine politics.[20] It too undermines citizens' faith in government and democracy. As with nepotism, favoritism, and unchecked control over government contracts, patronage inevitably leads to public corruption.

On October 17, 1969, Michael L. Shakman, a candidate for Illinois Constitutional Convention delegate, and Paul Laurie, his supporter, filed suit in federal court. The named defendants were the City of Chicago, the Democratic Organization of Cook County, Mayor Richard J. Daley, Illinois Republican Governor Richard B. Ogilvie, and Republican Party Chairman Edmund J. Kucharski.[21]

The Shakman case was initially dismissed by a federal district court on the grounds that Shakman could not prove that the defendants caused harm. Upon appeal, a majority of appellate justices found that taxpayers were indeed deprived, stating:

> The interest in an equal chance and an equal voice is allegedly impaired in the case before us by the misuse of official power over public employees so as to create a *substantial, perhaps massive,* political effort in favor of the ins and against the outs. . . . We conclude that these interests are entitled to constitutional protection from the injury of the nature alleged, as well as from injury resulting from inequality in election procedure.[22]

Shakman responded that the ruling "amounts to a political emancipation proclamation for government employees who are not protected by civil service."[23]

In April 1971, the Supreme Court of the United States agreed with the lower court that patronage hiring did violate the Fourteenth Amendment's equal-protection clause and the 1870 Civil Rights Act. The defendant political party and government officials tried unsuccessfully to argue that it was a political matter that should not be subject to judicial review.[24]

On October 20, 1971, fearing that they would have to disclose their secret political-party records in the discovery process, the Cook County Democratic organization reached an agreement with Michael Shakman and Federal Judge Abraham Marovitz known as the "Patronage Pact." Democrats agreed not to fire or demote government employees on the basis of political work or contributions. The agreement further stipulated that government employees cannot do political work on government time.[25] In various court testimony and rulings, estimates of the total number of patronage employees in state and local governments ranged from twenty to thirty-five thousand. In the Patronage Pact, signed on May 5, 1972, the defendants were enjoined from forcing employees to donate money or work for specific candidates, from being fired for refusing to do such work, and from requiring employees to do political work while they were on the clock.

While this dealt a blow to the machine, it did not immediately spell the end of patronage and machine politics. Conspicuously missing from the pact was any ban on the hiring of workers for political reasons. And it turned out that Mayor Richard J. Daley did not comply with the original order. He and the City of Chicago were found in contempt of court several times during the remainder of his tenure.[26]

Motivated by a 1976 U.S. Supreme Court case that prohibited politically motivated firing nationally, in 1977 the Democratic party of Cook County finally stipulated this fact in court.[27] Two years after the stipulation and ten years after the initial case was filed, Judge Nicholas Bua ruled that patronage hiring was indeed unconstitutional.[28] Judge Bua found that patronage hiring was an integral part of the way government workers got hired: not because they were qualified, but because they were "sponsored" by someone in the party or had otherwise "earned" the position by doing political work. He also found that this was blatant—he found that some people applying for these patronage posts were told by city officials that they must see first their Democratic party ward committeeman. Judge Bua found that this system unfairly advantaged Democrats to win elections in Chicago, disadvantaged Republicans and Independents, and kept the public from having a fair electoral system.[29]

The combined rulings and pact eventually came to be known as the "Shakman decree." The decision came with court-enforced monitoring of compliance. Little by little, agencies began to agree publicly that they would abide by the ruling. However, full implementation of the Shakman decree would not come until 1983, when Harold Washington was elected mayor. He had announced while campaigning that he would sign the decree, and in June 1983 he did just that.[30]

In 1989, Richard M. Daley was elected mayor. Patronage as practiced in Illinois was on its way out, as the U.S. Supreme Court ruled in 1990 in *Rutan v. Republican Party of Illinois* that the State of Illinois also could not hire, fire, promote, or transfer employees on the basis of political activity, save for a few policy-making positions and those that were confidential.[31] In this court case, it was the Republicans, not the Democrats, who were in power and used patronage hiring at the state government level. Patronage was proven to be a statewide problem, and it was clearly illegal after the ruling in the *Rutan* case.

At first, Daley did not challenge the Shakman decree. In fact, it looked like the 1990s would be a time when we would declare with Mayor Washington that patronage was "dead, dead, dead." By the end of 1991, the only county or city offices not to have signed the Shakman decree were the Cook County Board

President's Office and the Office of the Cook County Assessor.[32] In 1993, the President's Office would sign, and in October 1994, so would the Assessor.[33]

However, in 2002, U.S. District Court judge Wayne Andersen found Chicago in contempt of the court's order. According to the judge, Daley used temporary agencies and personal-services contracts to hire and fire employees that circumvented the Shakman requirements, creating a way for patronage to continue. Daley defended the use of contracts and agencies, calling them simply a management tool.[34]

Daley also argued that Shakman monitoring had cost the city between six and nine million dollars per year—and that taxpayers should not have to continue to carry that burden or the burden of another two million dollars on expanding Shakman monitoring.[35] Daley proposed instead writing the specifics of the decree into the personnel code. Daley was unsuccessful and ultimately was forced to comply with the order.

Then, in 2004, the Hired Truck scandal broke. In the resulting court cases it was revealed that private trucks hired to do city work were doing little or no work, had mob connections, were tied to city employees, and that trucking firms had to pay bribes to get contracts. The scandal also brought to light rigged hiring schemes. Shakman again took the city to court and asked a federal judge to hold Mayor Daley personally responsible for the violations.[36] Shakman and federal prosecutors alleged that the city had been violating the Shakman decree for years and that a new monitoring system was needed. In response, the court appointed its own monitor in 2005—just before the lid blew off the Robert Sorich scandal.

The Sorich Trial

Rigged hiring, it turned out, would be one of the biggest scandals in Daley's administration. It caused observers to declare that patronage was alive and well. Robert Sorich was assistant director of the Mayor's Office of Intergovernmental Affairs (IGA) from 1993 to 2005. Federal prosecutors would eventually prove that Sorich and his codefendants, Timothy McCarthy, John Sullivan, and Patrick Slattery, used their official city positions to hand out patronage jobs to those with political sponsorship and connections, in violation of the Shakman decree.

The IGA controlled many non-exempt jobs that were protected under the decree from political patronage hiring. These non-exempt jobs were required to be selected on merit, while a very few exempt jobs could be filled by political appointees who would carry out the policies of elected officials. The court found, in fact, that ward bosses, political officials, union leaders, campaign coordinators, and other politically connected people would nominate candidates to IGA for these non-exempt jobs. Sorich and McCarthy would determine which politically connected job candidates should be hired and then would forward lists of preselected candidates to the departments that did the actual hiring.

To avoid appearing to violate the Shakman decree, the city posted job listings and conducted interviews with those applying. But it was all a sham—the winners had already been determined. On July 5, 2006, Sorich, Slattery, and McCarthy were convicted of mail fraud in relation to the scandal. Sullivan was found not guilty on that count, but he was convicted of lying to the FBI. The following year, the city council approved a measure to create a twelve-million-dollar fund to compensate victims who had failed to be hired because of this patronage scheme[37]—another of the many costs of public corruption.

As far as can be determined, based upon Sorich's "clout list," it is believed that the number of patronage jobs had dropped from as many as thirty-five thousand under Richard J. Daley to as few as five thousand. The patronage jobs under Richard M. Daley were no longer distributed through the ward committeemen but through Daley-established political organizations like the Hispanic Democratic Organization. This pattern of patronage was later confirmed by further convictions in the Al Sanchez case and related cases that followed after Sorich.

End of the Chicago Hiring Monitor

After his election, Mayor Rahm Emanuel asked the U.S. District Court to dismiss the City of Chicago from oversight by the court-appointed Shakman hiring monitor. He asserted that the city had made great strides in fair hiring practices.[38] On June 17, 2014, the court agreed to do so but in essence said that "Mayor Emanuel has a long way to go to lift the 'cloud of mistrust' from a hiring scandal with a $22.9 million price tag."[39]

Judge Sidney Schenkier said that his finding of the city in "substantial compliance" with the Shakman decree "does not mean the city has 'achieved a state of perfection' but that it no longer needs the 'extraordinary restriction' of a federal hiring monitor."[40] After the decision, Mayor Emanuel wrote in an op-ed, "For the first time in decades, Chicagoans can be confident that we have the systems in place to ensure city employees owe their allegiance to residents and not to political sponsors. . . . We know that attempts to influence won't magically disappear. . . . We must remain vigilant about keeping political clout away from hiring decisions."[41]

Any future plaintiffs who allege that there have been abuses in patronage practices will still have access for redress. Shakman court cases continue as well against various other units of state and local government. While patronage has shrunk, it is still a part of the machine-politics tradition in Chicago and Illinois.

Nepotism

The more or less absolute power bestowed by the political machines controlling elections led not only to patronage but also to nepotism, the appointing of relatives to the government payroll. Most often it refers to sons and daughters, but Chicago and Illinois politicians have enlarged the idea to include husbands and wives, uncles and aunts, as well as cousins, nieces, and nephews. Aldermen Fred Roti (First Ward) and Vito Marzullo (Twenty-fifth Ward) used to brag about how they had twenty to twenty-five relatives on the city-government or related agency payrolls. Roti later went to jail for bribery, extortion, racketeering, and for fixing civil case and a zoning matter. His son, Bruno, while working for the police department in 1981 pleaded guilty to submitting ten thousand dollars in phony work orders for a friend's repair shop. Despite his conviction, in 1983 Bruno was given a job in the Water Department. Alderman Vito Marzullo was never indicted or convicted.

Mike Royko, in *Boss: Richard J. Daley of Chicago,* recounts in the "begats" section of his book how many of the most powerful politicians are relatives such that Alderman Joe Rostenkowski begat Congressman Dan Rostenkowski. Federal Judge Mike Igoe begat Cook County Board Secretary Mike Igoe. Thus it happens in elected and appointed offices in Illinois. Otto Kerner, a federal judge and Chicago Mayor Anton Cermak's confidant, begat a son, also named Otto Kerner, who became governor and then a federal judge after he married Cermak's daughter.[42]

One of the more famous clashes over nepotism occurred when Dick Simpson, who was then Forty-fourth Ward alderman, challenged the appointment of Tom Keane Jr. to a relatively obscure Zoning Board of Appeals in 1971. Tom Keane Jr. was the son of Mayor Richard J. Daley's floor leader, Tom Keane Sr. As an additional conflict of interest, Tom Keane Jr. was also a vice president of Arthur Rubloff and Company, the biggest real-estate company in Chicago. The Board of Appeals would affect the value of all the company's properties. On the council floor, Simpson challenged: "This appointment poses the problem of the faith of our citizenry in our city government. Why is it that members of the same family get appointments in several sections of government and only large firms seem to get representation on boards dealing with zoning and construction?"[43]

Mayor Daley asked how anyone could question "the idea that I made this appointment because a man's name was Keane and he was the son of a famous member of this council! I made this appointment because I have known Tommy Keane, the boy I appointed, since he's been a baby. . . . Should that boy be told . . . that he shouldn't hold office because his name is Keane?"[44] Tom Keane Jr.'s appointment was approved by a 44–2 vote.

One of the reasons that Daley was so adamant in his defense of the Keane appointment was that he was favoring his own sons with government contracts. The mayor gave no-bid city-insurance contracts to the firm of Heil and Heil, which employed one of his sons. And the local Cook County Circuit Court, whose judges Daley elected, gave an extraordinary number of profitable court receiverships to another Daley son. A 1973 resolution ordering Daley to account as to "whether he has unlawfully used his influence as Mayor . . . to receive undue preference" was defeated 35–7. A few days later, local newspapers reported that at a closed session of the Cook County Democratic Central Committee, Daley blurted out, "If a man can't put his arms around his sons, then what kind of world are we living in? I make no apologies. If I can't help my sons, [my critics] can kiss my ass."[45]

The more than twenty million Illinoisans who were not named Daley, Keane, Roti, Kerner, Madigan, or Rostenkowski, despite their ability, knowledge, or character, could not get equal treatment from the government they elected and to which they paid taxes. Even in the twenty-first century, the county assessor and chair of the Cook County Democratic Party Central Committee, Joe Berrios, has a number of relatives working for him in the assessor's office and won't get rid of them despite media exposés and public controversy.

In 2006, the *Springfield State Journal-Register* endorsed the Republican challenger to Democratic Secretary of State Jesse White and criticized White for nepotism. The editors said that although White's daughter was not hired by him, under her father her salary nearly tripled to $112,000 a year. "It doesn't stop there," they wrote. "A nephew, three nieces and a step-grandson all have landed jobs under White."[46]

There is no doubt that nepotism is alive and well in Illinois.

Is Machine Politics Evolving?

Machine politics, with its patronage, favoritism, nepotism, cronyism, and inflated contracts, fuels the continuing culture of corruption. Machine politics has evolved over the last century and a half. In the days when Mike McDonald was boss, the machine was split into multiple fiefdoms and rings of crooked aldermen in the city council. Mayors and party bosses Anton Cermak and Richard J. Daley centralized the machine into the form shown in figure 2.2. Paul Powell and others did so downstate as well.

In Chicago, Mayor Jane Byrne split the machine into pro-Byrne and pro–Richard M. Daley factions and helped to destroy the connection between the business elite, the political party, and the city-government bureaucracy. More destruction followed under the reform Mayor Harold Washington, who especially attacked patronage and the old-boy network of crooked contracts. He also instituted affirmative action in hiring and contracts, which opened up what had been a closed shop.

At the same time, machine politics in the state—which had flourished under the different fiefdoms, such as the one run by Secretary of State Paul Powell and those run by suburban politicians—continued. Political leaders like Governor George Ryan expanded modern machine politics statewide.

Back in Chicago, Richard M. Daley modernized machine politics much as his father had done forty years before him. His twenty-first-century machine operated with many of the same old elements in place, but with many new innovations and new players.

While longtime ward committeemen who still had patronage jobs from the old days continued to provide some precinct workers to get out the vote for the party candidate, Richard M. Daley, with the help of Sorich, Sanchez, and others at city hall, now gave patronage jobs to Daley political organizations. There was at least one such organization for each racial group in the city. But the Shakman decree and budget cutbacks, which meant eliminating city-hall jobs, limited the number of patronage jobs available.

While city contractors and unions—especially construction unions like carpenters and plumbers that depended upon government projects for work and sweetheart contracts for top wages—continued to provide money for Richard M. Daley's campaigns, the main money flow had changed from his father's day. When he was state's attorney, Daley received contributions from high-powered lawyers and major law firms, who also introduced him to the

Figure 2.2 Richard M. Daley Machine.

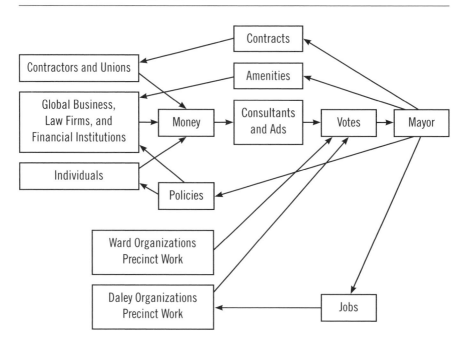

Source: Created by Dick Simpson.

top businessmen in the global economy. So Daley easily raised at least seven million dollars when he ran for mayor in 2003 and 2007, with more than a third of that coming from the global economy. All this money allowed him to run a presidential-style campaign, just like Clinton, Bush, and Obama. He hired the top consultants and fund-raisers in the country and did public-opinion polls, direct mail to voters, and television ads when needed. In return, global-economy businesspeople received policies they liked. So the city got Millennium Park, safety in the Loop, new buildings downtown, flowers in the parkway, and wrought-iron fences around parks and schools. Chicago became a place to bring their international clients and to keep their white-collar workers happy living here. This was no longer your grandfather's political machine.

Governor Rod Blagojevich tried to copy the Daley model. He had support from key machine wards like his father-in-law Alderman Dick Mell's Thirty-third Ward. He raised more than twenty million dollars twice to run for governor. And he got it primarily from businessmen. The big difference in Blagojevich's pay-to-play system is that many of his fund-raisers and large contributors got direct payoffs in the form of crooked contracts, bribes, and kickbacks. But that system came crashing down with his impeachment and later corruption conviction.

The big question in the post-Daley, post-Blagojevich era is: Are we able to change from machine politics, or are we still chained to the past? Governor Pat Quinn, particularly in comparison to Ryan and Blagojevich, has been a reformer. He appointed an Illinois Ethics Commission, which produced sound recommendations for curbing corruption. Pat Collins, the commission chairman, and other commission members like Lieutenant Governor Sheila Simon continue to push for adoption of these recommendations.

Rahm Emanuel, in his 2011 campaign, took the Richard M. Daley election tactics even further. He was supported by some Democratic ward commit-teemen and their precinct captains from the North Side white area of the city and by some black committeemen. But he raised even more money than Daley—roughly thirteen million dollars. Much of the money came not only from Chicago businesses and businesspeople in the global economy but from contacts he had made in the Clinton and Obama administrations. He got big contributions even from Californian movie moguls, and half his campaign funds came from out of state. So Emanuel's mayoral campaign was like the Daley campaigns on steroids.

On the positive side, he is even less dependent than Daley on patronage, party ward committeemen, and precinct captains. He has also broken up the old-boys club of Daley-connected contractors, but there are still allega-tions of favoritism in some contracts, and still no-bid contracts are given out. Emanuel has also dabbled in nepotism and crony contracting. He approved a multi-million-dollar bike-sharing program to a company run by a friend. He selected the sister of Alderman Pat O'Connor, his city-council floor leader, to direct the closing and transition of fifty-four public schools. In one of the bigger corruption scandals, John Bills, the former head of Chicago's red-light camera program, was arrested and charged in a two-million-dollar bribery scandal to help Redflex Traffic Systems obtain lucrative contracts. Emanuel later banned the company from further city contracts.[47]

On the other side of the ledger, since he has been in office, Emanuel has pro-vided more transparency in government, earning a 98 rating out of a possible 100 from the U.S. Public Interest Research Group for spending transparency. Chicago received its grade based "on how well 'checkbook level' information is presented online."[48] In addition, Chicago city clerks have posted ever more information on the city council, which has made tracking aldermanic voting records and legislation easier.

One thing that hasn't changed, or changed only for the worst, is that Emanuel continues mayoral control over the Chicago city council, just like his machine-boss predecessors. In fact, he has more control than ever.

We analyzed thirty city council divided roll-call votes from May 2011 through March 2013. (By definition, divided roll-call votes are those on which at least one alderman opposes the mayor's position.) We found that twenty-one of the fifty aldermen voted to support Mayor Emanuel's position 100 percent of the time, and another eighteen aldermen voted with him over 90 percent of the time. Only seven of the thirty controversial issues we studied drew six or more dissenting votes. Our conclusion was that Emanuel presides over a more compliant rubber-stamp city council than any mayor in Chicago history.[49] This means that the council does not act as a check and balance, nor does it initiate major new policies in the way we expect a genuine legislature to do in a democracy. It also makes it harder to break the culture of corruption and the expectation that aldermen and other public officials in Illinois are on the take.

The same complaint is made about the state legislature, which is not a "rubber stamp" for reform Governor Pat Quinn, but is a "rubber stamp" for the machine boss and Speaker of the House of Representatives Michael Madigan. He uses his long tenure, his ability to provide campaign staff and funds for his Democratic party members' reelection campaigns, and his control over the passage or defeat of their proposed legislation to keep their support on all important votes.

When the *Chicago Tribune* investigated the patronage army of Michael Madigan, who is also chairman of the Illinois Democratic party, they found more than four hundred current or retired government employees with strong political ties to him and "repeated instances in which [he] took personal action to get them jobs, promotions, or raises." He uses this patronage army, which also contributes money to his political campaigns, "to influence elections in every corner of the state, from suburban mayor to governor, from county board to Congress."[50]

The Challenge

Often it is assumed that machine politics and election fraud only occurred in Chicago in earlier centuries, but they are much more widespread and current than that. In 2005 in East St. Louis, Charles Powell Jr., the head of the local Democratic party, and eight accomplices in this thirty-one-thousand-person town were convicted of a vote-buying scheme. As Powell explained on a tape played at the trial, "We've been doing this so long in East St. Louis. We've been doing this for thirty years."[51]

In Cairo, Alexander County Clerk Louis Maze pleaded guilty to mutilating election materials, lost his job, and was sentenced to a year's probation and one hundred hours of community service. Among the charges against him were forged election ballots.[52]

In the small south-Chicago-suburban town of Burnham, the village clerk, Nancy Dobrowski, who had been elected and reelected for more than thirty years, stole seven hundred thousand dollars over more than a decade. The town has only 4,500 residents. She pleaded guilty and was sentenced to 18 months in prison in 2014.[53]

As long as political machines or big money control the outcome of elections, corruption will continue. And as long as machine politics dominates, patronage, ghost payrolling, nepotism, and crony contracting will prevail. It continues not only in Chicago and in the state capital in Springfield, but in county buildings, suburban town halls, and the smaller towns throughout the state.

If machine politics is replaced by big money provided by secret wealthy individuals and corporations, it will simply be replaced by an oligarchy. Under either political machines or oligarchies, citizens' control over and faith in their governments will not be achieved in Illinois. Government officials will continue to be in the thrall of private interests and unable to serve honestly in the public interest.

For democracy to prevail, honest elections and an end of machine politics and oligarchy must occur. Until then, corruption cannot be eliminated or controlled. Prosecutors can convict the few public officials they catch stealing from the public, but most will not be detected. Those few who are sent to prison will be replaced by other cogs in a new twenty-first-century machine.

In 2006, Republican Governor George Ryan was found guilty of eighteen counts of mail fraud, racketeering conspiracy, lying to the FBI, obstructing the IRS, and filing false tax returns. Since 1973, three other Illinois governors, all Democrats, were convicted and sent to federal prison. *Photo courtesy of Sun-Times Media.*

CHAPTER 3

The Sorry State of Illinois

ILLINOIS IS ONE OF THE MOST CORRUPT STATES in the nation. Not only is Chicago corrupt, but the suburbs, downstate towns, and statewide officials share in this corruption. Former Governor Rod Blagojevich is the undisputed champion of modern Illinois corruption. He is the only governor to be impeached and thrown out of office even before he was convicted.

One of the most unusual aspects of Blagojevich's case is that he was recorded on FBI wiretaps spelling out blatant details of his proposed deals. We hear him in his own voice talking about putting his private gain above public good and his duty as a public official. For instance, he tried to sell the U.S. Senate seat to the highest bidder because he could appoint the successor to Barack Obama after Obama had been elected president in 2008. Blagojevich declared over his wiretapped phone: "I've got this thing and it's fucking—*golden*. And I, I'm just not giving it up for fucking nothing."[1]

These audiotapes provide an inside look at crass and venal Illinois politicians. Blagojevich, like some of his predecessors, established a corrupt network of private businessmen, political appointees, and elected officials. In June 2011, he was convicted on multiple counts of corruption. In addition to attempting to sell the U.S. Senate seat, he was convicted of shamefully shaking down the CEO of Children's Memorial Hospital, a racetrack official, and a road builder for bribes and campaign contributions.

As a result, his sentence was very long. He received fourteen years in prison for his crimes. In his defense, two arguments continually get repeated, and they are similar to what many convicted officials have argued. First of all, his attorneys and supporters claim that he was no different from other politicians in what he did. He came up through the Chicago political machine and was simply a part of that pervasive culture of corruption. Second, his attorneys argue that there wasn't any cost to his misdeeds. His were victimless crimes.

Actually, what Blagojevich and other Illinois corruption crooks did is different from what other politicians do. As U.S. Attorney Patrick Fitzgerald said at the trial's conclusion, what he did "is not politics as usual. [What he did is] a crime."[2] The legal line is clear. When an official uses his or her government office for private benefit, it is illegal. Crooked politicians and their apologists have insisted that under the Illinois system of machine politics, everybody demands paybacks for favors, jobs, and crooked contracts—along with a little stealing. The illegal deeds of the late Congressman Dan Rostenkowski and many other convicted officials have been defended in the same way. Defenders of Blagojevich and Rostenkowski argue that they grew up in the system of machine politics and simply never adjusted to the modern era. But the truth is that Blagojevich and Rostenkowski stole from government and the public. As a lawyer, Rod Blagojevich knew that he was twisting and breaking the law. He was taking money in illegal ways, which is why he tried to disguise so many of his corrupt activities.

Blagojevich was convicted not only for trying to sell a U.S. Senate seat. What he did most frequently was to appoint his people to boards and commissions who then rigged contracts in return for payoffs for themselves and for campaign contributions for Blagojevich. It was a shakedown scheme for which many fellow conspirators, including Tony Rezko, Lon Monk, John Wyma, Stuart Levine, John Harris, William Cellini, and Ali Ata, have also been sent to jail. Blagojevich's friend and co-conspirator Christopher Kelly committed suicide rather than go to prison. Blagojevich led a wide-ranging enterprise of corruption—his was not a one-man show. Like former Governor George Ryan's scandals, which sent him to jail, they involved a lot of people.

After law school in California, Rod Blagojevich moved back to Chicago and began his legal and political career with the former Alderman Eddie Vrdolyak, who was later convicted of corruption in an unrelated case. At first, Blagojevich clerked on workman-compensation and personal-injury cases at Vrydolyak's law firm.[3] After several false starts as a lawyer, including running his own small firm, he became an assistant state's attorney in traffic court.

Blagojevich began to do political work on the side and met Thirty-third Ward Alderman Dick Mell. Soon he was dating Mell's daughter, Patti, whom he later married. He then joined Mell's aldermanic staff. "Rod Blagojevich slid easily into Mell's organization. City payroll records show he was being paid by as many as four different City Council committees in one year. But Blagojevich told the *Chicago Tribune* he never worked in City Hall; rather, he said, he worked in Mell's ward service office."[4]

When State Representative Al Ronan broke with Mell's organization in 1992, Mell slated his son-in-law, Blagojevich, to run for the state legislature. Mell had a strong political organization of experienced precinct captains used to turning out the vote, and Rod Blagojevich was really, really good at retail politics—going door to door meeting voters and greeting them at El stops in the district. He won handily.

He didn't stay in the state legislature for long. By 1996, he was elected congressman for the Fifth Congressional District of Illinois. By 2002, with Mell's help, guidance, and clout, he was elected governor. Ironically, he won as a populist on a campaign of promoting affordable drugs for seniors, providing jobs, raising the minimum wage, and ending the corruption of Governor George Ryan's administration. Along the way, he went from having to raise a few thousand dollars to raising millions of dollars for each campaign for higher office. He was steadily raising more than twenty million dollars for each of his gubernatorial races. He even set his sights on running for president, which would have required vastly more money. So he began to befriend crooked businessmen who could help with fund-raising.

During and after his gubernatorial campaign, Blagojevich surrounded himself with dubious characters like Chris Kelly and Tony Rezko. They gave the governor the names of those to be appointed to boards and commissions that gave out multi-million-dollar contracts. They then rigged the contracts to be given to the preferred bidder who paid a commission, finder's fee, or bribe to the board member or gave a large campaign contribution to the governor. In Illinois, it is called the "pay to play" system. Everyone in on the deals made a lot of money, and Governor Blagojevich got the campaign funds to run for reelection and, perhaps, president someday.

Everybody Does It

It is simply untrue that all public officials engage in corruption. The former U.S. Senator Paul Douglas and Alderman Leon Despres are two examples of government officials who were incorruptible. They had clear-cut rules to prevent bribery. They had a twenty-five-dollar limit on any gifts, so constituents might bring cookies or a cake to their staff as a thank you for helping to obtain legitimate government services, but they couldn't bribe these officials with money or gifts. Likewise, Senator Douglas and Alderman Despres didn't take campaign contributions from developers who had zoning issues in the past or pending in their wards. Thus, they avoided conflicts of interest. By contrast, Governor Blagojevich didn't want to be protected from corruption. He wanted to promote it. He simply sought not to be caught.

Blagojevich not only lacked clear nonbribery rules, but his campaign aides, government staff, and appointees shook down businessmen for large campaign contributions. He raised more money this way than any previous candidate for governor, including George Ryan.

These were not victimless crimes, as some Blagojevich apologists maintain. We were all his victims. For example, the first state bond issue after he was indicted cost taxpayers an additional twenty million dollars because the state's bond rating was downgraded. Blagojevich's pension-board appointees took bribes to give out the pension-fund-management contracts in return for kickbacks and contributions to his campaign fund. This contributed to the one-hundred-billion-dollar pension deficit, which remains the single biggest financial problem in state government today. Most of all, he undermined citizens' trust in their government. Why should they pay their taxes if Blagojevich and his allies were going to steal the money anyway?

The only positive outcome of this scandal was the reforms it spurred. After Blagojevich was indicted and impeached, Governor Pat Quinn quickly appointed a blue-ribbon Illinois Ethics Commission, which provided a blueprint of change. Unfortunately, their positive recommendations were only partially implemented. Thus, the Blagojevich scandal provided momentum for some reforms in campaign financing and later reforms in Chicago ethics ordinances. High-profile scandals frequently have this effect, but like vigorous federal prosecution of crooked politicians, they are never enough by themselves to change Illinois' culture of corruption.

Recent research has indicated that political scandals like the Blagojevich scandal can create propitious conditions for a change to a new regime characterized by alternative electoral coalitions and an alternate distribution of power and economic benefits of government.[5] However, a single scandal which allows the election of a reform mayor or governor for a term or two cannot by itself eliminate machine politics nor the corrupt political culture it creates.

Illustrating Corruption Theories

Illinois illustrates the theories of corruption all too well. Unfortunately, Illinois has corruption at all levels of state and local governments. As we discussed in chapter 1, Rasma Karklin's theory divides corruption into three types, all of which exist in Illinois: (1) everyday interactions between officials and citizens, which will be covered in later chapters; (2) interactions within public institutions including patronage and nepotism, which is described in this chapter; and (3) influence over institutions, which is the main focus of this chapter.

Robert Klitgaard's theory, which was also discussed in chapter 1, is demonstrated by top state officials who used their monopoly of power, discretion, and lack of accountability to create corruption on a grand scale. We use these egregious examples of corruption to show that public values in support of honest government have been too weak. If Transparency International were to rank states as it does nations, Illinois' corruption score would place it at the low level of corrupt third-world nations.

Most of all, Illinois' history of machine politics has led to public corruption, just as Richard Winters's study predicts. As Winters demonstrates, machine politics has led to a continuation of the culture of corruption. It has flourished within the dominant individualistic culture of Illinois' earliest settlers, who saw politics as a marketplace in which individuals and groups profit from government. This individualistic culture led to the establishment of a political-party machine in Chicago in 1871 and later throughout the state. The individualistic culture and institution of machine and machine-like political parties spawned a history of public corruption. This continuing corruption begat the culture of corruption that we are still struggling to eliminate.

A Brief History of Illinois State Corruption

Politics in the state of Illinois predates Chicago's pattern of corruption. Ninian Edwards, who served as territorial governor from 1809 to 1818 and as governor from 1826 to 1830, warned about the corrupting role of money in nineteenth-century elections. It was the common practice of the times to provide prospective voters with free whisky to win their votes.[6] He warned that the practice would "establish a school of vice and depravity. . . . All distinctions [holding higher office] will then be confined to the rich, for they alone will be able to meet the expenses of an election."[7]

There were a number of corruption scandals in the nineteenth century in Illinois. Governors and other elected state executive officials such as auditors and secretaries of state, as well as ever-eager state legislators, have engaged over the years in a great variety of corrupt practices. State executive officials have a monopoly of power; great discretion over granting jobs, contracts, and licenses; control over large sums of government money and campaign money; and a lack of accountability. Too many state officials over the decades have used their power to gain personal wealth. Their corruption encouraged lower-level, copycat corruption by state bureaucrats and local government officials. In the process, powerful state officials became not just a few "rotten apples" but helped to create the rotten-apple barrel that is Illinois politics.

As Governor Edwards feared, corruption started early. Although never indicted, Governor Joseph Duncan had legal troubles in 1841. Duncan, who resided in Brownsville and Jacksonville, Illinois, was the only Whig-party governor in the state's history. He had signed a surety bond, which made him liable for his brother-in-law, who failed to collect money for the U.S. government as he was supposed to do.

More seriously, Governor Joel Matteson from Kendall County, who served from 1853 to 1856, left office owing the state a quarter of a million dollars. While he was generally considered a good governor who contributed to the physical and economic development of the state, he was implicated in the false reissue of $224,183 in Illinois and Michigan Canal script.[8] The governor and his co-conspirators received cash for script to build the canal, which had been paid off first by a grant of land to the state from the federal government. Essentially, the state and its taxpayers paid twice for the same project, and the profits were pocketed by the governor and his allies. A lawsuit eventually recovered most of the funds, and there was no criminal trial.[9] Governor Matteson had used a sophisticated method of state funding to steal money, as would many other officials after him. The particulars of their schemes varied, and some were more sophisticated than others. His pocketing the funds from government script was the first big Illinois corruption scandal.

Corruption in Illinois became worse, not better, by the twentieth century. Charles T. Yerkes, the urban-transportation baron and Chicago grain broker, bought votes in the state legislature as well as in the Chicago city council. A journalist, mistaken for a state legislator by a nearsighted old state senator, was offered $2,500 for his vote on a Yerkes public-transportation bill.[10]

In one of the most celebrated cases of corruption in the early twentieth century, supporters of Congressman William J. Lorimer paid one hundred thousand dollars in bribes to forty lawmakers to elect him to the U.S. Senate. Newspaper records of the times show that "[b]ribes of up to $2,500 per bribed lawmaker were split between pre-vote payments and then as part of a post-session 'jackpot' of payments. . . . At the time a new Model T Ford cost $850."[11] However, in 1912, Lorimer was expelled from the U.S. Senate for winning his seat through bribery. In 1913, this scandal helped pass the Seventeenth Amendment to the U.S. Constitution, which provides for the direct election of senators—an example of the way in which corruption scandals in Illinois have led to reforms. But somehow, corruption continues. Chicago and Illinois remained well known in the twentieth century for the practice of bribing voters to vote for preferred party candidates. Stolen and rigged elections became a frequent occurrence, even when the presidency was at stake.

In the 1920s, Illinois Governor Lennington (Len) Small, a Kankakee Republican, was accused of embezzling over one million dollars in state funds. The governor was later acquitted. Not coincidentally, after his trial, four jurors received state jobs as a reward for their decision.[12]

State officials other than governors and legislators have also frequently engaged in corruption. In 1956, Illinois auditor Orville Hodge from Granite City pleaded guilty to stealing at least $1.5 million from the state. That was a huge amount of money back then. Ironically, he was responsible for auditing Illinois spending to make sure that all expenditures were legitimate.

Hodge was a tall, burly, back-slapping man who was "the model of a successful small-town businessman and politician."[13] He created a false report that his office was insolvent and convinced the legislature to provide a $525,000 emergency appropriation, which he kept for himself. In his position, he was also able to issue state "warrants" for payment to people who had done business with the state. However, they never received the payments, nor were they entitled to them. Rather, in a pattern similar to Governor Matteson's misuse of script a hundred years earlier, Hodge cashed the warrants himself. With this money he was able to purchase two private jets, thirty automobiles, and multiple properties in Illinois and Florida. For his thefts, he served six and a half years in prison. As a result, the new state constitution of 1970 abolished the office of state auditor and replaced it with the office of comptroller. None of the comptrollers elected since have been accused of fraud, much less gone to prison.[14] A number, like former state comptroller Dawn Clark Netsch, have served with distinction.

In 1965, former Governor William Stratton from Lake County was indicted but later acquitted on charges of tax evasion similar to those that convicted later Illinois politicians such as Congressman Jesse Jackson Jr. When first elected, Stratton was the youngest governor in the history of the country and was seen as a rising star in the Republican party just as Congressman Jesse Jackson Jr. would become a rising star in the Democratic party. Stratton was acquitted of failing to report $83,069 to the IRS. He claimed that the funds were campaign contributions and therefore not taxable. He spent the funds on oil paintings of himself and his second wife, a European trip for his daughter, household furniture, expensive clothes for his family, and a lodge at Centralia, Illinois. These were hardly campaign expenses, but he beat the charges in a jury trial.[15] U.S. Senator Everett Dirksen testified at the trial, citing an IRS opinion on the use of campaign contributions he had received: "I think it is a matter of donation intent. If [the donor] places no restrictions on them, then the recipient is free to use them as he sees fit. . . . If they were contributions, they would not be taxable as such."[16] Despite the clear use of the funds for personal gain rather than state benefit or legitimate campaign expenses, the jury acquitted Governor Stratton.

Although Governors Small and Stratton were indicted, and Governor Matteson had to make restitution of funds in a civil case, Governor Otto Kerner from Chicago, who succeeded Stratton, was the first Illinois governor to be convicted of corruption and serve time in prison. Kerner was convicted in 1973 on bribery, conspiracy, and income-tax evasion involving racetrack stock acquired while in office. Like other politicians of the time, he got the stock at a deep discount for providing additional racing dates and pro-racing legislation while he was governor. He was serving as a federal judge at the time of his conviction and had been the author of the famous Kerner Report on the 1968 Democratic Convention. He always maintained his innocence, declaring at his sentencing, "I shall always be satisfied that my conscience and my record of loyal and dedicated service as governor of this state were never tarnished or my integrity bought."[17]

In addition to Judge Kerner, state supreme-court judges were caught up in corruption scandals. In 1969, Illinois Supreme Court Chief Justice Roy Solfisbug from Aurora and former Chief Justice Raymond Klingbiel from East Moline were forced to resign from the court because of similar gifts of stock.[18] They received stock in a bank run by Theodore Isaacs, who made the Kerner stock arrangements. This occurred at the same time that the Illinois Supreme Court dismissed charges against Isaacs in a decision authored by Klingbiel.

Continuing the parade of convicted governors, former Governor Dan Walker from suburban Cook County was found guilty of making $1.4 million in fraudulent loans after he left office. He was the head of a savings and loan at the time.

In addition to the governors and auditors, the secretary of state's office has been frequently involved in corruption. When he died in 1970, Secretary of State Paul Powell from Vienna, Illinois, had an unexplained eight hundred thousand dollars in his hotel room! He had served in the state legislature since the 1930s, rising to become Speaker of the Illinois House of Representatives before being elected as secretary of state in 1965. The money, in one-hundred- and one-thousand-dollar bills, was found after Powell's death in his hotel apartment closet in a shoebox, two leather briefcases, and three steel strongboxes hidden behind old whisky cases and covered with old clothing. Much of this money came from state contracts awarded without competitive bidding to friends and political allies. The rest came from unrecorded campaign contributions. His gravestone is appropriately political. It reads, "Here Lies a Lifelong Democrat."[19] Perhaps an even better epitaph for Powell was his often-quoted quip, "I smell the meat a-cooking."[20] Besides being a downstate party boss, he was thoroughly corrupt.

Continuing the corruption parade, the Chicago Republican and Illinois Attorney General William Scott was also convicted in 1981 on income-tax charges involving misuse of campaign funds. Scott was once the most popular Republican in Illinois. He had made environment protection, antitrust enforcement, and consumer issues priorities in the attorney general's office, which made him popular with the voters. He was convicted of converting five thousand dollars in campaign funds for personal use and not reporting it on his income-tax returns.[21]

In one of the most serious cases of corruption, which ended in deaths as well as bribes, another secretary of state and later Kankakee Republican Governor George Ryan was convicted of racketeering, mail fraud, filing false tax returns, and lying to investigators. A fatal truck accident in 1994 led to an investigation into a scheme to trade truck operators' licenses for political contributions. The ensuing massive investigation, named Operation Safe Roads, resulted in seventy-nine people being convicted, including Ryan.

Certain patterns and trends become obvious. Both Republican and Democratic officials have been corrupt. Suburban mayors as well as Chicago aldermen have been convicted. Downstaters have engaged in corruption just like their big-city brethren. Illinois' culture of corruption has been fostered by political machines and machine-like political parties throughout the state.

Downstate Corruption

Obviously, not all corruption happens in Springfield, nor involves high-level state officials like governors. More corruption than is usually realized also occurs in smaller cities, towns, and counties. Nearly three hundred of the more than 1,913 corruption convictions since 1976 were of lower-level state officials and local government officials.

One of the most extreme cases occurred in Dixon, Illinois, where the long-time Comptroller Rita Crundwell stole $53.7 million between 1991 and 2012, at the same time that town debts multiplied and town workers were let go. She used the money to purchase a home in Florida, more than four hundred prized quarter horses, dozens of vehicles, and hundreds of pieces of jewelry. In 2010, one of her largest fraud years, Crundwell stole $5.6 million by transferring city funds into her own bank account while the town ran a $3.7 million deficit, despite personnel and expense reductions undertaken to balance the budget.[22] Due to the money she stole, there was less money for the street department and for upgrades in police radios, as well as cuts in city employees. For her crimes, the sixty-year-old comptroller was sentenced to nineteen and a half years in prison.[23]

She began working for the town in 1970, while she was still in high school, and she became comptroller/treasurer in 1983. *Forbes* reported that the accountant Joseph Petrucelli said that the problem was that Crundwell was given a monopoly of power over the town funds without accountability: "Ms. Crundwell was in a powerful position without proper oversight (she was the only signatory on an account). Twenty-two years is a long time to leave someone unchecked. While she may have once been trustworthy, it appears that she developed the perspective that she could get away with fraud and put her own self-interests ahead of the interests of others."[24]

Rita Crundwell is not the only small-town and downstate special-district official to be convicted of corruption. In Woodford County, Sheriff Bill Meyers was sent to prison in 2002 for stealing more than $233,000. Like Crundwell, he spent public money on personal items like guns, a camera, motorcycle equipment, and hotels.[25]

In Pekin, Illinois, Mayor Lynn Howard used his city credit card to obtain fraudulently $1,400 to gamble, in a case similar to that of Cook County Commissioner William Bevers. Howard was forced to resign his position as mayor in 2005, and his conviction was upheld by the state supreme court in 2007.[26]

In nearby Peoria, Benice Drake, interim director of the Peoria County Historical Society, told reporters that city officials turned "a blind eye on prohibition and gambling operations. . . . In the '20s, '30s, and '40s, we were a Las Vegas. It just wasn't legal like Las Vegas."[27]

More than two hundred miles south of Peoria, Gallatin County Sheriff Raymond Martin was found guilty in 2010 for selling marijuana from his sheriff's vehicle, drug dealing while carrying his firearm, and witness tampering for trying to hire hit men to kill a witness.[28] His wife, Kristina Martin, pleaded guilty to harassing a witness against her husband.[29]

In 2013, Madison County Treasurer Fred Bathon pleaded guilty in federal court in East St. Louis to rigging the auction of property-tax liens to benefit three securities dealers who were also contributors to his reelection campaign.[30] Bathon, a Democrat, was first elected in 1998. Shortly after he was reelected in November 2002, Bathon was criticized for nepotism for hiring his daughter as his chief deputy for sixty-two thousand dollars per year.[31] Two securities dealers and a businessman pleaded guilty to conspiring with Bathon to fix at 18 percent, a very high rate, the fee that property owners would have to pay to redeem property liens.[32]

In Edwardsville, the seat of Madison County, the chief of police, James Bedell, pleaded guilty in federal court to embezzling $138,600 from a police-department lock box in 2013. The box contained fees paid by vehicle owners whose cars had been impounded for various violations.[33] He had to resign his position, pay restitution of $138,600, and serve eighteen months in prison.[34]

Corruption in Springfield

The state legislature has also been involved in various bribery schemes. Over the last forty years, nineteen state legislators have been convicted of corruption. Most recently, four state legislators have been on trial. They are State Senator Donne Trotter and State Representatives LaShawn Ford, Derrick Smith, and Connie Howard.

Senator Trotter tried to board a plane at O'Hare Airport with a loaded Beretta handgun and was arrested and charged with a felony. He claimed to have worked at a part-time security job and said that he forgot that the weapon was in his garment bag. He had also failed to report his second job on economic-disclosure forms. Senator Trotter is chairman of the Senate Appropriations

Committee and a major political figure on the South Side of Chicago. At the time of his arrest in 2012, he was running for the Second Congressional District seat vacated by Jesse Jackson Jr. The arrest forced Trotter to drop out of the election. The judge accepted his guilty plea to reckless conduct, a misdemeanor. He received a sentence of community service, court supervision, and a fine.[35] But in the process he lost his chance to run for Congress.

LaShawn Ford was accused of lying about his income to Shore Bank in order to get a $1.5 million loan for his business and then using some of those funds to cover personal expenses.[36] He had the 17 felony counts dismissed, but pleaded guilty to filing a false federal tax return.

Derrick Smith was charged with the more garden-variety corruption of attempting to extort a seven-thousand-dollar bribe in exchange for a letter of support for a day-care center's fifty-thousand-dollar state-grant application. The prosecutor said, "Smith made it clear he wanted the bribe in cash, not a cashier's check, saying, 'I don't want no trace of it. . . . ' He also said he wanted to 'keep . . . everything clean,' even making sure that the people providing the bribe wouldn't see him turning over the money."[37]

Based upon the indictment and the wiretap evidence, Smith was impeached and expelled from the General Assembly, only to be reelected handily in the November 2012 election. He was the first member of the state house to be expelled in 107 years. In the debate to expel Smith, State Representative Barbara Flynn Currie declared, "Using one's office for personal gain, not for the public good, is an affront to the core reputation of every legislator. To act in this way [to solicit and accept the bribe] is, to me, a stunning violation of the oath of office each of us has promised to uphold."[38]

Party leaders backed Smith in the Democratic primary in the belief that he would then resign, and they would be able to replace him. However, after he won 77 percent of the vote in the primary election, he refused to resign. He went on to win the general election with 63 percent of the vote, despite opposition by some Democratic party officials and all of the mass media. Illinois voters are often very forgiving of corrupt politicians. When he ran for reelection in March 2014, Derrick Smith was defeated in the Democratic primary. He was convicted of bribery in June 2014.[39]

After she resigned, State Representative Connie Howard pleaded guilty to skimming tens of thousands of dollars from her charity golf outing for personal and political use.[40]

In 2013, New York had a major scandal in their state legislature. More than thirty-two New York state officials have gotten into deep trouble over a very few years, including four former Senate majority or minority leaders. However, New Yorkers can always point to worse examples from Illinois. "'We used to say—thank God for Illinois,' said Gerald Benjamin, a former Albany hand who is now an executive at the State University of New York in New Paltz."[41] It is part of the shame of Illinois that officials in other states take solace that Illinois is worse than the corruption in their cities and states.

Patterns in State Corruption

As the accounts of some of the more visible and egregious cases of state corruption demonstrate, several general patterns of corruption emerge. A repeating pattern is to use grants and contracts to gain campaign contributions, kickbacks, and bribes from businesses and businesspeople. Small bribes can be readily understood in simple cases like Paul Powell's. But as more and more money is needed to fund ever more expensive campaigns, the "pay to play" method of coercing contributions becomes more essential. Lorimer's supporters paid one hundred thousand dollars to legislators to buy his seat in the U.S. Senate at the beginning of the twentieth century. Jesse Jackson Jr.'s supporters pledged millions of dollars to Governor Blagojevich to buy a Senate seat a century later. Today's races for governor in Illinois cost more than twenty million dollars. Buying TV ads to convince voters to elect Rod Blagojevich cost a lot more than Lorimer bribing legislators. The price of corruption has gone up.

The corrupt state-grant and contract-fraud pattern continues long after big-name defendants like Ryan and Blagojevich are convicted and removed from power. At the end of 2013, at least thirteen people had been charged or convicted by U.S. prosecutors of embezzling more than sixteen million dollars from the state treasury in a variety of contract and state grant schemes.[42]

Another common way that has been used to steal money from the state is to issue fake warrants or script, effectively a state IOU, which the office holders then cash for themselves. It is fancier than simply taking money from the till. Some of these schemes can be very subtle and elaborate, even though there are simpler ways to steal state funds. Governor Joel Matteson and State Auditor Orville Hodge used more elaborate methods. As far as we know, officials throughout the state are no longer using fake warrants, but they have simply moved on to other schemes, like Comptroller Crundwell depositing government funds in her own bank accounts.

A common third method of corruption is the theft of campaign contributions. While the donations have been obtained legally, the candidates or office holders use the funds to pay for personal expenses, as Governor Stratton, Attorney General Scott, Congressman Jackson, Cook County Commissioner Beavers and many others have. Since campaign funds aren't government funds, some officials think of them as their own private piggy bank that they can spend on jewelry, airplanes, cars, or homes as they want. Usually they don't pay taxes on these funds, which often leads to their tax-evasion convictions in federal court.

Conclusion

As shown in Table 3.1, Illinois is the third most corrupt state in the nation.[43] A public-opinion poll of one thousand respondents across the country taken in 2012 by Jim Nowlan shows that the American public correctly identifies Illinois as a corrupt state. One-third of all those surveyed and 45 percent of those over thirty-five years old identified Illinois, unsolicited, as one of the most corrupt states in the nation.[44] Our corrupt reputation is bad for business. In another Nowlan survey in 2011, three-fourths of seventy economic-development professionals surveyed said that "corruption in Illinois had a negative impact on their business recruiting."[45]

There are tangible costs to corruption. It is estimated that corruption in Illinois costs taxpayers as much as five hundred million dollars a year. Worst of all, corruption undermines faith in government. A Gallup public-opinion poll found that only 28 percent of Illinois citizens trust their state government.

Table 3.1 Total Federal Public Corruption Convictions by State 1976–2012

Rank for Convictions Total	State	Convictions 1976–2012	Convictions Per Year
1	New York	2,631	71
2	California	2,498	67.5
3	**Illinois**	**1,913**	**52**
4	Florida	1,865	50.5
5	Texas	1,742	47
6	Pennsylvania	1,597	43
7	Ohio	1,454	39
8	District of Columbia	1,101	29.5
9	New Jersey	978	26.5
10	Louisiana	965	26

This is the lowest level of citizen trust in state government in the country. By contrast, 72 percent of Texans trust their state government.[46]

As Jim Nowlan describes, it undermines citizens' and officials' sense of political efficacy: "Why apply for a city or state job if you think that only friends of political insiders will be hired anyway? Why report corrupt officials if you think they won't be punished and that the system may turn the powers of government on you instead? Voters may laugh at times at the antics of corrupt public officials but in the end they feel powerless, lose faith in their government and vote less often because they believe the 'fix is in.'"[47] This corruption is pervasive, infecting all levels of government. While public attitudes have changed from an easy tolerance of corruption, and incremental reforms have been adopted, there is much still to be done if Illinois corruption is to be curbed.

In his more than thirty-five-year political career, Edward "Fast Eddie" Vrdolyak's shady activities were investigated numerous times, but he always avoided indictment. That ended in 2008 when the former alderman pleaded guilty to conspiring to take a bogus finder's fee in a corrupt real-estate deal with Blagojevich's crony Stuart Levine. *Photo by Paul Merideth*.

CHAPTER 4

Aldermanic Corruption

WHILE PUBLIC CORRUPTION IS A PROBLEM throughout Illinois, its epicenter is Chicago and Chicago's suburbs. The six-county Chicago metropolitan region contains nearly two-thirds of the state's population, so naturally more corruption occurs there. Moreover, machine politics and corruption appeared first in Cook County and were then copied in other parts of the state. As the cases of aldermanic corruption illustrate well, machine politics provides the institutional base for corruption.

Former Alderman Edward "Fast Eddie" Vrdolyak is the poster boy for that aldermanic corruption. He is one of the colorful rogue aldermen in the tradition of "Bathhouse" John Coughlin, "Hinky Dink" Kenna, and Johnny "Da Pow" Powers from the heyday of the Council of the Gray Wolves one hundred years ago. Crooked Chicago aldermen have been media favorites and leading characters in books on public corruption because they have provided many colorful news stories, political cartoons, and history lessons.

Vrdolyak grew up working in his family bar in the Tenth Ward at the extreme southeastern corner of Chicago, a steel-mill, working-class neighborhood. He was known as "a tough street fighter" despite his University of Chicago law degree, humorous banter, and urbane exterior. He was smart, arrogant, and gregarious. As he asserted in a 1978 interview with Milton Rakove, "I don't lack for confidence. I never did that, rightly or wrongly."[1]

He fought his way to power in the Tenth Ward by first defeating the political machine's ward committeeman and taking over as head of the local Democratic party. In 1971, before he was elected alderman, his brother, Peter, and seven other men pleaded guilty to conspiracy to promote prostitution and gambling in connection with stag parties arranged at the Tenth Ward Democratic Club.[2] Fast Eddie was the Tenth Ward committeeman and president of the club at the time. From that seat of political power, he was able to elect himself alderman.

As he moved up the political ladder, he became a millionaire lawyer with his own law firm specializing in personal-injury lawsuits and was dismissively called an "ambulance chaser." In 1975, a federal grand jury investigated allegations that Alderman Vrdolyak received free work from contractors to build his two-hundred-thousand-dollar home in the ward.[3] No charges were filed. In 1990, he was censured for representing injured city workers in lawsuits against the city. In 2005, his law license was suspended for a month for concealing legal fees from a judge.[4] By the time of his conviction, he had expanded to much bigger deals than personal-injury cases.

In the 1970s, Fast Eddie was one of the city council's "young turks." He even had the audacity to imitate Mayor Richard J. Daley's fractured language behind his back, to the amusement of his fellow aldermen. Unsurprisingly, this did not endear him to the old man. Even so, like other machine aldermen, Vrdolyak had to toe the line in his council votes as long as Daley was the Boss. He, of course, put a more positive spin on his relationship with Daley: "I didn't like everything he did. But he was my friend and if he asked me to do anything in particular before I made a commitment, I would do it."[5]

After Daley's death, Jane Byrne in her race for mayor in 1979 denounced Vrdolyak as part of the "evil cabal" surrounding Daley's successor, Mayor Michael Bilandic. She revealed Fast Eddie's role in the secret meetings that set higher taxi-cab fares. But after her election, she turned to Vrdolyak and Alderman Ed Burke to run the city council for her. She went on to engineer Vrdolyak becoming the chairman of the Democratic party of Cook County—ousting the senior statesman and County Board President George Dunne, who had succeeded Richard J. Daley in this supreme political post.

Vrdolyak repaid his patron. He supported Mayor Jane Byrne in her reelection bid against State's Attorney Richard M. Daley and Congressman Harold Washington. However, Democratic party chairman Vrdolyak helped to racially polarize the election when he spoke to white precinct workers on the Northwest Side. He bluntly told them the Saturday before the February primary: "A vote for Daley is a vote for Washington. It's a two-person race. It would be the worst day in the history of Chicago if your candidate . . . was not elected. It's a racial thing. Don't kid yourself. I'm calling on you to save your city, to save your precinct. We're fighting to keep the city the way it is." When Vrdolyak's racist quote became front-page news, it rallied Washington supporters to show up and vote against Byrne. However, it also aptly summarized what the election was about: protecting the status quo politically and leaving the white power structure in control of the city.[6]

When Harold Washington became mayor in 1983, Aldermen Vrdolyak and Burke became the leaders of the faction of twenty-nine aldermen in the "Council Wars" that followed. Fast Eddie was such an unrelenting, forceful anti-Washington nemesis that the comedian Aaron Freeman dubbed him "Darth Vrdolyak," after Darth Vader of the *Star Wars* movies. In 1986, to help his preferred candidate in the upcoming aldermanic elections, Vrdolyak hired two former gang members and campaign workers so they could be paid government salaries by a city-council committee he chaired and whose budget he controlled.[7]

When Mayor Washington finally overcame Vrdolyak's forces and won city-council control through court-ordered redistricting elections in seven wards in 1986, Vrdolyak switched from the Democratic party to running for mayor on the short-lived Solidarity party in 1987. After losing that election badly, he became a Republican candidate for county office—an election he also lost. And then in a step that is unique in Chicago political history, he became chairman of the Republican party after being chairman of the Democratic party of Cook County. After all, Chicago politics isn't really about ideology or policy; it is about power and the division of spoils. Political-party labels only denote which political machine is in power. Republican and Democratic party machines have ruled Chicago in different historical eras.

In general, Fast Eddie was a political opportunist. He was always portrayed as crafty and smart, if not necessarily principled. After losing these elections and switching back and forth between political parties, he left electoral politics and returned to his lucrative law practice. He also became a popular radio talk-show host in the 1990s, some twenty years after he began his aldermanic career.

But he continued to be a deal-maker. Throughout the decades he was investigated many times and called before several grand juries, but prior to 2007 he avoided being convicted or indicted for corruption, in spite of frequent media stories that suggested he was politically corrupt. He even became the lawyer representing the town of Cicero, the most corrupt Chicago suburb since the days Al Capone and the mob took it over after they were run out of Chicago. In 2003, while representing Cicero, Vrdolyak privately had a silent interest in the development of the town's Sportsman's Park, a well-known track for horse and auto racing. In a court filing, Vrdolyak was accused of operating on both sides of a potential half-billion-dollar development. The deal collapsed, and no charges were filed.[8]

In April 2008, according to the *Chicago Tribune,* the power broker and deal maker Stuart Levine testified in another trial, not Vrdolyak's, that he, Levine, paid bribes through Fast Eddie to gain city contracts, used Vrdolyak and bribes to obtain contracts for his insurance firm from the Chicago Board of Education, and on behalf of Vrdolyak funneled money from straw contributors to political candidates.[9]

Despite these previous allegations, what finally tripped up Vrdolyak was a real-estate sale in a trendy Near North shopping and dining area. Most aldermen who have been convicted since 1970—twenty-six of the thirty-three convicted aldermen and former aldermen—were found guilty of bribery, extortion, conspiracy, or tax-fraud schemes that essentially extracted bribes from builders, developers, or business owners. The Vrdolyak scheme differs from the general pattern in the magnitude of the sale and in that he was no longer alderman. He was to profit from a shared commission from a crooked sale of a building, the Dr. Scholl School of Podiatric Medicine. It was being sold for fifteen million dollars to a condominium developer. Another politically connected lawyer, Stuart Levine, was involved. Levine was a trustee of the Chicago medical school that owned the property. He conspired with Vrdolyak to arrange the sale using his position as trustee in exchange for a kickback from the $1.5 million dollars (10 percent of the sale price) that Vrdolyak was to get for arranging the sale.[10]

While Vrdolyak, until convicted, declared his innocence, he believed in doing business—his political and law business—the old-fashioned "Chicago way." "'That's the way life is,' he said in 1974. 'You do for one, he does for you.'" He also said, "If you're good to people, they reciprocate. They send business your way. So you get jobs for people. That's the way it's done. Me—it's the only place these people can go. I'm the committeeman, alderman, father confessor, cop, lawyer, employment agency. Me. I'm the man."[11] In the end, "the man" was convicted of felony conspiracy fraud for his role in the real-estate kickback scheme. At first he received only probation and a small fifty-thousand-dollar fine instead of prison time. After the prosecution appealed, he was sentenced to ten months in prison and fined $250,000.[12]

Corruption in the Council of the Gray Wolves

Vrdolyak was hardly the first alderman to be convicted of corruption. The history of public corruption in the Chicago city council goes as far back as 1869, when Chicago was growing rapidly. The growth and disorder provided ample opportunities. This time was characterized by several corruption cases in the city, including a city-council ring of aldermen on the take known as McCauley's Nineteen. These aldermen and their county-commissioner allies were involved in a city-hall contract scandal, as described in the first chapter. Of the fourteen aldermen and public officials indicted in that scandal, four were convicted, and several lost reelection bids in the 1871 elections.

Other historical examples of brazen corruption include two aldermen who ruled Chicago's First Ward from the late nineteenth century until the 1940s. (In this period, there were thirty-five wards, each of which was represented by two aldermen.) First Ward Alderman "Bathhouse" John Coughlin won election in 1892, and his fellow First Ward Alderman "Hinky Dink" Mike Kenna was first elected in 1897. As they were reelected for decades and delivered the vote for party candidates, they came to control police, zoning, prostitution, and gambling in the city's Levee District along the Chicago River for decades. Along the way they enriched themselves and their allies. They employed extortion, personal favors, and voting fraud to stay in power. As described in chapter 2, in the First Ward, getting out the vote on election day involved saloon patrons being given a free lunch and beer to vote multiple times in different precincts.

In the 1890s, the business tycoon Charles Yerkes offered Aldermen Coughlin and Kenna a $150,000 bribe (worth more than one million dollars today) to support a fifty-year extension of his streetcar franchise. They turned him down, but not for moral reasons. Bathhouse told Mayor Carter Harrison II: "Mr. Maar, I was talkin' a while back with Senator Billy Mason and he told me, 'Keep clear of th' big stuff, John, it's dangerous. You and Mike stick to th' small stuff; there's little risk and in the long run it pays a damned sight more.' Mr. Maar, we're with you. And we'll do what we can to swing some of the other boys over." With their backing, the mayor defeated Yerkes's ordinance by a vote of 32–31 in the then-seventy-member city council.[13] And in general, Bathhouse and Hinky Dink did stick to the small corruptions in their Levee District, shaking down more than one thousand salon and brothel keepers. Of course, they were also running one of the two rings of aldermen in the council, to whom they freely distributed bribes for their votes on legislation and budgets.

The Council of the Gray Wolves' character was summed up most colorfully by one of its members, Ninth Ward Alderman Nathan T. Brenner, who said of the seventy-member council that perhaps only three were not "able and willing to steal a red-hot stove."[14]

Corruption in the Rubber Stamp Council of the Late Twentieth Century

Just as Vrdolyak epitomizes twenty-first-century aldermanic corruption on the grand scale, the Thirty-first Ward Alderman Thomas E. Keane symbolizes late twentieth-century aldermanic corruption. He was Mayor Richard J. Daley's floor leader from the 1950s until the 1970s. When he "ascended with Daley's backing to chair the Finance Committee, Tom Keane was already Daley's floor leader. The combination of the two posts made him the most influential alderman in Chicago's history."[15]

Tom Keane was born into politics in the usual Chicago way. His father, Thomas P. Keane, had served as alderman from 1931 until his death in 1945. Thomas E. Keane took over his father's Thirty-first Ward seat from 1945 until his 1974 conviction. In 1971, he won council approval of an appointed position for his son, Thomas E. Keane Jr., on the powerful Zoning Board of Appeals. And when Alderman Thomas E. Keane was sent to jail for corruption, mail fraud, and conspiracy, his wife Adeline Keane held the family aldermanic seat from 1975 until 1979, when the Keane political dynasty ended. However, he reemerged behind the scenes as an advisor to Mayor Jane Byrne. He drew the ward-redistricting map of 1981 for her, and he even regained his law license in 1984.[16]

Journalists and historians of the Daley era provide a similar description. "Keane was confident and sometimes ruthless. His brilliance was unquestioned. He grabbed for power in the city council and played a key role in dumping . . . Martin H. Kennelly as mayor in 1955, clearing the way for . . . Richard J. Daley to win the office. Keane and Daley worked well together—the mayor interested in amassing great local and national political power and Keane in becoming chairman of the important Finance Committee and floor leader of the council."[17] As Keane would later tell the journalist Mike Royko, "Daley wanted power and I wanted money; we both got what we wanted."[18] But later, Keane's greed and arrogance would bring his downfall.

The journalist Jay McMullen, who later became the husband of Mayor Jane Byrne, described Keane's powerful role in the city council this way:

> Keane is the mayor's chief City Council confidante and hatchet man. . . . As the mayor's floor leader, Keane must push administration measures through the Council, easy work considering the lopsided 38 to 12 majority that the administration can command on a party-line vote [in the 1960s]. . . . Keane conducts Council debates like a symphony director, often with an accompanying cacophony of discordant sound that leaves television viewers aghast. He confers with his cronies before each meeting at which controversial measures are coming up. They marshal their arguments and Keane parcels out little batchings of them to the men he wants to back him up in floor debate.
>
> When the voting starts, he looks over to Ald. Fred Roti (1st Ward) [who would later be convicted of corruption] and gives the signal—sometimes a mere nod of his head—on how to vote. The others follow Roti. When it is a particularly obnoxious measure presented by a Republican or independent, Keane might turn thumbs down to Roti, like some Caesar dispatching a fallen gladiator.[19]

Keane was the brightest alderman in the Chicago city council, with the possible exception of the Independent Alderman Leon Despres (Fifth Ward). But Keane was also terribly arrogant. Because of his extreme self-confidence, Keane was willing to fight it out, especially with the machine's more-than-thirty-vote majority to insure victory for his side. He knew he would win. He thought he was smart enough and experienced enough to beat anyone. And usually he was right.

But in October 1974, Keane's career ended ignobly with a conviction in federal court for mail fraud and conspiracy to commit fraud. He was charged with directing a scheme to buy tax-delinquent properties, moving ordinances through the city council to improve their value and then selling the tracts to various government agencies. He made lush profits on a 148-acre tract of prime Chicago-owned land in suburbia after pushing the sale through the council. He also got an associate a property-tax-assessment cut of $229,248 and managed an improper $2.7 million property-tax-assessment reduction for the Hyatt Regency O'Hare Hotel. He sold off a city street so that the Sears Tower could be built, for which he received a commission.[20]

Keane also used his influence to get rich in ways that might not have been totally illegal at the time. For instance, when O'Hare Airport was built, he represented several of the companies that obtained lucrative concession contracts.

Table 4.1 Convicted Chicago Aldermen1973–2013

Date Convicted	Name	Ward	Years Served	Crime
1/6/1973	Fred Hubbard*	2	1969–71	Embezzlement
4/12/1973	Joseph Jambrone*	28	1966–70	Bribery, income-tax evasion
6/25/1973	Casimir J. Staszcuk	13	1967–73	Bribery for zoning changes
10/30/1973	Joseph Potempa	23	1971–73	Extortion, mail fraud, tax evasion
9/4/1974	Frank J. Kuta*	23	1967–71	Extortion, mail fraud, tax evasion
10/9/1974	Thomas E. Keane	31	1945–74	Mail fraud, conspiracy
10/10/1974	Paul T. Wigoda	49	1959–74	Tax evasion, bribery for zoning change
3/14/1975	Donald T. Swinarski*	12	1967–72	Tax fraud
12/2/1975	Edward T. Scholl*	41	1963–73	Extortion, bribery, tax evasion
10/22/1980	Stanley Zydlo*	26	1963–79	Bribery related to fixing fire-department exam
8/23/1983	William Carothers	28	1980–83	Conspiracy, extortion
5/24/1983	Tyrone T. Kenner	3	1971–83	Bribery, extortion, fraud
12/7/1983	Louis P. Farina	36	1980–83	Conspiracy, extortion
3/19/1987	Chester Kuta*	31	1979–81	Fraud, tax evasion, civil rights violation
4/23/1987	Clifford P. Kelley	20	1971–87	Extortion, mail fraud, racketeering
10/13/1987	Wallace Davis	27	1983–87	Bribery, extortion
9/28/1989	Perry Hutchinson*	9	1983–87	Bribery, insurance fraud
5/1/1989	Marian Humes*	8	1977–87	Bribery
1/15/1993	Fred Roti	1	1968–93	Bribery, extortion, racketeering
1/10/1996	Ambrosio Medrano	25	1991–96	Extortion, bribery, ghost payrolling
4/17/1996	Allan Streeter	17	1981–96	Bribery, extortion
1/23/1997	Joseph A. Martinez*	31	1981–83	Ghost payrolling
6/16/1997	Jesse Evans	21	1987–97	Extortion, racketeering
12/4/1998	Lawrence Bloom*	5	1979–95	Tax fraud, bribery
4/30/1998	John Madrzyk*	13	1973–94	Ghost payrolling, bribery, extortion
1/28/1999	Virgil Jones	15	1991–99	Bribery
11/9/1999	Percy Z. Giles	37	1986–99	Bribery, tax evasion
8/6/2008	Arenda Troutman*	20	1990–2007	Mail fraud, tax fraud
2/1/2010	Isaac Carothers	29	1999–2010	Tax fraud, bribery for zoning change
3/21/2013	William Beavers*	7	1983–2006	Tax evasion
2/29/2013	Sandi Jackson	7	2007–13	Filing false tax returns
9/24/2013	Ambrosio Medrano*	25	1991–96	Wire Fraud

Indicted and convicted of acts unrelated to service

4/9/1997	Joseph Kotlarz	35	1983–92	Theft by deception
6/13/2006	James Laski	23	1990–95	Bribery, mail fraud, wire fraud
11/3/2008	Edward R. Vrdolyak	10	1971–87	Conspiracy to commit mail and wire fraud

Table 4.1 Continued

Date Convicted	Name	Ward	Years Served	Crime
Indicted but died before trial				
1974	Mathew J. Danaher*	11	1964–68	Conspiracy to defraud, accepting bribes Died 12/15/1974
1992	William C. Henry	24	1983–91	Extortion, racketeering, mail fraud Died 5/7/1992
1995	Anthony Laurino	39	1975–94	Ghost payrolling Died 3/25/1999

*Indicates aldermen who were indicted or convicted after their aldermanic service ended. In most cases the criminal acts began while they were alderman.
SOURCES: *Chicago Tribune, Chicago Sun-Times, Chicago Defender,* and Chicago Public Library.

The Republican state's attorney Ben Adamowski charged that "[t]he airport was being run as a private concession for Tom Keane."[21]

When Keane was sent to jail, Mayor Richard J. Daley stood by him, saying, "I've known him for many years. He represents one of the finest families. I know his wife and children. I'm shocked that anything like this could happen."[22] He skipped over the part about Tom Keane being corrupt and stealing from the citizens of Chicago.

The Pattern of Aldermanic Corruption

Specific aldermanic crimes have differed over the last century and a half, but there is an underlying pattern, as demonstrated in table 4.1. The guilty aldermen include bumblers and some of the most brilliant politicians of their eras, such as the real-estate manipulators Tom Keane and "Fast Eddie" Vrdolyak.

In the past forty years, a total of thirty-three Chicago aldermen have been convicted of federal crimes such as bribery, extortion, embezzlement, conspiracy, mail fraud, and income-tax evasion. Alderman Ambrosio Medrano was convicted for three different corruption schemes, once in 1996 and twice in 2013. Three additional aldermen were indicted for similar offenses, but two died before federal prosecutors could bring them to trial, and one, Anthony Laurino (Thirty-ninth Ward), was too sick to stand trial. Several other aldermen, who were not indicted but were targets of news-media investigations, resigned their positions after the public learned of their questionable behavior. One was Eleventh Ward Alderman Pat Huels, Mayor Richard M. Daley's Bridgeport alderman. He was forced to step down after the media disclosed that he took loans for his private security firm from a politically connected trucking contractor whom he had helped to get city contracts. Aldermen taking loans from city contractors would later be made illegal under an amendment to the city's ethics ordinance.

Of the thirty-three convicted aldermen since 1970, three were Republicans and twenty-nine were Democrats. Vrdolyak is more difficult to categorize: he was a Democrat, a Solidarity party mayoral candidate, and then a Republican party chairman. Thus, his party label was a matter of convenience and remains ambiguous. Most aldermen in the last forty years have been Democrats of one stripe or another, and therefore, most convicted aldermen have also been Democrats.

Although aldermen run for office in nonpartisan elections, nearly all of these convicts were products of the vaunted Cook County Democratic organization machine. The exceptions were the three Republicans plus Lawrence Bloom (Fifth Ward) and Fred Hubbard (Second Ward), both of whom were Democrats but were independent of the machine. Hubbard ran for election as an independent, but almost immediately after taking office, he was embraced and co-opted by Mayor Richard J. Daley's administration. However, Bloom remained an independent and a strong ally of Mayor Washington. The large majority of convicted Democratic aldermen held political patronage positions before they were appointed or slated for election.

If you set aside the Democratic-machine identity, the class of convicted aldermen approaches real diversity. Four of the thirty-three are women; sixteen are African American and nineteen Caucasian; two are Hispanic or Latino. Among the Caucasians, two are Jewish, five have Polish ancestry, three Italian, one Irish, one Lithuanian, and one had Croatian ancestors.

An extraordinary case involved a father and son, with the son inheriting the aldermanic seat when the father went to jail. They were both convicted of essentially the same crime. William Carothers was alderman of the Twenty-eighth Ward when he was indicted for extorting office-remodeling work from a contractor at a local hospital, accepting bribes to get patronage jobs for constituents, and a cash bribe from nursing-home operators for help with health-code violations.[23] His son and successor, Twenty-eighth Ward Alderman Isaac Carothers, accepted cash to help a businessman win lucrative airport-concessions contracts. He also accepted bribes of forty thousand dollars in home repairs for pushing through a zoning change for a developer, nearly the same type of remodeling bribe for which his father had been convicted two decades earlier.[24]

After he got out of jail, Isaac Carothers sought unsuccessfully to run for the Cook County Board of Commissioners, but he lost his 2014 election bid.[25]

Another curious case is that of Ambrosio Medrano (Twenty-fifth Ward). He is the only alderman in Chicago's long corrupt history to be convicted three times for different corruption schemes. He was convicted first in the 1990s in Chicago's infamous Silver Shovel federal probe, in which he took a bribe from a federal mole posing as a businessman. Then in 2013 he was convicted again, this time of plotting to bribe a Los Angeles County public official to obtain a government contract for a mail-order drug contract for business colleagues. Finally, he was convicted for a third time for a scheme with County Commissioner Joseph Moreno to sell bandages to public hospitals, including Cook County's Stroger Hospital. As the prosecutors put it, Alderman Medrano is "incorrigibly corrupt."[26] After serving his first prison sentence, Medrano unsuccessfully attempted to regain his Twenty-fifth Ward aldermanic seat. He is famous for saying on tape, "Hogs get slaughtered, pigs get fat." He strove to be a pig, not a hog, in his corruption, but he was caught and convicted three times. For his latest convictions, he was sentenced to ten and a half and two and a half years, respectively.[27]

There also is some diversity in the occupations and career paths that the lawbreakers took prior to becoming alderman. A large number were lawyers. But one was a union official, and others included a community organizer, postal worker, school teacher, insurance salesman, sports editor, and campaign consultant. Four of the rogue aldermen were small businessmen.

Real estate and law, two fields often considered ideal for attracting "clean graft," provided opportunities—legal and illegal—for twelve of the perpetrators. Four were real-estate brokers or salesmen, and seven were attorneys. At least one practiced both of these professions, and another one had a law degree but never practiced law.

The most traveled route of convicted alderman was up through the ranks of political machines. A total of twenty of the aldermen who got caught had previously held patronage jobs with the City of Chicago, Cook County, or the State of Illinois.

In most cases, the Chicago political machine taught the crooked aldermen, in one way or another, the fine art of graft. These men—only 11 percent were women—were schooled in the importance of political campaigns and precinct election work. They understood the connection between patronage jobs and the political work that got them their jobs. On their way up through the ranks, they learned the importance of political fund-raising dinners and events. They bought tickets and sold tickets. They watched as precinct captains who turned out the highest votes for party candidates got promoted to better jobs. They noticed when ward bosses placed their sons, daughters, and other relatives on the city payroll. They petitioned their aldermen to get traffic tickets fixed for constituents or to get shoplifting charges against a neighbor's teenager dropped. They saw political officials amass power and get rich over time by playing the game, keeping quiet, and delivering votes and campaign funds for the party.

They came to know what was going on in front of their noses in their own ward organizations. They could easily extrapolate to the other forty-nine wards. What they didn't see, or rarely saw, was anyone getting caught. All sorts of infractions and abuses were never or rarely punished by supervisors or department bosses. Heads only rolled if the news media got involved. In these cases, the offenders were often severed from the payroll only to reappear later in other, less-visible patronage positions. The Cook County state's attorney or Illinois attorney general almost never investigated or prosecuted political corruption. The few exceptions were on the rare occasions when Republicans held those offices—an increasingly rare occurrence in recent years.

The task of rooting out and prosecuting political corruption was left to the U.S. Attorneys, postal inspectors, the FBI, and IRS agents. The U.S. Attorneys for the Northern District of Illinois have prosecuted thirty-four Chicago aldermen and former aldermen in the past forty years. Thirty-three were either convicted by a jury or pleaded guilty to charges. Only one in four decades, Alderman Rafael "Ray" Frias, was found not guilty. Three others were indicted but died before they could be tried.

The total list of all convicted aldermen is too lengthy to discuss in detail. Here are some examples beyond the ones already discussed. Stanley Zydlo resigned as Twenty-sixth Ward alderman some eighteen months before he pleaded guilty in 1980 to paying a thousand-dollar bribe to fix the firefighters' test for two relatives. Joseph Martinez (Thirty-first Ward) pleaded guilty to illegally receiving more than ninety thousand dollars in wages and benefits for doing little or no work as a ghost payroller on three city-council committees after he lost a reelection bid. John Madrzyk (Thirteenth Ward) also pleaded guilty to ghost payrolling, placing his daughter in a "no-show" job with the Committee of Special Events, which he chaired. He pleaded guilty as well to receiving kickbacks from two other individuals he placed in ghost jobs. Madrzyk also admitted that he accepted payment for helping people obtain zoning changes and favorable results from city inspections.

Almost all—twenty-six of thirty-three convicted aldermen—were guilty of bribery, extortion, conspiracy, or tax fraud involving schemes to extract bribes from builders, developers, or business owners. That has been the main pattern of aldermanic corruption going back to the days of the famous Council of the Gray Wolves. Businesspeople often have been willing accomplices and abettors. The bribe payers either were told or assumed that payment was necessary to receive zoning changes, building permits, or similar city action. Usually the tax-evasion or tax-fraud charges on which they were technically convicted stemmed from the failure to report income from these bribes.

In current parlance, such bribery-extortion schemes are labeled "pay to play," but it's an old game. Sometimes an envelope stuffed with cash is handed directly to an alderman, and sometimes it's picked up by an aide. These days, the payment often comes in the form of a campaign contribution. But regardless of how payment is made, there usually are no willing witnesses and no hard evidence that the payment was made in exchange for specific official actions. The bribe payer and the recipient have reasons to keep quiet and to hide any evidence of the transaction. It is extremely difficult to prove the "quid pro quo."

Friends and supporters of some convicted aldermen point to the pared-down charges to argue "he only took a five-hundred-dollar gift," or "he was only guilty of one tax charge." Sometimes they argue that these are only petty crimes. They leave unsaid their belief that political corruption is not a serious matter that must be corrected.

Many convicted aldermen have been involved in many acts of graft, corruption, and payoffs over the years. Aldermen like Tom Keane and "Fast Eddie" Vrdolyak became millionaires not only by their legal law-office activities but also by unethically exploiting their conflicts of interest and by highly profitable corruption schemes. The same was true of earlier rich aldermen like the known crook "Bathhouse" John Coughlin.

If you look at the indictments as well as the convictions, and study the charges, the number of people involved—underlings, relatives, business associates—and the fact that these crimes continue to occur over a long period of time, it is clear that in Chicago and in Illinois there is a thriving culture of corruption. Accepting the evidence of a culture of corruption can only lead to the realization that major changes are needed. The problem won't be solved by piecemeal measures. It will require a comprehensive effort over decades to change the political culture in which we have been mired for over a century and a half.

Lessons from Aldermanic Corruption

Aldermanic corruption has been at the center of Chicago's and Illinois' culture of corruption since the first court case in 1869. As we have seen, this is because aldermen occupy the nexus between machine politics and government. The vast majority of aldermen have worked their way up from precinct captain to government employee to alderman. Earlier in Chicago history, they were as likely to be part of the Republican party machine as the Democratic party machine. But as the Democrats gained dominance after the Great Depression and consolidated their hold on Chicago during the reign of Richard J. Daley, more Democrats than Republicans were convicted of corruption. In fact, the last convicted Republican alderman was Edward Scholl in 1975. When this book was written in 2014, not a single Republican was serving in the Chicago city council. There are no longer Republican aldermen to be corrupted.

In the past, the usual aldermanic convictions were for what Coughlin correctly characterized as "the little stuff." The most common offense was taking about a five-hundred-dollar bribe to fix a zoning case or grant a building permit to a developer. For those with the ambitions for higher office, such as Fifth Ward Alderman Larry Bloom, who was running for state's attorney, bribes in the form of campaign contributions were greater than ten thousand dollars. And for the big-time lawyer/aldermen like Tom Keane and "Fast Eddie" Vrdolyak, bribes and kickbacks were much more substantial, sometimes involving more than a million dollars.

Even when not convicted of corruption, smart aldermen like Ed Burke are able to parlay their clout into legal fees that make them millionaires. They practice what the New York City party boss George Washington Plunkitt called "honest graft."[28] And as long as aldermen have the political clout to control zoning, licenses, permits, property-tax reductions, city contracts, and patronage jobs, corruption will continue to send aldermen to prison.

Nonetheless, things are changing down at city hall for the better. When Mayor Harold Washington was elected in 1983, he signed the first freedom-of-information ordinance allowing citizens, media reporters, and reform organizations access to some of the government information needed to curb corruption.

Over the last several decades, the laws regarding freedom of information have improved access. Mayor Washington also appointed an Ethics Commission, and in 1987, the first ethics ordinance in Chicago's history was adopted.

During Mayor Richard M. Daley's twenty-two-year reign, various corruption scandals caused the ethics ordinance to be amended with more stringent restrictions. More significantly, because of the continuing scandals, Daley began appointing former assistant U.S. attorneys as city inspectors general. Those inspectors general began to investigate and curb corruption in new ways—issuing reports to the public, recommending employee sanctions and prosecutions, and uncovering waste and inefficiencies.

In the same time period, former Alderman James Laski, who would himself be convicted of corruption, was elected city clerk and created a very useful Web site. His city clerk's site provides more and better information than in the past on city-council proceedings, aldermanic voting, and legislation. But the transparency added by Laski and subsequent city clerks has been insufficient to curb aldermanic corruption.

With the election of Mayor Rahm Emanuel in 2011, a chief technology officer was appointed, and city government provided a flood of information that previously was not easily available. The city's own Web site allows online access to information on city employees, lobbyists, and city contracts.

Other changes are helping to reduce corruption, sometimes inadvertently. Budget cuts, which limited new personnel hiring, and the mayor's lack of dependency on a patronage army to get elected have severely curtailed new patronage hiring. Thus, over the years, the number of patronage employees in local governments has decreased. It is presumably even less under Mayor Emanuel, whose administration has achieved "substantial compliance" with the Shakman decree and no longer requires a court-appointed lawyer to monitor its job hiring.[29]

Hope increased for better checks and balances when, in the 2011 elections, eighteen new aldermen were elected. Yet, there were not enough independent aldermen to defeat mayoral initiatives. Unfortunately, the city council has become even more of a rubber stamp. Mayor Emanuel enjoys more aldermanic support than any mayor before him, including the Boss, Richard J. Daley, and his son, Richard M. Daley. Emanuel's opposition is confined to a handful of regularly dissenting aldermen and has split into two separate caucuses rather than acting as a uniform bloc. Thus, the average level of aldermanic support for Mayor Emanuel is 93 percent on all divided roll call votes, and he has not lost a single vote since he has been mayor.[30]

Trading votes for government services, precinct work for government jobs, and campaign contributions for government contracts was accepted and incorrectly thought to be legal in the past. Moreover, it usually wasn't prosecuted. So members of the party, and especially aldermen who worked their way up through the machine, had trouble distinguishing between standard machine operating procedures and taking bribes. Machine politics thus bred corruption, nowhere more than among aldermen in the Chicago city council. Only about two hundred men and women have served as aldermen in the last forty years. So thirty-three convicted of federal crimes has produced a higher crime rate than ghetto communities in the city.

While the Chicago Democratic machine has weakened, it has not disappeared. It lives especially at the ward and precinct levels. And until the grip of machine politics is broken, too many aldermen will be corrupted and corruptible. Unfortunately, the Chicago political machine is not yet, as Mayor Harold Washington declared three decades ago, "dead, dead, dead."[31]

Ambrosio Medrano served as State's Attorney Richard M. Daley's administrative assistant. In 1989, he was Hispanic coordinator for Daley's successful mayoral campaign. Medrano was elected alderman in 1991 and served until 1996, when he pleaded guilty to accepting bribes and arranging ghost payrolling jobs. In 2013, he was convicted twice more in separate bribery cases, making him Illinois' first three-time loser. *Photo courtesy of Sun-Times Media.*

CHAPTER 5

Chicago City Haul

PUBLIC CORRUPTION IN CHICAGO has a long history, dating from the first scandal involving Chicago aldermen and Cook County commissioners in the 1860s. Often, elected officials such as Governor Rod Blagojevich, Alderman "Fast Eddie" Vrdolyak, or Congressman Dan Rostenkowski attract the most media and public attention, but the legion of appointed officials at city hall, the County Building, suburban city halls, and the state capitol carry out more pervasive levels of patronage, nepotism, machine politics, and corruption.

We begin with the cautionary tale of the former Chicago alderman and city clerk James Laski, who relates how machine politics drew him into a corrupt contract deal. In a similar way, many machine minions get drawn into corrupt actions in their everyday government jobs. Laski was an up-and-coming politician who had won citywide election as city clerk—still young, handsome, well-liked, and energetic. Back at the end of the twentieth century, there was talk that maybe he might even become the mayor after Daley.

Laski had been a law student when he joined the Regular Democratic party and worked his precinct as a precinct captain. Then, he became the alderman's successor. Later, he moved up the political ladder. As city clerk, he kept the official city-council records and sold motor-vehicle registration stickers.

In his book, mostly written during his prison stay, Laski describes his role in the Hired Truck scandal in which he accepted bribes from a trucking company to obtain crooked city contracts for trucks the city didn't even need.

I was campaigning for City Clerk at that time, and one day, [his friend and precinct captain] Mick [Jones] told me about a program he was interested in for himself and his partners. At that point in my life, I had known Mick Jones for over sixteen years. ... [Mick] told me that the city had a Hired Truck Program that employed private trucking companies to work for various city departments. ...

That following week, I had an appointment with Alderman Pat Huels, who was not only chairman of the transportation committee, but the mayor's number one guy. If anyone needed anything from the mayor and his office, Alderman Huels was the one to see. ...

After the pleasantries, I asked Pat about the Hired Truck Program, and told him I had a very good friend who was interested in being part of the program. I also told him that this would be a personal favor to me if he could put some of Mick's trucks on the payroll. When I finished, the alderman answered nonchalantly, "No problem." ...

It wasn't long after the trucks were on, maybe a month or so, that Mick stopped by the house one evening. ... Before too long, he leaned over to shake my hand, and said, "Take care of the family."

As I extended my hand and we shook, I knew, though we never spoke about it in any detail, he had just handed me money—how much, I didn't know. As soon as we transferred the money, I quickly put it in my pocket. During the course of the evening, Mick used my bathroom, and I went into my pocket and counted five $100 bills. I knew at this point that we were starting a wonderful, but illegal, business relationship, because this was technically bribery. However, I told myself the money wasn't for me, but for my family—my loved ones.[1]

In the introduction, we discussed theories of corruption that are relevant to the kind of bureaucratic corruption—the day-to-day stealing from the taxpayers—that takes place in Chicago government. As Rasma Karklins explains in *The System Made Me Do It!*, corruption occurs with (1) the everyday interactions between officials and citizens; (2) interactions within government, such as patronage, nepotism, and favoritism; and (3) influence over political institutions, such as when machine and machine-like political parties take over government. All three levels of corruption occur at Chicago's city hall.[2]

This chapter also vividly illustrates Robert Klitgaard's theory that "illicit behavior flourishes when agents have monopoly power over clients ... great discretion, and [weak] accountability."[3] Multiple corruption schemes at city hall, like the Hired Truck scam, show that when city employees have the power to grant contracts and licenses, along with discretion to rig bids and let no-bid contracts with little supervision or accountability, then corruption will abound. So it was with Jim Laski and hundreds of other city-hall bureaucrats who saw their opportunity to profit illegally and took it.

Most of all, the examples of corruption in this chapter illustrate the principal theory that animates this book. The individualistic political culture that pervaded Illinois since its founding has begat machine and machine-like political parties. Machine politics has enabled the takeover of city hall and other Illinois governments over time. This has created a history of political corruption that, in turn, begat the culture of corruption that still exists today.

In chapter 2 we discussed the connection between political machines and the rigged and sometimes stolen elections that granted them the keys to city hall and the state house. In chapter 3 we gave examples of corruption at the highest levels of state government. In chapter 4 we provided a detailed analysis of more than thirty aldermen and former aldermen convicted of public corruption since 1970. In this chapter we tell of some other major scandals at city hall. These corruption schemes resulted in hundreds of convicted individuals and the loss of hundreds of millions of dollars.

Many of the corruption cases in Illinois center around Chicago City Hall, or as some journalists call it, "Chicago City Haul." These abuses nearly always lead back to the Chicago Democratic machine.

The first political machine was created by Michael Casius MacDonald after the Chicago Fire of 1871. His style of machine politics was modernized under Mayor Anton Cermack in the 1930s, Richard J. Daley in the 1950s, and Richard M. Daley at the birth of the new millennium. All of these political machines, from the nineteenth century to the twenty-first, run on patronage jobs, crony contracts, and government services delivered as favors.

All political parties seek to control the government by electing their candidates to office. Under Richard J. Daley, the party provided city services (in the form of favors such as getting a tree trimmed, extra garbage pickup, street repair, getting your kid out of jail, or fixing a parking ticket) in return for a family voting for the party's candidates at election time. In Chicago, loyal Democrats got better services than Republicans or Independents. The political machine also provided patronage jobs with the city, county, or state government for party precinct workers who delivered a strong vote for party candidates.

The third essential component of machine politics was money. Businesses and businesspeople who gave campaign contributions to the mayor and the Democratic party were rewarded with city government contracts. Of course, these contracts at inflated rates yielded a substantial profit. Business contributors to the party also got help with zoning changes, building permits, and licenses to operate their businesses.

Under Richard M. Daley, favors, jobs, and contracts continued, but they were distributed differently. Instead of giving out jobs to precinct captains through the party ward committeemen, city-hall jobs were given to those who worked for Daley's own political organizations, such as the Hispanic Democratic Organization. And while some businesses still received rigged city contracts, much of Daley's campaign contributions now came from global businesses, law firms, and financial institutions that didn't want to sell widgets to city hall. Rather, these businesspeople wanted certain policies and conditions, such as a safe, beautiful city with cultural amenities for executives, professionals, and business clients from abroad. They wanted policies that promoted Chicago as a global city and a world-class tourist attraction. So the old-style machine politics was upgraded to a twenty-first-century political machine.

Machine politics inevitably leads to public corruption, because if government workers have been trading favors for votes, jobs for precinct work, and contracts for campaign contributions, they can't tell the ethical difference between these exchanges and taking bribes for government services or for fixing contracts. Machine politics inevitably feeds a culture of corruption in government and among the public.

Despite new ethics laws and inspectors general to investigate corruption, it continues at city hall. We begin with two scandals that are emblematic of political corruption in Chicago government during the Richard M. Daley era: the Hired Truck corrupt-contract scandal investigations, in which Laski was involved, followed by the Robert Sorich trial. The Sorich trial exposed the extent of Chicago-style patronage hiring. Patronage continued even though it had been outlawed by court agreements and decrees. Subsequent scandals and court cases exposed ghost payrolling, bribery, ties to the mob, and fake women and minority companies bidding for city contracts.

Hired Trucks

Problems with the city's Hired Truck program go back to at least 1992. The City's Fleet Management Department decided that rather than purchase enough trucks and staff them with permanent truck drivers for seasonal efforts, like winter snow removal or summer asphalt paving, it was better to lease the trucks as needed from private trucking firms. In principle, this made sense as a way to save taxpayers' money. But no-bid contracts for leasing the trucks were given to political insiders. For instance, the department's records show that from 1992 to 1997, Michael Tadin, a friend of Daley's, received more than fifty million dollars' worth of city truck-leasing business.

The costly Hired Truck program did not cause major scandals until the *Chicago Sun-Times* published its "Clout on Wheels" series in January 2004.[4] Investigative reporters documented that privately owned dump trucks and drivers were paid under no-bid contracts even though they often sat idle all day, doing no work. Follow-up stories documented that the forty-million-dollar-per-year program involved payoffs, sweetheart deals, connections to organized crime, and ties to Daley's family and friends. Money for the leased trucks went to fifteen firms owned by mobsters or their families. It was estimated that the program resulted in ten to fifteen million dollars stolen each year for at least ten years.

Some of this easy money went to political cronies and to trucking companies in the Eleventh Ward, who in return over a ten-year period gave $840,000 in campaign contributions to the mayor and other politicians.[5] For seven years the program was run by key members of the Hispanic Democratic Organization, a political army that operated across ward boundaries to elect candidates backed by the mayor.[6]

Following the huge public outcry about hired trucks, Mayor Daley fired his cousin from a top job in the Water Department after it was discovered that the cousin helped his mother cash in with a truck in the program.[7]

In the scandal's wake, besides firing the mayor's cousin, the city fired Angelo Torres, who ran the program. Then Bill Abolt, director of the mayor's budget office, resigned, and trucking companies were forced to reapply to keep their contracts. Later still, some firms were dropped from the program, and the city made other changes to prevent future abuse.[8]

Forty-six people were indicted in the Hired Truck scandal, and nearly all pleaded guilty or were convicted. Prosecutors first arrested Angelo Torres, who was convicted and sentenced to two years in prison for shaking down trucking-firm owners for cash. He also solicited campaign contributions for the Hispanic Democratic Organization, which supported Mayor Daley. At his sentencing hearing, Torres said, "I worked very hard in my life to get where I got, and I unfortunately abused my authority, and for that reason I am apologetic. . . . When that money came to me, I accepted it."[9] So did Laski, the forty-four others who were convicted, and many more who didn't get caught.

Numerous other city officials, particularly in the Water and Streets and Sanitation Departments, participated in the trucking scheme. The commissioner of the Water Department, Donald Tomczak, was convicted for heading up the scheme in the water department. This was a bribe scheme in which many insiders benefited until they were caught.

Patronage at City Hall

In addition to convictions of many individuals, the Hired Truck probe eventually led to the investigation of the Mayor's Office of Intergovernmental Affairs. From this office, the mayor's patronage chief Robert Sorich, his assistant Timothy McCarthy, along with the Department of Streets and Sanitation aides Patrick Slattery and John Sullivan, managed the illegal dispensing of city jobs and promotions to reward political workers in the mayor's organization.[10] All four were convicted of mail fraud as part of the patronage scheme. Sullivan was also convicted of lying to the FBI.

Patronage jobs in which government employees are hired for their political work at election time rather than their skills and ability to do government work are central to political-party machines. In this way, political parties obtain the armies of precinct workers necessary to convince voters to vote for party candidates. By winning elections, political parties gain control of the government and acquire spoils, including patronage jobs.

Despite the fact that both Republican and Democratic parties in Illinois have been dispensing patronage jobs since the nineteenth century, this practice was only seriously challenged in the 1970s with the case of *Shakman v. Democratic Organization of Cook County*.

Michael Shakman had run for Illinois Constitutional Convention delegate in 1969 in the Hyde Park neighborhood on the South Side of Chicago. His lawsuit claimed that he had been defeated in his election bid by Democratic party patronage workers and that this denied patronage employees their First Amendment rights to support whichever political candidates they chose. It also deprived voters of the right to select candidates of their choice and denied candidates a fair chance to be elected.

The court case and its successors have dragged on for more than four decades and ended in a variety of consent decrees and court decisions that permanently changed patronage politics in Chicago and throughout the country. Reforms in Illinois have often come from court cases such as the Shakman cases, Bernie Weisberg suing Secretary of State Paul Powell for equal access to the ballot, and ACLU plaintiffs suing to dismantle the Red Squad in the Chicago police department, which spied upon the machine's political opponents.

At the first stage of the Shakman case, witnesses testified that there were as many as thirty-five thousand patronage employees in local and state government in Chicago and Cook County. In the Shakman consent decree of 1972, the parties, including local and state governments and political parties, agreed that they would not fire, demote, transfer, or use other punishments for any employee who failed to support a particular political party or candidate. In short, political parties could no longer force government employees to work precincts or give campaign contributions.

In 1983, it was further agreed that it was unlawful to take any political factor into account in hiring public employees. The one exception was a small number of employees specifically exempted because of their political, policy, or administrative roles, such as department heads. Various political officials and governments signed these consent decrees, which meant that they could now be sued in federal court if they hired or fired people for political reasons.

In ordering the decision that led to the 1983 consent decree, Judge Nicolas Bua described how the patronage system worked:

> For a number of City jobs persons normally can be hired only with regular Democratic *political sponsorship*. . . . The City often informs Democratic Party officials of City job openings of which public notice is not otherwise given. Persons applying for some City patronage jobs have been told by City officials that to get a job or learn about job openings the applicant must see the Democratic Party Ward Committeeman. . . . [Patronage] employees of the City are [then] coerced into political work and support for the regular Democratic organization. This support helps the Regular Democrats win elections in the City of Chicago and Cook County. It provides them with a significant advantage in those elections.[11]

Harold Washington was the Chicago mayor who, as a reformer, signed the Shakman consent decree outlawing patronage. It was one of his first acts when he took office in 1983. He famously declared at the time that machine politics was "dead, dead, dead." The state and other local governments, such as Cook County and the Chicago Park District, have over the years also agreed to end patronage politics and signed the decrees. Over time, the number of government patronage jobs has decreased, but they have not yet entirely disappeared, even in the second decade of the twenty-first century.

A 1985 federal lawsuit, *Cynthia Rutan et al. v. The Republican Party of Illinois et al.,* led the Supreme Court of the United States in 1990 to reaffirm that patronage hiring and firing is unconstitutional, as the Shakman cases had determined earlier. In the Rutan case, the patronage employees were state- and not city-government employees. Patronage is an Illinois-wide phenomenon, not just a Chicago one. The court ruled that firings "based on political affiliation or support are an impermissible infringement of public employees' First Amendment rights." The court further ruled that "conditioning hiring decisions on political belief and association plainly constitutes an unconstitutional condition."[12]

The later criminal court case, *U.S. v. Robert Sorich, Timothy McCarthy, John Sullivan, and Patrick Slattery,* proved that patronage continued in the Richard M. Daley reign from 1989 to 2011. Part of the evidence was a "clout list" of 5,700 people recommended for hire by ward committeemen, aldermen, and other party officials. Further evidence proved that the Office of Intergovernmental Affairs (IGA), under the mayor's direct control, determined who should be hired based upon political considerations. IGA then instructed officials in each department to rig civil-service test results so that they would get hired. At the time, the city was bound by the court-sanctioned Shakman decree, which required the city to hire based upon objective criteria. The Daley administration ignored the court and illegally maneuvered around those requirements.

Robert Sorich was assistant director of the Office of Intergovernmental Affairs from 1993 to 2005. He, along with McCarthy and Slattery, coordinated the scheme, but many other city employees were involved. The federal prosecutor's proffer of evidence described the scheme this way:

> Politically connected people nominated job candidates to Sorich and McCarthy. After participating in the decision to predetermine the winners for these particular jobs, Sorich and/or McCarthy communicated with personnel directors and other employees of the Operating Departments and then provided the personnel directors with lists of preselected candidates that IGA wanted the Operating Departments to place in those positions. . . .
> Interviewers from the Operating Department then conducted sham interviews. . . . [T]he highest scores were assigned to favored candidates on the basis of their IGA designations, without regard to the Operating Department's evaluation of the candidates' relative qualifications. . . . Members of the scheme falsely signed "Shakman certificates" attesting that particular hiring sequences had not been influenced by political patronage.[13]

The Sorich case and the later convictions of former Streets and Sanitation Commissioner Al Sanchez and others were meant unequivocally to enforce the restrictions against patronage hiring. It is now clear to everyone that government employees convicted of rigging job hiring or firing and covering it up could be sentenced to federal prison.

Nepotism

On July 21, 1971, as a young, newly elected alderman, Dick Simpson rose in the Chicago city council to question Mayor Richard J. Daley's proposed appointment of Thomas Keane Jr. to the Zoning Board of Appeals. Keane was both the son of Daley's city-council floor leader and the vice president of the Arthur Rubloff Company, the largest real-estate firm in Chicago.

Simpson was hesitant to oppose this appointment because Keane's father, Alderman Thomas E. Keane, was at the time a powerful ally of Mayor Daley's. Alderman Simpson knew that opposing the son's appointment would be seen as a personal insult to Alderman Keane, who could thwart future legislation proposed by Simpson. Nonetheless, this appointment of Tom Keane Jr. was not only a case of nepotism but also favored the city's largest real-estate firm by putting their vice president on the board that directly controlled zoning. Since zoning determined the value of his firm's real-estate properties, the younger Keane's membership on the Zoning Board of Appeals was a direct conflict of interest.

In questioning Keane's appointment, Simpson said: "This appointment poses the problem of the faith of our citizenry in our city government. Why is it that members of the same family get appointments in several sections of government, and only large firms seem to get representation on boards dealing with zoning and construction?" Interrupting Simpson, Mayor Daley challenged, "Who's going to ask those questions and make those charges?" Simpson replied, "My students will." Daley countered, "And you'll encourage them."[14]

After other aldermen had spoken in Tom Keane Jr.'s defense, Daley read a sentimental poem by Grace Nowell Crowell entitled "Sons." He then launched into the longest and most emotional tirade of his colorful career. It came only three years after the 1968 Democratic National Convention and the clash between student protestors and the Chicago police.

I hope the halls of all the great educational institutions will stop being places for agitation and hatred against this society. And talk about the young people! With their cynical smiles and their fakery and polluted minds, and the idea that I made this appointment because a man's name was Keane and he was the son of a famous member of this council!

I made this appointment because I have known Tommy Keane, the boy I appointed, since he's been a baby. And I know his mother, Adeline Keane, one of the greatest women I know, not only in the city but in any city in the United States . . . a fine Polish-American woman, who raised a fine boy. And should that boy be told by any professor or faker that he shouldn't hold office because his name is Keane and she's his mother?

Where are we going with this kind of society? Where are we going with these kinds of educators? You are doing this to the young people of our country! . . . A teacher is supposed to be dedicated to tell the truth. What kind of truth is that? . . .

Let's look at the record of the universities and what they are doing to the minds. Is that what's being told to them? I made the appointment because he is the son of the Chairman of the Finance Committee? . . . That is what we have too much of in education today—hypocrites and fakers—afraid to face the truth, afraid to let the young people to go into the combat of election contests.

They want to stand behind the cloak of a great university and tell us how wrong our country is, how wrong our society is, and they know nothing about it and they refuse to take any steps to correct it. They haven't got the guts to tell what's wrong.

That what's being taught today. And [Simpson] is not the only one. He's typical of the large numbers in universities polluting the minds of the young people . . . and if this is the society in which we live, that we're afraid to appoint any member of our family because of what? Of fear of what might be said? Not the truth. But the fear.

Who creates fear? Who creates these phony issues? The very people we're talking about. Let me say to you very frankly, if you're a teacher, God help the students that are in your class, if this is what is being taught.[15]

It seems strange that a simple challenge to a minor government appointment should provoke such a great outcry from the all-powerful mayor and his allies. When the vote came, Tom Keane Jr.'s appointment was approved by an overwhelming vote of 44–2, with only Forty-third Ward Alderman William Singer joining Simpson in opposition.

It is a curious fact that a political machine not only promotes patronage politics but nepotism as well. Usually, nepotism is not considered a crime. Thus, party bosses throughout Illinois feel free to appoint or elect their sons, daughters, and other family members to important government positions.

A current star nepotism practitioner is the party boss Joseph Berrios, Cook County assessor and chairman of the Cook County Democratic Central Committee. More than a dozen of his close family members are, or have been, employed by government agencies. Many are directly on his assessor's payroll. In 2012, his sister received $108,000 as deputy assessor, and his daughter and son, Vanessa and Joey, each earned more than seventy-two thousand dollars.[16] Nepotism didn't end with the death of Richard J. Daley. It is alive and well in Chicago.

In *Boss: Richard J. Daley of Chicago,* Mike Royko gives a roll call of nepotism that could be duplicated today with new names of the politically powerful:

There was Otto Kerner, Cermak's confidante and a federal judge, and he begat Otto Kerner, governor, federal judge and husband of Cermak's daughter; . . . Dan Ryan ward boss and County Board President, begat Dan Ryan, ward boss and County Board President; . . . Joe Rostenkowski, ward boss, begat Daniel Rostenkowski, congressman; . . . Thomas Keane, ward boss and alderman, begat Thomas Keane, ward boss and alderman.[17]

Names like Daley, Madigan, Stroger, and Berrios would top Royko's begats list if the columnist were alive today.

Operation Haunted Hall

Another side effect of machine control is ghost payrolling. In one investigation, four aldermen, the Cook County treasurer, and an Illinois state senator were among those convicted in a federal investigation of ghost payrolling at city hall. Ghost payrolling is the practice of giving government jobs to political workers or family members who never, or rarely, show up at work. They take their salary but deliver no work in return. They are ghost employees.

The federal investigation into ghost payrolling was called Operation Haunted Hall. It resulted in thirty-eight indictments and thirty-five convictions.[18] Among them, Aldermen John Madrzyk, Joseph Martinez, and Ambrosio Medrano were convicted for putting relatives and cronies on the city payroll in jobs that required no work.[19] Former Alderman Anthony Laurino was also indicted in 1995, but he died in 1999 before his trial, which had been delayed because of his poor health, could be held.

Before the investigation was completed, thirty-four officials and employees pleaded guilty, including Illinois State Senator Bruce Farley. Marie D'Amico, Alderman Laurino's daughter, at various times held ghost jobs at the Cook County Sheriff's Office, the Clerk's Office, and the Chicago City Council Finance Committee. She pleaded guilty, as did her husband, John D'Amico. Cook County Treasurer Edward Rosewell also pleaded guilty but died before sentencing.[20] Former State Representative Miguel Santiago was acquitted in a jury trial.[21]

Most of those convicted were Democrats, but the probe began with an investigation of the hiring practices of the Cook County sheriff's office, run by Republican James O'Grady. His undersheriff, James Dvorak, who coordinated most of the corruption schemes, was convicted.

The *Chicago Sun-Times* reported that the ghost payrolling schemes involved in the Haunted Hall investigation cost the taxpayers an estimated three million dollars a year. But ghost payrolling in local, county, and state government was more widespread than these few convicted individuals. It cost taxpayers tens of millions annually in wasted salaries for politically connected employees who did little or no work.

Operation Incubator

Straight-out bribery remained at the center of much corruption at city hall. Operation Incubator centered on several bribery schemes. One was designed to take Chicago's parking-fine collection contract from one New York company and to give it to another. In another case, Cook County Circuit Court Clerk Morgan Finley was convicted for taking twenty-five thousand dollars in bribes, and his chief investigator, Michael Lambesis, pleaded guilty to passing bribes and selling machine guns and silencers.[22]

Clarence McCain, a former top aide to Mayor Harold Washington, was convicted for taking fifty-seven thousand dollars in bribes from a government mole,[23] as were former Aldermen Wallace Davis Jr. (Twenty-seventh Ward),[24] Marian Humes (Eighth Ward),[25] Perry Hutchinson (Ninth Ward),[26] and Clifford Kelley (Twentieth Ward).[27]

Michael Raymond, the FBI mole who used the assumed name Michael Burnett in Chicago, operated out of an expensive apartment in Lake Point Tower with a beautiful view of the lakefront. The FBI occupied the adjacent unit. In fourteen months, Raymond dispensed $307,100 in cash and gifts to the public officials, while the FBI tape recorded many of the payoffs.[28]

The Incubator bribery investigation also resulted in convictions or guilty pleas by another dozen lower-level officials.[29] These convictions demonstrated once again how city and other local government contracts were given out for campaign contributions or outright bribes by legions of public officials. The crooked and inflated contracts cheated taxpayers out of better and less expensive services and, therefore, lower taxes.

Mirage Inspections

In 1977, investigators from the *Chicago Sun-Times* and the Better Government Association opened the Mirage tavern in the River North neighborhood. Working undercover, these investigators, without the involvement of the federal government, documented bribery of city inspectors who failed to conduct legitimate inspections of the bar. The Mirage appeared to be a normal, just-opened local tavern, so it attracted numerous inspectors from all agencies charged with inspecting new taverns. Nearly all of the inspectors, cops, firemen, and other officials solicited or accepted bribes. As a result, the Mirage became a major scandal.

Lieutenant Benjamin Jungman, a fire inspector, was the first of dozens of corrupt inspectors, police officers, and garbage collectors to take Mirage's documented bribes. According to reports, he ignored a number of code violations, including exposed electrical wiring, missing ceiling plaster, and a makeshift partition that mocked the city fire code.[30] Lieutenant Jungman accepted an envelope containing ten dollars as he marked the Mirage as passing inspection. He was suspended for failing to enforce fire and building regulations at the Mirage.[31]

The Mirage investigation also documented the practice of Chicago firefighters assigned to sell tickets for charitable causes, leaving firehouses understaffed. On-duty firefighters came into the Mirage tavern selling the tickets, stayed drinking beer for hours, and divulged the workings of the ticket scheme to the undercover journalists. As relayed to investigators, firefighters were given tickets and pressured by superiors to sell them. The more tickets sold, the more paid time off a firefighter could take. Resulting news stories alleged that these tickets, supposedly being sold to benefit a fund for widows and orphans of firefighters, were actually a secret funding source for City Fire Commissioner Robert J. Quinn's pet project, a ceremonial marching band.[32]

For the most part, reforms proposed by the Better Government Association after the Mirage scandal were not adopted. Bribing inspectors, including fire inspectors, remained a Chicago tradition, part of the "Chicago way" that continues the culture of corruption throughout city government.

City Treasurer's Office

Corruption occurred in city offices other than the city council and departments and administrative units under the mayor's control. One example was the city clerk's office. James Laski and several previous city clerks were convicted of corruption. Corruption in the city treasurer's office came to light in 1999, when Treasurer Miriam Santos was accused of illegally soliciting campaign contributions. She ran an unsuccessful campaign for Illinois attorney general against the incumbent, Jim Ryan.[33] The investigation began in May 1998 with allegations that Santos threatened to end city business with banks and other large firms if they did not contribute to her campaign.[34]

According to evidence presented at trial, Santos pressured Citibank to contribute and attempted to force the bank to hold a fund-raising event for her. Samuel Borwoski, a high-level Citibank official, testified that he received a threatening phone call from Santos, demanding that the bank contribute $1,500 to her campaign instead of the five hundred dollars that Citibank was willing to contribute. Santos called the smaller contribution unacceptable, implying that Citibank had to come up with the full $1,500.[35] During the trial, the jury learned that Patricia Errera, chief investment manager in the treasurer's office, filed a complaint with the Chicago's Board of Ethics charging that Santos had ended business with several brokerage firms due to their reluctance to contribute approximately ten thousand dollars each to the Democratic party on Santos's behalf.[36]

The allegation that Santos withheld business was particularly scandalous because she was responsible for overseeing the investment of $2.5 billion in city funds in banks that provided the highest rate of return with the lowest possible risk. U.S. Attorney Scott Lassar said, "Santos's blacklisting of investment firms cost the city at least $16,000 in interest."[37]

During her trial, a tape-recorded phone call between Santos and a Fuji Securities executive was played in which she tells him that it is time to "belly up," since the firm has "no other choice."[38]

The indictment against Santos included the use of city workers to do political work for her campaign. In July 1999, Santos was found guilty of one count of attempted extortion and five fraud charges. She was sentenced to forty months in prison.[39] However, there were various hiccups in the trial and a "veritable avalanche of errors" in cross-examining witnesses and obtaining evidence. Santos appealed and won the right to a retrial.[40]

On October 26, 2000, nearly two weeks before the scheduled start of her retrial, Santos pleaded guilty to only one felony count of mail fraud. Her bargain with the prosecutors included serving time in prison, paying restitution of twenty thousand dollars to the city, and a one-thousand-dollar fine. In her plea agreement, Santos also confessed that she did "direct and cause employees of the treasurer's office to engage in campaign activities while they were on duty at their city jobs."[41]

Santos was initially appointed to the treasurer's position in 1989 by Mayor Richard M. Daley. She won election to a full term as treasurer in 1991. Ironically, early in her appointed term, Miriam Santos got to play corruption cop when she joined with the city inspector general to uncover a check-cashing scam among lower-ranking employees that began under the previous treasurer.

In this scheme, six treasurer employees wrote personal checks on closed bank accounts and then cashed the checks. Once the checks bounced and were returned to the treasurer's office, they were retrieved by the employees and destroyed to remove evidence of the embezzlement.[42]

Procurement Contracts

The Duff family and their employees defrauded the Chicago city government of over one hundred million dollars in Minority-Owned Businesses (MBE) and Women-Owned Businesses (WBE) set-aside contracts.[43] This has happened often, since the city created a set-aside program to advantage minority- and women-owned businesses during Mayor Harold Washington's administration. In this particular scheme, the head of the Duff family, James M. Duff, used his elderly mother, Patricia Green Duff, to create a sham WBE front by claiming that she owned and controlled at least 51 percent of Windy City Maintenance. James Duff also convinced an African American employee to pose as the majority owner and controller of Remedial Environment Manpower. James Duff pleaded guilty and was sentenced to nearly ten years in prison. He and his companies paid more than twenty-two million dollars in fines for defrauding Chicago by illegally taking contracts meant for minorities and women.[44]

Duff family members held at least two fund-raisers for Mayor Richard M. Daley to insure that they were favored at city hall. In addition, Duff family members, their businesses, and a union they controlled contributed at least thirty-two thousand dollars to Daley's campaigns.[45] It has also been alleged that in 1989, Mayor Richard M. Daley instructed a top aide to ensure that the Duffs received a city contract. Shortly afterwards, the Mayor's Office of Special Events awarded Windy City Maintenance a no-bid contract to clean up after the Taste of Chicago, which brought the firm roughly five hundred thousand dollars annually.[46] Additional evidence of Daley-Duff collusion was brought forward by Bruce DuMont, president of the Museum of Broadcast Communications, who told the *Chicago Tribune* that Daley personally instructed DuMont's wife, then a top city-hall staffer, to make sure that the Duffs got a share of city work.[47]

The Duff family scandal is a good example of government fraud at city hall, not only in minority- and women-owned business contracts, but of how insiders with clout and bribes get crooked contracts that cost taxpayers millions of wasted dollars a year.

Silver Shovel

Consider the further example of John Christopher, a mob-connected construction contractor who had served time for bank fraud and for submitting phony snow-removal bills to the city in 1979. He became an undercover mole for the FBI in 1993 and spent three years bribing numerous public officials in Chicago and the suburbs. He secretly recorded his payoff conversations.

In addition to documenting public officials accepting bribes to facilitate illegal dumping and siting of landfills, Christopher gathered evidence about drug trafficking, organized-crime activity, and labor-union corruption. He paid off city aldermen, the president of the Metropolitan Water Reclamation District, and two city inspectors.[48]

Christopher's "Silver Shovel" scooped up and delivered to federal prosecutors a total of eighteen convictions and guilty pleas from six aldermen and numerous public employees. Thomas Fuller, the former president of the Metropolitan Water Reclamation District (MWRD), was found guilty of receiving two bribes, totaling nine thousand dollars, from Christopher to help lease land from the district and to acquire a contract.[49] Fuller further pleaded guilty to separate tax-fraud charges. Fuller's codefendant, James Blassingame, a campaign consultant, was also found guilty of arranging bribes for Fuller and MWRD Commissioner Joseph Gardner, who died before he could be indicted.[50]

Before he began working for the FBI, Christopher was the principal businessman behind an illegal dump site at Roosevelt Road and Kildare Avenue in Chicago. Christopher and others piled up more than seven hundred thousand tons of concrete, asphalt, and other construction material.[51] The pile, which was about six stories high, aggravated neighbors and prompted calls to the U.S. Attorney's office. The cost of cleaning up the site was twenty-one million dollars.[52] Taxpayer money was lost to public corruption, and a hazard was created for residents in every neighborhood where Christopher's other illicit construction dumps were located.

The Mob and City Hall

One of the darkest sides of the crooked deals at city hall is the connection between some politicians and the crime syndicate. Operation Family Secrets—the most successful organized-crime investigation in Chicago history—is not usually considered an example of public corruption. However, two of those involved in the murder, conspiracy, and racketeering scandal were a former

Chicago police officer and a deputy U.S. marshal. Another defendant previously ran McCormick Place,[53] and yet another had worked for the city in the 1960s.[54]

While working in the police-evidence section, Anthony "Twan" Doyle acquired key investigation information and passed it on to the Outfit. Doyle was found guilty in the conspiracy and was ordered to pay more than forty-four thousand dollars in restitution.[55]

Michael Ricci, also a former Chicago police officer, was charged with passing messages from the jailed Frank Calabrese Sr. to other members of the mob while he was a Cook County sheriff's officer.[56] Ricci, who had heart problems, died before being tried.[57]

The deputy U.S. marshal, John Ambrose, was convicted of telling the Outfit about a mobster he was guarding in the federal witness-protection program.[58] Ambrose's father, a Chicago police officer, had been convicted earlier in the Marquette Ten trial. He served jail time with another former police officer and family friend, who also passed information to the mob.[59]

The Family Secrets probe took direct aim at Chicago's three dominant mob chapters: the Grand Avenue crew of Joey "the Clown" Lombardo, the Melrose Park crew of brothers Jimmy and Michael Marcello, and the Twenty-sixth Street crew of the imprisoned mobsters Frank Calabrese Sr. and his brother, Nicholas.[60] Nicholas Calabrese, who became an FBI informant, was a former mob hit man himself who admitted to killing fourteen people. He was the only made member of the Chicago Outfit ever to testify against his superiors and his testimony was crucial in prosecuting mob leaders in the Family Secrets trials.

Frank Calabrese Sr., Joey Lombardo, and Jimmy Marcello were found guilty of racketeering and held responsible for ten murders. The jury deadlocked on eight other murders.[61] Five of the defendants in the trial were ordered to pay more than $4.3 million in restitution to the families of the murder victims. U.S. District Judge James Zagel also held Marcello, Lombardo, Calabrese Sr., and Paul "the Indian" Schiro responsible for the lost wages and earnings of the murder victims.

However, there are even more extensive connections between the mob and city hall. Operation Gambat, another federal investigation, was named for a gambling attorney who worked for the crime syndicate for more than ten years before going undercover for the FBI. He was able to expose the symbiotic relationship between the First Ward Democratic Organization and the mob. Over the years, there had been many rumors that organized crime was a player in Chicago politics. Operation Gambat, which is described in detail in chapter 9, removed all doubts.

The connection between the mob, city hall, and the court system led to racketeering and the fixing of court cases, including murder trials. Politicians and mobsters are, to some extent, still in bed together in a tradition that goes back to the founding of the Chicago political machine. That history includes the infamous crime boss Al Capone, who gave large campaign contributions to Republican Mayor "Big Bill" Thompson in the 1920s. Mayor Thompson, in return, had city officials overlook gambling and liquor operations during the Prohibition era.

The Cost of Corruption

The extent of corruption at city hall helps us understand the cost of corruption in wasted tax dollars, in lives ruined or lost, and in citizens' loss of faith in our government. We now know that more than 1,900 individuals have been convicted of myriad forms of public corruption since the 1970s. Based on testimony before the Illinois Ethics Commission, Mayor Emanuel's Ethics Reform Task Force, and our own research, we believe that the cost of corruption or "corruption tax" to Illinois taxpayers is at least five hundred million dollars a year.

Examples of some of the costs of corruption in a few major scandals include the costs of the Jon Burge police-brutality scandal, which has already reached eighty-five million dollars and counting.[62] The cost of Chicago police corruption averages forty-seven million dollars a year, as we will detail in chapter 7. The Better Government Association has calculated that police misconduct cost a total of $521 million between 2004 and 2013 alone.[63]

The Hired Truck scandal cost more than one hundred million dollars over the decade it operated. The ghost-payroll scandals in the Haunted Hall investigation cost more than three million dollars a year. The Incubator bribery cases involving Chicago aldermen cost more than $239,000, and the cleanup of the dumps cost an additional twenty-one million dollars. Bribery cases with building inspectors cost more than twenty-three thousand dollars, not counting the lives lost when porches collapsed or fires occurred in unsafe nightclubs. These costs do not include tens of millions of dollars for investigating, prosecuting, and imprisoning these public-corruption criminals. Since there have been 1,597 convictions of officials in the Chicago metropolitan region for bribery, tax evasion, lying to the FBI, and obstructing justice from 1976 to 2012, the total cost of corruption has been enormous.

Calculating a precise dollar amount of corruption is difficult and fluctuates from year to year. However, we can begin to make a rough estimate of the costs. The greatest financial costs are from (1) patronage and no-show jobs, (2) fraudulent government contracts, (3) lawsuits for damages, such as in police abuse cases, and (4) embezzlement of funds or stealing government property.

The federal government's False Claim Act gives us an idea of how costly government corruption can be. Since 1986 when the law was amended, the federal government has recovered over twelve billion dollars in settlements, with some individual settlements reaching $731 million.

The Haunted Hall court documents indicate that employees with no-show, ghost-payrolling jobs cost the city more than three million dollars a year in wages and benefits.[64] Similarly, the diverted public funds, public property, and wages and benefits from Governor George Ryan's licenses-for-bribes scandal cost state taxpayers another five million dollars.[65]

Based upon the "clout-list" in the Robert Sorich trial, we know that there are at least five thousand patronage employees in Chicago city government, and we can presume that there are at least five thousand more in the other state and local governments. If they are only working at half capacity in their government jobs and earn on average fifty thousand dollars a year in wages and benefits, then patronage employees cost Illinois taxpayers more than twenty-five million dollars a year, because more employees have to be hired to get the work done.

However, in dollar terms, the greatest cost is from crooked contracts "with thievery written between the lines."[66] The head of purchasing for the Illinois prison system testified to the Illinois Ethics Commission that because of corruption, the inflated costs of all state contracts were at least 5 percent of the total. A sizeable portion of Chicago's seven-billion-dollar operating budget and the state's sixty-one-billion-dollar budget are spent on contracts for outside goods and services. Five percent of every billion dollars of government contracts is fifty million dollars. The costs of crooked contracts escalate quickly, as the Hired Truck scandal demonstrates.

In the most recent study of the cost or corruption in states, the authors found that the most corrupt states, like Illinois, averaged $1,308 per capita in state expenditures over what states with only an average corruption level spend. This cost citizens in corrupt states like Illinois an additional per capita expenditure of more than twenty-five thousand dollars from 1997–2008.[67]

In addition to outright bribes to government employees to obtain overpriced contracts, there is a costly nexus between campaign contributions and winning government contracts. Dana Heupel and the journalists at the *Springfield State Journal-Register* were able to document that at least one-third of the state contracts following the elections in 1990 (fourteen thousand contracts, worth $1.6 billion) went to individuals or businesses that contributed to the campaigns of statewide office holders.[68]

As Illinois Auditor General Robert Cronson put it, "The people involved know that contributing pays. I don't think it's usually said that blatantly . . . it's just the raising of an eyebrow, an environmental attitude. . . . The general feeling (among state contractors) is that you are infinitely better off if you contribute. And the feeling in government is that you've got to reward your friends or you don't get reelected."[69] Or, as the former state legislator James Nowlan said, "There is an appearance that you have to pay in order to play in the game of doing business with the state."[70]

These are some of the findings of the *State Journal-Register's* study of Illinois contractors' campaign contributions:

- At least 14,500 contracts and purchase orders worth up to $1.61 billion went to 1,300 people or firms that contributed to statewide campaigns.
- Contractors who made political donations averaged $1.2 million each in state business.
- Governor Jim Edgar's campaign contributors landed 30 percent to 70 percent of the business done by some state agencies under the governor's control.
- About 150 contributors donated to both Democrats and Republicans—thereby guaranteeing they would back a winner—and landed almost four thousand state contracts worth some $225 million.
- Contractors who gave money to Edgar and the state Republican party landed contracts worth eight times more, on average, than firms or individuals who do not make contributions.
- About $335 million in no-bid contracts and purchases that did not require competitive bidding under state law were awarded by the administration to firms or individuals who donated money to Edgar and the Republican party.[71]

In response to the original newspaper exposés, Illinois attorney general Roland Burris asked: "It's legal, so what's the problem?"[72] The problem, of course, is that if those who contribute to political campaigns can gain government contracts and jobs for their contributions, they facilitate corruption in the political system.[73] And the taxpayer is stuck with overpriced contracts that add millions of dollars to their tax bills.

Then there are cases of graft and embezzlement, such as when clerks in the city treasurer's office simply cash checks to the government for themselves. The largest known case of this sort is not a Chicago case but the Comptroller and Treasurer of Dixon, Illinois, who managed to steal fifty-three million dollars from that local government. A similar case involved a former suburban Burnham village clerk who stole more than seven hundred thousand dollars over a decade.[74] There are lots of other cases as well such as the ex-Country Club Hills Police chief who stole nine hundred thousand dollars in state grant money or the Chicago Public Schools local tech coordinator who stole four hundred thousand dollars.[75]

All these forms of graft and corruption, large and small, add up. To paraphrase U.S. Senator Everett Dirksen, a million stolen here and a million stolen there, and you are soon into real money.

Has anything changed after all these scandals? Have the reforms after the convictions of Governors Ryan and Blagojevich made any difference? Has the election of Pat Quinn as governor or Rahm Emanuel as mayor signaled a new "Post-Daley era" in which corruption will be curbed?

There have been new ethics commissions appointed and some new state laws and city ordinances adopted. In our estimation, however, it will still take decades to root out the existing level of bribery, theft, and unethical exploitation, and it will take decades to change the culture of corruption that has been created over the last 150 years.

Former Chicago police officer William Beavers served as alderman of Chicago's Seventh Ward for twenty-three years before being elected Cook County commissioner in 2006. He was convicted in 2013 for failing to pay income taxes on thirty thousand dollars he took from his campaign fund to gamble at a casino and for using another sixty-eight thousand dollars in campaign donations to boost his City of Chicago pension. *Photo courtesy of Sun-Times Media.*

CHAPTER 6

Crook County

CORRUPTION—LIKE PATRONAGE WORKERS, favor seekers, and lobbyists—flows easily back and forth between Chicago city hall and the Cook County side of the building that the two governments share. It hardly matters on which side of the building a particular scandal erupts, since both the city and county governments are integral parts of a single system of machine politics.

Lead roles in the "Crook County" saga were played by three political powerhouses: County Board Presidents George W. Dunne and John Stroger, and the ultimate Boss, Richard J. Daley, mayor of Chicago and chairman of the Cook County Democratic party. These three, plus Daley's and Stroger's sons, were involved in, or tacitly permitted and tolerated an astonishingly long parade of political-corruption scandals.

How Chicago's Democratic machine controlled Cook County government and politics was aptly explained in the 1975 book *Clout*, by Len O'Connor:

> By statute, the County Board president holds an autonomous office; in fact, since ten Democrats who dominate the board are dependent for slating upon the Democratic machine, the president is required to defer to the desires of the mayor of Chicago when the mayor is also the Democratic czar. . . . [I]t would have been unthinkable for [County Board President] Dunne to challenge Daley in any way. Even when a Republican is Cook County Board President, . . . a politically strong mayor like Daley can frustrate him with a two-thirds majority.[1]

While city and county officials have engaged in corruption as far back as the first corruption trial in 1869, this chapter focuses on a more recent era, during the reigns of Dunne, the Daleys, and the Strogers. Their records, and those of their underlings, tell a tale of corruption, waste, and mismanagement that plagued both sides of the city/county building.

We pick up the story in 1962, when George Dunne's friend and ally, Mayor Richard J. Daley, asked him to leave his position in the Illinois House of Representatives to fill a vacancy on the County Board of Commissioners. After seven years as a commissioner and chair of the board's powerful finance committee, Dunne—with Daley's backing—was chosen by the commissioners to be County Board president, a position he held for twenty-one years, from 1969 until he retired in 1990.

George Dunne and Dick Daley were heads of supposedly separate units of government, but Daley had superior power. By holding the dual positions of mayor of the nation's second largest city and Democratic party chairman, Daley controlled city and county patronage. Moreover, he directed the slating of the party's candidates for county office as well as for city, state, and congressional races. Publicly, George Dunne never crossed or challenged Daley. He seemed satisfied with his role as second fiddle.

In addition to serving as a state legislator, county commissioner, and eventually County Board president, Dunne was for forty-three years Democratic committeeman of the Forty-second Ward. His ward was split between the rich, all-white "gold coast" side surrounding the Magnificent Mile shopping area and the poor, all-black Cabrini Green CHA housing project on the west side of the ward. He managed to rule the rich and poor sections and to deliver the vote for his party.

When Daley died in 1976, Dunne succeeded him as Democratic party county chairman. Although he never wielded power comparable to Daley's, he did become wealthy over the years. George Dunne was ousted as county party chairman in a power struggle in which Mayor Jane Byrne installed Alderman Edward Vrdolyak in his stead soon after her 1979 election.

George Dunne's public image contrasted sharply with Daley's tough Boss persona. George Dunne walked to work without an entourage. He was affable and easy to talk to. News reporters liked him. He was "Gentleman George" to the media, and he held a wider vision of the role of government than Mayor Daley.

While George Dunne was County Board president, more than a dozen major corruption scandals erupted, involving almost every major unit of county government. But Dunne's reputation escaped damage until the end of his career. He was not blamed for any of the numerous scandals that occurred on his watch, one after another, for almost the entire time he led the County Board. However, in his last term, news reports disclosed that Dunne had sexual encounters with several female Cook County employees. He admitted indiscretions but denied that he exchanged jobs for sex. At the time he was a seventy-five-year-old widower.[2] News reports treated the scandal as a harmless aberration.

When George Dunne died a few years later, obituary writers heaped praise on him. They repeated his boasts of saving taxpayers money and, for the most part, ignored the corruption that thrived while he was in charge. But a closer look reveals that George Dunne's ethical record was far from spotless. In 1964, shortly after he joined the Cook County Board, Dunne purchased five thousand dollars' worth of racetrack stock and sold it two years later for twenty-five thousand dollars.[3] Dunne and numerous public officials, including Governor Otto Kerner, State Revenue Director Theodore Isaacs, Congressman Dan Rostenkowski, and other insiders were given special access to racetrack stock, which they purchased and then quickly sold for huge profits. Dunne and most of the others bought their stock after receiving advice from Secretary of State Paul Powell, who had the final say in the assignment of racing dates. Favorable dates could increase the profitability of the racetracks and racing associations.[4] Even though their stock purchases and resale were highly suspicious and hidden by complex transactions, neither Dunne nor Rostenkowski was indicted in the racetrack scandal. Apparently, there wasn't proof that they took any official action in return for their bargain racetrack stock. But they were certainly among the connected politicians that benefited from the stock deals.

Sometimes attractive business deals just landed in George Dunne's lap. In 1973, a joint Better Government Association (BGA) and *Chicago Tribune* investigation revealed that Dunne and numerous other political leaders took advantage of a favorable opportunity to invest in two luxury, high-rise apartment buildings in the Lincoln Park neighborhood of Chicago. The deal was offered by James McHugh, president of James McHugh Construction Company, whom Dunne described as a "good friend." McHugh invested $14,930 in one of the buildings for a 1 percent share of the profits, while Dunne invested only $4,590 for a 3 percent share of the profits. Dunne received a similarly generous deal on the second building. In the decade preceding the Lincoln Park deal, McHugh Construction was awarded at least thirty million dollars in county and city construction contracts. As Finance Committee chairman and then Board president during that ten-year period, Dunne had the ability to approve, expedite, delay, or kill major county construction projects. Despite the obvious conflict of interest, George Dunne denied any impropriety.[5]

George Dunne was also owner and then co-owner of Near North Insurance Agency. During Dunne's reign as County Board president, Near North was awarded, often without competitive bidding, millions of dollars in contracts to insure government buildings.[6] Near North also had a no-bid contract to broker workers' compensation and liability insurance for O'Hare International Airport.[7] Over the years, Near North was given contracts for brokering insurance for McCormick Place, Chicago Public Schools, Chicago Housing Authority, Chicago Transportation Authority, Metra, Pace, Midway Airport, Chicago Skyway, Cook County Hospital, Navy Pier, and City Hall.[8]

In 1985, George Dunne sold his Near North Insurance stake to his partner, Michael "Micky" Segal, a well-liked friend of many powerful politicians and celebrities. For instance, Cook County commissioner and Mayor Richard M. Daley's brother, John Daley, was on the Near North board of directors. Segal invested in property in Wisconsin with Congressman Dan Rostenkowski, Alderman Ed Burke, and former Aldermen Terry Gabinski and Joseph Kotlarz.[9] Of course, Segal was as well a fund-raiser and contributor to the campaign funds of powerful politicians, including Governor George Ryan. And Governor Ryan's son, George Ryan Jr., once worked with Segal setting up insurance deals.[10]

By exploiting his political connections, Segal grew Near North into the second largest insurance brokerage in Illinois. By 2002, Near North recorded sales in excess of one hundred million dollars annually and had one thousand employees in eight U.S. cities, an office in London, and a corporate jet.[11] During the ten years prior to his indictment, Segal's Near North Insurance also contributed more than $150,000 to various Illinois politicians. In January 2002, Micky Segal's high-flying, big-spending life ground to a halt when he was indicted by the federal government for insurance and mail fraud and for misappropriating more than twenty million dollars from a trust fund for customers' premiums.

Segal's indictment exposed some of the loans, deals, discounts, and contributions he provided to his friends. Some journalists expected that Segal would succumb to the pressure and squeal on his political cronies. Segal's lawyer suggested that the feds were on a fishing expedition when they indicted him.[12] Micky Segal was convicted in June 2004 for racketeering, mail fraud, and embezzlement. The jury also convicted Near North Insurance and returned a thirty-five-million-dollar forfeiture judgment against Segal.[13] After his conviction, Segal said, "No one should be nervous about me cooperating" to get a reduced sentence.[14] The long sixteen months he spent in the federal detention center awaiting sentencing may have been designed to loosen his tongue, but he didn't succumb to the pressure and was sentenced to ten years in federal prison. At the end of May 2012, after serving about eight years, he was let out of prison early.

George Dunne, like Richard J. Daley, rarely uttered the slightest critical comment when county officials were accused of violating the public's trust. Throughout his twenty-one-year reign as County Board president, there were a series of scandals involving the Cook County treasurer, zoning commissioner, assessor, Board of Tax Appeals, and two county commissioners. Top office holders and assistants faced a torrent of investigations, indictments, and convictions. Dunne was not held responsible by the media or the voters, even though the scandals occurred on his watch. He almost never took any action nor publicly criticized county officials who violated the law or unethically used their positions to make money at the expense of county taxpayers.

The County Tradition of Corruption

A long series of county scandals was sparked by an unusual event on the night of March 6, 1969, when George Dunne first became County Board president. It could have been scripted by a Hollywood film-noir screenwriter. The deputy Cook County tax assessor, Borrie Kanter, was arrested by a sheriff's policeman as he left Acoustics Development Corporation in Northbrook with a five-hundred-dollar bribe in his pocket. Sheriff Joseph Woods was a Republican, and assessor P. J. Cullerton was a Democrat, which may have encouraged Sheriff Woods to act in this case.

The sheriff's police and the government watchdog organization, the BGA, had received a tip from the company's president that the bribe had been solicited a month earlier during an assessment inspection of the company's personal property. Acoustics' president said that he was told that the bribe would reduce the company's tax bill from seven thousand to five hundred dollars per year. At the time, the county taxed the personal property of individuals and corporations. There were numerous complaints that the assessor's inspectors had too much discretion in determining the value of inventories, cash holdings, and other property and that the assessments were not uniform or fair. In the early 1970s, the personal property tax on individuals was eliminated, but it continued on businesses until it was replaced in 1979 by an increase in the corporate income tax.

Following the tip from the company's president, Sheriff Woods ordered his police to set up a sting with the BGA to document evidence of the bribe being paid. Kanter was arrested as he left Acoustics Development with twenty-five marked twenty-dollar bills. He was indicted by a county grand jury for bribery and official misconduct. A judge threw out the charges, but Kanter was reindicted by a different judge.[15] In December 1970, Kanter was found guilty of soliciting a bribe and official misconduct in a bench trial in Circuit Court.[16] Borrie Kanter, like Congressman Mel Reynolds years later, shared the unusual distinction of being convicted in both state and federal courts. In 1971, Kanter admitted cheating on his federal taxes and pleaded guilty to extorting a $750 bribe from an auto dealership.[17]

After Kanter's arrest, but before his conviction, the *Chicago Tribune* reported that a federal grand jury was investigating "a ring of personal property tax fixers in the county assessor's office."[18] Philip Armento Sr., county supervisor of personal property-tax assessment, was charged with evading taxes on fifty-three thousand dollars of income.[19] Armento was convicted and later hanged himself while in jail.[20] The indictment of Armento, the guilty plea by Kantor, and numerous newspaper articles charging impropriety in the assessor's office caused huge political problems for the incumbent Parky Cullerton, who was in a battle for reelection with Benjamin Adamowski, a popular Republican.

After Cullerton was reelected, the scandal continued to gather momentum as another half-dozen city and county officials were convicted, along with two businessmen who had offered bribes for assessment reductions.

While the property-tax investigation was under way, another of George Dunne's conflicts of interest attracted scrutiny. The BGA charged that thirty million dollars in county funds had been deposited in non-interest-bearing accounts and that some County Board members and other public officials were among the banks' stockholders or directors.[21] George Dunne himself was a stockholder and director of Amalgamated Trust and Savings Bank and a shareholder of Oak Trust Savings Bank, and Metropolitan Bank and Trust Company. All three banks held public funds.[22] Two other County Board members—Floyd Fulle, a Republican, and Charles Bonk, a Democrat—had similar conflicts of interest.

Dunne called for a study of the situation, but his proposal was safely sent to die in the Finance Committee, which he controlled. Months later, the county state's attorney Edward Hanrahan filed suit in state court in an attempt to recover back interest for $18.8 million that Cook County had deposited in non-interest-bearing accounts in thirty-two banks.[23] Even though Hanrahan was a Democrat, he was feuding with Dunne while running for reelection so he was willing to attack Dunne's government.

During the campaign, Republican Bernard Carey upped the ante. He called on Hanrahan to bring "criminal conflict of interest" charges against the public officials who were stockholders in the banks.[24] Criminal charges weren't filed, and Carey won the election in November. Less than a month later, Judge Joseph A. Power, a Democrat and Mayor Richard J. Daley's former law partner, refused to extend the county grand jury and thus dismissed the investigation into the connections between the banks and county public officials.[25]

Bribes and Kickbacks

In September 1972, U.S. Attorney James Thompson indicted Cook County Clerk Edward Barrett for accepting $180,000 in kickbacks for the purchase of nine hundred voting machines from the Shoup Company, a Philadelphia firm. The seventy-two-year-old Barrett was also charged with income-tax evasion and accepting about six thousand dollars in kickbacks for insuring the voting machines with Centennial Insurance Company.[26]

Eddie Barrett was convicted but escaped prison time because of ill health.[27] He died on April 4, 1977, after a long illness. Barrett had been a powerhouse in Illinois Democratic politics for more than forty years. He first won election in 1930 and became the youngest state treasurer in Illinois history. He was elected state auditor in 1932 and reelected in 1936. When Richard J. Daley was elected mayor in 1955, he arranged for Barrett to replace him as Cook County clerk.[28]

Bribes also played a role in property-tax appeals. George Keane, brother of Alderman Tom Keane, resigned as chairman of the Cook County Board of Tax Appeals. This caused observers to speculate that the resignation was related to the federal probe of the county's handling of tax assessments. George Keane gave no reason for his decision.[29] His resignation was followed by a score of convictions of Board of Appeals employees from 1973 through 1983.

Five months later, the *Chicago Tribune* reported that federal prosecutors were investigating politicians who held stock in Chicago banks and "have been able to maneuver tax breaks for prime bank customers."[30] George Keane and Alderman Tom Keane became stockholders in Jefferson State Bank in 1965, sixteen days after the bank's president, Bernard Feinberg, and his partners were allowed to buy a city-owned ten-foot alley for $19,920, despite an assessment showing that the alley was worth sixty-eight thousand dollars.[31] Keane and another alderman, Edwin Fifielski, were indicted but not convicted for voting to place city deposits in Jefferson State Bank while owning its stock. Feinberg was then indicted for sending false information through the mails to obtain reductions in tax assessments.[32] Subsequently, he was convicted of the mail-fraud charges involving two Loop buildings, but not for the alley deal.[33]

As the federal investigation of the assessor's office continued, the pressure to resign increased on P. J. Cullerton. Mayor Daley and the Cook County Democratic Committee didn't want the assessor's scandal to drag down the rest of the ticket in the next year's elections. So Cullerton agreed to step aside and not run for reelection in 1973. The seventy-six-year-old Cullerton made his offer on the condition that the committee slate Thomas Tully, Cullerton's protégé and former deputy.[34] Tully had been credited with professionalizing the assessor's office and raising the low assessments of many of the Loop's largest buildings. It was expected that he would clean house. But taxpayers would eventually discover that Tully was no reformer.

As Cullerton served out his fifth term in office, the scandals continued to fester. Oscar Tucker, the assistant chief of the assessor's real-estate tax division, pleaded guilty to bribery and income-tax evasion.[35] In addition, Robert Moran, Cullerton's office manager, was found in contempt in federal court for telling employees to work in Tully's campaign.[36]

After retiring in 1974, Cullerton became a partner in an insurance business and continued as Thirty-eighth Ward Democratic committeeman until his death in 1981.[37] He left an estate valued at four hundred thousand dollars,[38] which, according to the Bureau of Labor Statistics, is the equivalent of $1,043,221 in 2014.[39] P. J. Cullerton's family had been a part of the political machine and various local governments, and Cullertons are still in state and local government today. P. J. Cullerton was part of a political family dynasty that didn't end with his removal from the assessor's office.

The Irish patriarch Edward Cullerton was elected as a Chicago alderman back in 1871, just before the Chicago Fire. He served until 1920 and long held the record for the longest-serving alderman in Chicago history. He was followed by P. J. Cullerton, who lost his first aldermanic bid in 1931 but was successfully elected in 1935 from the Northwest Side's Thirty-eighth Ward, which the family still controls eighty years later. The other Cullertons who have been Thirty-eighth Ward alderman include Bill Cullerton, Tom Cullerton, Tom Allen, and Tim Cullerton. Patricia Cullerton, who worked in the assessor's office most of her adult life, is currently Thirty-eighth Ward committeeman. John Cullerton has the most powerful position of all as president of the Illinois Senate.[40]

Tom Tully followed P. J. Cullerton when he was elected assessor in November 1974, but three years later he befuddled political observers when he announced that he wouldn't seek reelection. In 1980, a federal grand jury began an investigation after the *Chicago Tribune* reported that Tully "became wealthy as a result of real estate deals with property developers for whom his office cut taxes while he was assessor."[41] In 1982, the U.S. Attorney closed the federal probe of Tully without any indictments.

Earlier, U.S. Attorney Jim Thompson and his team of federal prosecutors indicted a number of elected officials for extorting and accepting bribes to obtain favorable zoning changes. In February 1975, Thompson charged two Cook County commissioners, Floyd Fulle and Charles Bonk, with extorting eighty thousand dollars in bribes to influence zoning cases before the County Board.[42] John Daley, Mayor Richard J. Daley's cousin, was a zoning attorney and Eighteenth Ward Democratic committeeman. At Bonk's trial, Daley testified under a grant of full immunity that he gave Bonk seventeen bribes totaling $46,500 from 1966 to 1972.[43] Despite John Daley's testimony, the jury found Bonk not guilty. Bonk died a year later from a heart attack.[44]

John Daley was also mentioned as an official who needed to be bribed in the trial of Stanley Zima, executive secretary of the City Council's Building and Zoning Committee. Zima was found guilty of extortion and failing to report a twenty-thousand-dollar payoff on his tax returns. John Daley was not indicted in this case either.[45]

When Bonk and Fulle were indicted, George Dunne remarked to the *Tribune*: "What can a guy say? As colleagues on the board they demonstrated a dedication to their duties."[46] While Bonk was on trial, Dunne reappointed him to the chairmanship of the Zoning and Tax Delinquency Committees.[47] Dunne and former Governor Richard Ogilvie were character witnesses for Fulle. It didn't help; Floyd Fulle was found guilty of perjury, income-tax evasion, and extorting sixty-nine thousand dollars to approve zoning changes.

Favoritism and Corruption

Paul Marcy, secretary of the Cook County Board of Appeals, was found guilty of failing to pay taxes on a fifty-five-thousand-dollar bribe he received in the same zoning scheme for which Fulle was convicted.[48] Paul Marcy's brother, Pat Marcy, was the secretary of the mob-controlled First Ward Democratic organization. A dozen years later, Pat Marcy, a "made member of the Chicago mob, was indicted for trying to fix two murder trials and rigging zoning cases."[49] He died before he could be tried.[50]

In 1978, the *Chicago Tribune* published a series of articles about favoritism and corruption at the Board of Tax Appeals. The elected two-member board considers appeals of property-tax assessments and decides to sustain or reduce them.[51] Two years later, the U.S. Attorney indicted fourteen individuals in a bribery scheme involving more than thirty-three million dollars in real-estate assessment cuts.[52] More than two dozen individuals were indicted before the investigation was completed. According to the *Tribune* reporter Ed McManus, it was the largest corruption scandal in Cook County history: "The scope of the scandal is massive. Twenty-nine persons have been indicted and 23 have been convicted, so far, for fixing 5,000 cases in the late 1970s involving a whopping $140 million in property tax assessment reductions and $80 million in actual tax revenue lost."[53]

McManus quoted an FBI official, saying, "[W]henever one person's tax is cut, everyone else's tax goes up a bit to fill the gap." A deputy U.S. Attorney estimated that because of the fraud, every Cook County property owner had to pay an extra one hundred dollars in taxes.[54] Harry Semrow, one of two commissioners on the Cook County Board of Tax Appeals, escaped indictment even though Robert Berger, a multimillionaire real-estate magnate, testified that he paid bribes to Semrow.[55] Berger and a deputy commissioner of the board were found guilty of bribery, however.[56]

Corruption in the Sheriff's Office

When corruption is caught and beaten back in one area of Cook County government, it breaks out in another department. It broke out in the Sheriff's Office during the reign of Sheriff James O'Grady (1986–90). O'Grady was a former superintendent of the Chicago Police Department and a former Democrat who switched to the Republican party to run for sheriff in 1986. O'Grady's campaign was run by James Dvorak, another former Democrat and a former homicide detective. After O'Grady named Dvorak undersheriff, Dvorak became chairman of the Cook County Republican party.

Under the O'Grady-Dvorak administration, there were at least three major overlapping federal investigations, resulting in dozens of convictions in various city and county offices. It is difficult to separate these scandals or to determine which investigation came first and which clue, tip, or incident got the ball rolling. But before the smoke cleared, federal prosecutors investigated not only the sheriff's office but also the city and county clerk's offices, the county treasurer's office, and the Board of Tax Appeals.[57]

In November 1989, as O'Grady's reelection campaign was getting under way, the *Chicago Tribune* published a two-part series alleging that "Sheriff O'Grady has demanded thousands of dollars in campaign contributions from deputies and given sensitive law-enforcement jobs to political cronies." At least four high-ranking employees in the sheriff's office, including Undersheriff Dvorak, ran political organizations that solicited contributions from colleagues and subordinates.[58] Dvorak resigned, and the next day, Richard Simon, who ran the sheriff's part-time deputy program, also resigned.[59] Simon was another former Chicago police officer whose ties to organized crime came to light in 2012, after his janitorial company was awarded a contract to clean O'Hare Airport.[60]

In early 1990, federal prosecutors played a tape in federal court containing statements by a witness that Dvorak was paid off to protect mob-run gambling operations. The next year, that witness testified that the mob boss Rocco Infelise made monthly protection payments through Dvorak to O'Grady.[61]

For several years after he left the sheriff's office, allegations of corruption under O'Grady continued to surface. In 1992, James Novelli, the chief investigator for the Sheriff's Merit Board, pleaded guilty to accepting bribes to fix test grades and alter applications for corrections-officer jobs. Subsequently, Novelli pleaded guilty to additional charges of bribery and conspiracy.[62] Novelli admitted that he accepted bribes from two additional bagmen in return for giving thirty individuals passing grades on the sheriff's entrance exam. Prosecutors also suggested that under O'Grady 1,500 applicants were given a pass on the exam and that 367 persons had obtained jobs with the sheriff despite failing scores.[63]

Later, Dvorak pleaded guilty to accepting the use of eight rental cars as a payoff for steering a contract to the car-rental agency's owners. He also admitted that he hid bribe proceeds and gambling winnings from the IRS. However, Dvorak flatly denied that he accepted bribes of $175,000 to protect mob-run gambling.[64] The federal judge who presided in the Infelise case ruled that prosecutors did not prove that Dvorak took mob payoffs.[65]

Ghost Payrollers

While in prison, Dvorak pleaded guilty to selling jobs and placing friends and relatives of public officials in ghost jobs where they received pay but did little or no work. Although the sheriff's personnel director pleaded guilty to similar corruption charges, O'Grady was never indicted.[66]

Then the U.S. Attorney began searching for "ghosts" on the staff of Edward Rosewell, the Cook County treasurer and Forty-sixth Democratic Ward committeeman. Rosewell was one of the Democratic machine's most energetic cheerleaders, fund-raisers, and patronage facilitators. He had a diverse political career, serving as executive director of the Illinois Tollway and as a Chicago Park District commissioner. In the private sector, he had been vice president of Continental Bank's public funds division. In 1974, he was handpicked by Richard J. Daley to become Cook County treasurer.[67]

In 1995, federal prosecutors delivered subpoenas to Rosewell's office and obtained time sheets and payroll records.[68] A week later, Rosewell's close friend and roommate, Rodney Zobjeck, resigned from his job as deputy treasurer. Before he was hired in 1994 as a thirty-five-thousand-dollar-per-year clerk, Zobjeck was a window washer. In less than a year his annual salary nearly doubled to $63,616.[69]

Rosewell and his chief deputy, James Fuglsang, were indicted and charged with giving special ghost jobs to Chicago Democratic State Senator Bruce Farley and State Representative Miguel Santiago.[70] The indictments said that the two legislators received $320,000 in wages and benefits for which they did little or no work.[71] Fuglsang cooperated with investigators and pleaded guilty to two misdemeanor charges.[72]

Rosewell was very ill in 1998 when he faced the likely possibility that Fuglsang would testify against him. Calculating his chances to win his case, or even survive the trial, Rosewell pleaded guilty to a single charge of mail fraud. Senator Farley also pleaded guilty.[73]

Miguel Santiago was acquitted. He testified that he did do work for the treasurer and that he verbally reported directly to Rosewell. Even though Rosewell had pleaded guilty to giving Santiago a no-work job, Rosewell was too ill to testify at Santiago's trial. Thus the jury heard no evidence to counter Santiago's claim of actually working.[74] Six months later, Rosewell died in a Kankakee hospital in 1999. He was seventy-two and had suffered from hepatitis C and liver and kidney ailments.[75]

Earlier in his term, Rosewell, the former banker and ward boss, had been charged with bank fraud for giving false statements to five banks to obtain personal loans totaling $168,000.[76] Although Rosewell was acquitted, his administrative assistant was convicted of conspiracy and bank fraud for lying to receive more than seven hundred thousand dollars in loans from banks with millions of dollars in county deposits.[77]

Even though the investigation of ghost payrolling began in the sheriff's office, it was dubbed "Haunted Hall" because of the involvement of city hall, numerous aldermen, and city-council committees. By the time the probe ended in 1999, a total of thirty-four individuals pleaded guilty, one defendant was convicted, and one was acquitted.[78]

The Stroger Era

Following the George Dunne era, Cook County government was controlled by John Stroger. Stroger was a genial African American politician who was thoroughly rooted in and completely loyal to the Cook County Democratic machine; he even supported Mayor Richard M. Daley over Harold Washington in the 1983 election. He rose from a foot soldier in Ralph Metcalfe's Third Ward Democratic political organization to become a powerful two-term president of the Cook County Board of Commissioners. In that position he was a champion accumulator of patronage jobs for his relatives and supporters and the dean of African American politics in Chicago.[79]

For most of his time in public office, Stroger's conflicts of interest, dispensing of contracts to cronies, and tainted campaign donations attracted little attention. But at his career's end, the secrecy around his disabling stroke and the backroom maneuvering to appoint his son, Todd, to succeed him as board president outraged the public. The ineptness of Todd Stroger, and the many scandals that erupted during his short four years as board president, further damaged the Stroger name.

In 1968, John Stroger, then working for the State of Illinois, was named Eighth Ward Democratic committeeman. Two years later, with Mayor Richard J. Daley's help, he was elected to the Cook County Board, a position he held for thirty-five years. In 1994, in the final month before the March primary, Daley's son, Mayor Richard M. Daley, contributed a much-needed one hundred thousand dollars to Stroger's campaign, enabling him to win nomination for board president over two strong opponents. In the same last-minute fund-raising blitz, the businessman Antoin "Tony" Rezko, who would later be convicted in the Governor Blagojevich scandals, gave Stroger's campaign $69,500.

Back in 1990, before he was board president, Stroger was paid more than two hundred thousand dollars in fees for serving as co-counsel for bond deals for the Chicago Park District, O'Hare Airport, the Water Reclamation District, the Public Building Commission, and other local government agencies, according to a *Sun-Times* report. Two of the Public Building Commissions' eleven members were confirmed by Stroger and the other members of the County Board.[80] While Stroger was the Finance Committee chairman, the committee voted to invest $6.5 million in a low-interest home-loan program. Legal work on the bond issue for the loan program was assigned to Chapman and Cutler, whose co-counsel was Stroger. In denying that politics was involved, Stroger told the *Chicago Sun-Times,* "The fact is that I do a lot of bond work for a lot of companies. I have a lot of friends that are lawyers. To imply that something is wrong here is wrong. I have looked at it and I don't believe there is a conflict."[81]

In 1997, Stroger was shamed into reimbursing six hundred dollars to Michael Segal, the president of Near North Insurance, who gave Stroger two front-row seats to a Chicago Bulls basketball game. The county ethics ordinance prohibited Stroger and other county employees from accepting any gift worth more than $125 from anyone with a financial interest in county business. Six months earlier, the board had awarded Near North a no-bid contract to place twelve million dollars in construction insurance for the new Cook County Hospital. Stroger tried to explain that he should not be criticized for accepting the free tickets from Segal, who was a friend for twenty-five years, and that he bought his own insurance from Near North Insurance.[82]

"Crony contracting" was again an issue in 1997, when Stroger said that he had selected two of his largest fund-raisers to manage the county's new office building. According to the *Chicago Sun-Times,* Stroger selected U.S. Equities and East Lake Management and Development Corporation to save money for the county, not because their top executives headed up a Stroger campaign event that brought in three hundred thousand dollars in donations.[83]

Early in 2005, Stroger told the County Board that a federal grand jury was looking into a contract for radiology services at the new county hospital. The county awarded the contract in 2001 to a joint venture of Siemens Medical Systems and a minority contractor, Faustech Industries, even though Faustech had no experience in radiology. The president of Faustech, Faust Villazan, had contributed to Stroger's political fund and to campaigns of three other commissioners.[84] Villazan received a five-hundred-thousand-dollar cut but didn't do any work as required by the contract. In 2007, he pleaded guilty to fraudulent bidding. He also admitted paying a twenty-thousand-dollar bribe to the county employee responsible for making sure contracts adhered to minority-participation rules.[85]

In addition to crony contracting, Stroger practiced two forms of patronage:

crony hiring and nepotism. In 1990, Stroger admitted that five members of his family were working in county jobs and that his godson, Orlando Jones, was deputy director of Cook County Hospital.[86] In 1994, when he became board president, Stroger hired Jones as his chief of staff. Jones left his county job in 2001 to become a lobbyist and Tony Rezko's business partner.

Often Stroger's political cronies were placed in high-paying jobs. In 2004, after two years of layoffs of hundreds of Forest Preserve workers, Sam Simone, head of the Palos Township Regular Township Democratic Organization, was hired as an assistant superintendent for $68,820 per year. He worked with Thirty-eighth Ward Democratic committeewoman Patricia Cullerton, who received an annual salary of ninety thousand dollars from the Forest Preserve.

After the Hired Truck scandal broke in 2004, federal prosecutors indicted John Cannatello and charged him with fraudulently running a minority-owned trucking company while holding down a full-time county job as a regional superintendent with the Forest Preserve District. Cannatello got his county job in the early 1990s, after he became the first suburban committee-man to endorse Stroger for board president.[87] Cannatello pleaded guilty to paying bribes to get contracts.[88]

Before the 2006 Democratic primary, the *Chicago Sun-Times* reported that "at least 17 of the party's 80 ward and township committeemen were on the county payroll, some in jobs directly under Stroger."[89] Patronage hiring and crony contracting paid off politically for John Stroger. Between 1999 and mid-2005, his campaign committee raised $624,543 from county employees and $611,278 from county contractors, according to the BGA.[90] The watchdog group followed up with a report that the Cook County inspector general, auditor, and ethics director—three supposedly independent investigators of county misdeeds—contributed a total of more than $7,300 to Stroger's campaigns.[91]

Two of John Stroger's most important relationships were with his godson Orlando Jones and with the power broker Tony Resko, a businessman and bipartisan fund-raiser. In the last seven years of Stroger's life, Jones and Rezko were business partners. These relationships between Stroger, Jones, and Rezko were a tangled web of nepotism, patronage, and crony contracting.

In 2003, a no-bid thirty-million-dollar contract for telephone service at the county jail was awarded to the telephone company SBC Illinois and Crucial Communications, a minority subcontractor with ties to Rezko and Jones.[92] An African American woman, Deloris Wade, was a special assistant to the president of Rezko Enterprises for six years before becoming chief operating officer of Crucial Communications in April 2003.[93]

In 2004, Orlando Jones received a $212,000 fee from William Blair and Company for helping it obtain a contract to invest $294 million of state pension funds.[94] In 2005, Stroger reappointed Rezko's wife, Rita, to the Cook County Employee Appeals Board, which paid her thirty-seven thousand dollars annually.[95] Five other Rezko relatives were on the county payroll at the time.[96]

Stroger's conflicts of interest, patronage hiring, and crony contracting drew criticism during his twelve years as board president, but he avoided direct personal scandal. He was never indicted; however, his reputation was damaged.

He had recovered from prostate cancer in 1994 and quadruple-bypass heart surgery in 2001. Despite his health problems, the seventy-five-year-old John Stroger decided to seek reelection as board president in 2006.[97] What followed was a series of maneuvers that exposed the undemocratic, voters-be-damned machinations of the Daley-Stroger political faction as they fought to keep control of the county's three-billion-dollar budget and its twenty-seven thousand employees.

A month before the 2006 primary, John Stroger was hospitalized and in intensive care after suffering a stroke that left him with slurred speech and unable to walk. His doctor was hopeful for a full recovery and said that it would be a month or two before Stroger could return to work.[98] Before the election, Stroger's aides put out the word that his health was improving. Although Stroger was unable to campaign, neither the media nor the voters could gauge how extensively he was impaired. Stroger won the primary election, benefitting from low voter turnout, Mayor Daley's backing, and radio commercials featuring former President Bill Clinton.

In the months that followed, there were many rumors and questions about Stroger's health. It was uncertain if he would return to work and remain on the ballot for the November general election. By July, a quiet backroom deal was engineered by party leaders. They chose Stroger's son, Eighth Ward Alderman Todd Stroger, to replace his father as the Democratic nominee. Bobbie Steele would serve as interim board president until Todd Stroger was sworn in as the new president on December 4, 2006. In the game of musical chairs, Alderman William Beavers (Seventh Ward), who would be convicted of corruption in 2013, was slated to run for John Stroger's commissioner's seat. Mayor Richard M. Daley would then appoint Beavers's daughter, Darcel, to his aldermanic seat.

After the election, but before being sworn in as a commissioner, Bobbie Steele resigned as board president so her pension would be based on the president's $170,000 annual salary rather than on the commissioner's eighty-five thousand. Then, Democratic committeemen from Steele's district selected her son, Robert Steele, a Chicago Park District administrator, to replace her on the County Board. The game of County Board musical chairs benefited everyone but the taxpayers.

Other Scandals

In 2005, before this big "switcheroo" and before his stroke, John Stroger was gearing up for his reelection campaign. But a major scandal rocked the Cook County Board President's Office of Employment Training (POET), a fourteen-million-dollar annual program funded primarily by federal government funds for employment training, education, and job placement.

Shirley Glover, the financial manager of POET, was arrested and charged with embezzling more than $180,000 from the agency. According to the state's attorney, Glover's appointment to the position was ordered by Gerald Nichols, a former patronage chief for John Stroger. Glover was in charge of the county program despite ten prior felony convictions.[99] A year later, the *Chicago Sun-Times* obtained memos indicating that Orlando Jones, Stroger's godson and chief of staff, had recommended that Glover be interviewed for the POET job.[100] Two days after the FBI attempted to interview him, Orlando Jones was found dead on a Michigan beach with a gunshot wound to his head. Police determined that it was a suicide.[101] Eventually, Glover pleaded guilty to stealing more than one hundred thousand dollars from POET.[102]

POET scandals didn't stop after Todd Stroger became board president. In 2008, three former POET officials were charged with a scheme to siphon off more than two million dollars from banks and the jobs program. They were charged with stealing $1.6 million in federal funds and bank loans, which were intended to help disadvantaged individuals get jobs as carpenters.[103] Charges against two were dropped for health reasons, but the other official pleaded guilty.[104]

In 2009, Brendolyn Hart-Glover, acting director of POET at the time, told staffers to doctor files to avoid losing federal funding.[105] Hart-Glover, a sister-in-law of Shirley Glover, pleaded guilty to federal charges that she told workers to fake birth certificates and other documents.[106]

After Todd Stroger took office, he imitated his father's practice of crony hiring. In January 2007, he appointed Cedric Giles, son of a corrupt former alderman, to a $103,000-per-year job and promoted the wife of a lifelong friend to be the county's new purchasing agent with an annual salary of $126,000. He appointed another friend to be chief of human resources, and he appointed his first cousin, Donna Dunnings, as the county's chief financial officer.[107] Dunnings was a twenty-year county employee who had spent the last eight years as deputy chief financial officer and budget director.[108]

In the three years that followed his father's death, Todd Stroger accomplished very little as he stumbled from one scandal to another. Todd Stroger's most notorious example of crony hiring was Tony Cole, a former University of Georgia basketball player. Cole was working as a restaurant busboy when Stroger hired him as an administrative assistant with a fifty-eight-thousand-dollar annual salary. On his job application Cole failed to disclose his criminal background, including a conviction for writing bad checks and rape charges, which were later dropped.[109] While he was on the county payroll, Cole was arrested twice for violating an order of protection. Cole was convicted of violating bail conditions set after an earlier arrest for domestic battery of a former girlfriend.[110]

The negative ripple effects of crony hiring and political patronage continue long after clout-connected individuals get added to the payroll. In 2009, a BGA and *Chicago Sun-Times* investigation revealed that twenty-eight Shakman-exempt patronage workers at the Cook County Forest Preserve District were given huge pay raises after making political contributions to campaign committees controlled by John and Todd Stroger.[111] When patronage workers are hired or kept in their jobs because of their political work or campaign contributions, they often cut corners in their government jobs or fail to work a full day for their pay. This has continued into the twenty-first century.

In 2009, Dane Placko of Fox News Chicago teamed up with the BGA to investigate waste of taxpayer money in the Cook County Highway Department. After observing county employees for several days, they found Alex Moreno, the brother of Commissioner Joseph Mario Moreno, sleeping at the desk of his eighty-eight-thousand-dollar-per-year job, and the county highway supervisor Mike Ponticelli, who is paid seventy-four thousand dollars annually, spending the first five hours of a workday eating at his desk, getting cash from a bank, and then meeting a friend for lunch.[112]

Under the Strogers, some businesses obtained county contracts after making political contributions. In 2008, eleven Cook County contracts worth a total of $11.8 million were awarded to companies that made campaign donations to county officials. Andy Shaw, the executive director of the BGA, said, "This investigation, like so many others, confirms the toxic 'pay to play' culture that infects every level of Illinois government."[113]

The *Daily Herald* and BGA also reported that:

- Cook County commissioners often voted on contracts despite having received political donations from the firms awarded the business.
- County Board President Todd Stroger received $47,920 in campaign donations over a twelve-year period from companies or employees that won business through the personal service contracts.
- Commissioner William Beavers and his daughter Darcel received $16,075 from the firms or employees involved in the contracts. Beavers voted to approve a contract for a parking-lot design in which the winning bidder gave his campaigns ten thousand dollars.

Crony contracts also caused the downfall of two of Todd Stroger's top aides. In 2010, Carla Oglesby, his deputy chief of staff, was indicted by the Cook County state's attorney for felony theft of government services, official misconduct, and money laundering.[114] Earlier that year, Oglesby had been a spokesperson for Stroger's failed campaign for renomination. After the campaign, she was given a county job with an annual salary of $120,000. She then steered a series of $24,900 contracts, one to her own firm, CGC Communications, and allegedly to others for work that wasn't done.[115] County contracts of less than twenty-five thousand dollars do not have to be approved by the County Board and usually escape scrutiny. In 2013, Oglesby was found guilty in state court of theft and money laundering for steering more than three hundred thousand dollars in fraudulent county contracts to her own public-relations company and to her friends.[116]

In a related case, Eugene Mullins, the former chief spokesperson for board president Todd Stroger, was arrested by the FBI in 2012. He was charged with accepting $34,700 in kickbacks for improperly steering four less-than-twenty-five-thousand-dollar county contracts for disaster relief, energy grants, and census work to four codefendants. He was also charged with steering fifty thousand dollars in census grants to two individuals.[117] Mullins, a former Chicago police officer, is Todd Stroger's best friend since childhood. In 2013, he was found guilty after federal prosecutors presented evidence that he received nearly thirty-five thousand dollars in kickbacks for steering the contracts to unqualified pals who did not plan to do the work required by the contract.[118]

When William Beavers was convicted and sentenced to six months in prison in 2013 for filing false tax returns, he became the first Cook County commissioner to be found guilty since Martin Tuchow was convicted in 1983.[119] Beavers, a former Chicago alderman, failed to pay taxes on thirty thousand dollars in campaign funds that he spent gambling on slot machines at the Horseshoe Casino in Hammond, Indiana. Beavers also neglected to report and pay taxes on $1,200 per month in county expense money that he spent personally and sixty-eight thousand dollars in campaign funds that he paid to boost his city pension.[120] According to the U.S. Attorney, "Between 2006 and 2008, Beavers allegedly paid himself more than $225,000 from three campaign accounts and used at least a portion of those funds for personal purposes, including gambling."[121]

In 2012, the former Cook County commissioner Joseph Mario Moreno, former alderman Ambrosio Medrano, and six businesspersons were charged with bribery, extortion, conspiracy, and wire fraud. According to the U.S. Attorney, Moreno and Medrano used bribery and kickbacks to sell bandages to public hospitals, including the county's new John H. Stroger Hospital. They were also charged with federal crimes for their involvement in two other bribery schemes.[122] A former aide to Moreno disclosed that she kept a secret "clout list" for him. There were more than 180 people on the list, and about half of them held or had held government jobs.[123] Machine politics, patronage, and corruption still go together in Cook County.

In July 2013, Moreno pleaded guilty to extortion conspiracy for pressuring a company to hire a minority contractor who had given Moreno one hundred thousand dollars. Moreno also admitted to pushing Stroger Hospital officials to purchase bandages from a company that agreed to pay kickbacks to him.[124]

Like Moreno, Cook County Circuit Court Clerk Dorothy Brown had a bad year in 2013. Three days before Thanksgiving, the BGA and Fox TV 32 reported that in 2011 a suburban businessman gave, or sold for one dollar, a Southwest Side building worth one hundred thousand dollars to Dorothy Brown's husband, Benton Cook III. A few months later, Brown's consulting business got the title and then sold the building for one hundred thousand dollars. The transactions were not reported on campaign fund-raising reports or on Brown's statements of economic interest as required by law.[125] Naren Patel, the businessman who gave or sold the building to Brown's husband, also contributed more than eighty-five thousand dollars to Brown's campaigns since 2003.[126] While these transactions raise ethical and legal questions, as of the present writing, there are no reports that any investigations are under way.

Earlier in 2013, court records were unsealed showing that one of Dorothy Brown's campaign contributors was a subcontractor on a $1.7 million Cook County contract for software upgrades and computer-system maintenance. He was convicted in 2011 of bribing the chief technology officer of New Orleans.[127]

The subcontractor, Mark St. Pierre, gave a five-thousand-dollar campaign donation to Brown, and one of his companies contributed ten thousand dollars.[128] In 2006, St. Pierre hosted, and Dorothy Brown chaired, a fund-raiser in Chicago for New Orleans Mayor Ray Nagin, who was indicted in 2013 for allegedly accepting free trips and more than two hundred thousand dollars in bribes from St. Pierre and other contractors.[129] Early in 2014, Nagin was found guilty of accepting bribes, wire fraud, and money laundering.[130] There are no charges or any indication that Dorothy Brown's dealings with St. Pierre violated any laws.

Ever since she took office in 2000, Brown has come under fire for her handling of money. Early on, she announced that she would accept campaign contributions from her employees, but years later, under pressure from the BGA, she discontinued the practice. She also ran into trouble for a "jeans day" program allowing her employees to wear jeans to work if they contributed small amounts of money to an office charity fund.[131] The BGA and Fox TV reported in 2010 that thousands of dollars were unaccounted for. She then canceled that program.[132]

Lack of Accountability in Crook County

Even in the reform era of County Board President Toni Preckwinkle, too many county employees have gone to jail. They include a revenue inspector for taking bribes to alert merchants to upcoming inspections, a thirty-five-year veteran of the sheriff's department, a Forest Preserve worker who took bribes to fix contracts, and two employees of the Cook County Board of Review for taking bribes to reduce property taxes.[133]

Cook County government and politics remain a stew of public corruption, with three main ingredients: monopoly power, near-total discretion, and a lack of accountability. As we discussed in chapter 1, Robert Klitgaard argued that these ingredients allow corruption to flourish.

Through his unchallenged control of Chicago city government and the Cook County Democratic party, Richard J. Daley was able to slate candidates for all offices, to contribute or withhold campaign resources, and to appoint or remove appointed officials. Of course, he listened to his more powerful allies, paid attention to public opinion, and had a keen sense of what and how much the public would tolerate.

County Board Presidents George Dunne and John Stroger, and certain Democratic elected officials such as county treasurer Rosewell and assessors

Cullerton and Tully, were able to exercise great discretion in their domains. They were able to do what they wanted as long as they didn't challenge Daley's control and didn't endanger the viability of the Democratic party. Even though Cook County has a huge budget and tens of thousands of employees, it attracts relatively little news-media attention, and the public is not sufficiently engaged to hold its officials accountable.

The Sheriff's Office, under the control of Republicans O'Grady and Dvorak, was not controlled by the mayor or the Democratic machine, but they enjoyed relatively unfettered discretion in the dispensing of jobs and the awarding of contracts. As long as political machines are able to control the election of a sizeable majority of Cook County commissioners and the board president, county government will remain a major source of patronage, nepotism, and corruption.

The Democratic machine's control of some county offices has weakened over the past two decades. The election of reformers like Cook County Clerk David Orr and County Board President Toni Preckwinkle has begun to curb stolen elections, patronage hiring, and rigged contracts. The Cook County Forest Preserve, long a bastion of patronage and cronyism, has been cleaned up sufficiently that a federal judge has discontinued oversight of hiring by the court-appointed Shakman case monitor.

While it will still take decades to uproot all the conflicts of interest in the various offices and fiefdoms of county government, progress is being made, with high-profile trials of county officials. The turnaround of county government indicates that progress in rooting out corruption is achievable.

Before Betty Loren-Maltese became Cicero town president in 1993, her husband, Frank Maltese, was the town's assessor, a city-hall insider, and a bookie. He helped shield the mob's criminal activities from police interference. In 2002, Betty Loren-Maltese was convicted for her role in a mob scheme that stole twelve million dollars from Cicero's insurance fund. *Photo courtesy of Sun-Times Media.*

CHAPTER 7

Suburban Scandals

CHICAGO ATTRACTS LOCAL, NATIONAL, and even international attention for its long and salient culture of corruption, but the media and the public tend to overlook the abundant political corruption that also exists in many of the region's suburbs. Patronage, nepotism, cronyism, abuse of power, and criminal activity flourish, sometimes for decades, in numerous town halls, police stations, and special-purpose government agencies in the suburbs. Public corruption has afflicted the north, south, and west suburbs. It impacts upper-income and lower-income villages, towns, and cities.

More than 130 individuals have been convicted of corruption-related schemes in the suburbs since the 1970s. One hundred public officials have been convicted in the last two decades. Far from being an escape from the corrupt practices of the big, bad city, many of the suburbs seem determined to imitate them.

There are six categories of corruption-related convictions in suburban Chicago:

1. Public officials with ties to organized crime
2. Nepotism
3. Police officers aiding or extorting criminals
4. Kickbacks and bribes to officials
5. Bribes from large development projects
6. Stealing of funds by leaders of school and other special purpose districts.

Figure 7.1 Corruption in Chicago-Area Suburbs

In some suburbs, corruption found a home. In others, it just paid a visit.

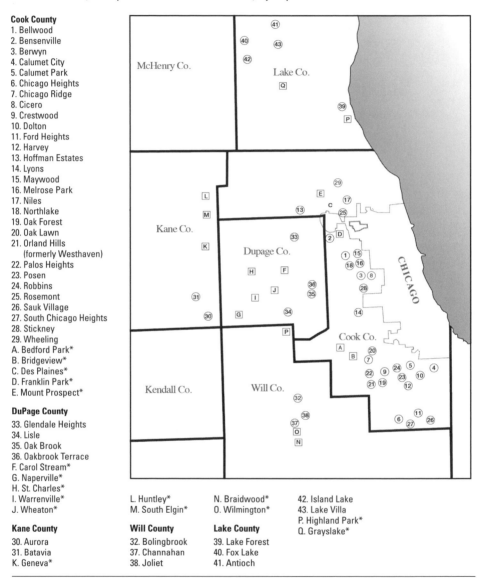

Cook County
1. Bellwood
2. Bensenville
3. Berwyn
4. Calumet City
5. Calumet Park
6. Chicago Heights
7. Chicago Ridge
8. Cicero
9. Crestwood
10. Dolton
11. Ford Heights
12. Harvey
13. Hoffman Estates
14. Lyons
15. Maywood
16. Melrose Park
17. Niles
18. Northlake
19. Oak Forest
20. Oak Lawn
21. Orland Hills
     (formerly Westhaven)
22. Palos Heights
23. Posen
24. Robbins
25. Rosemont
26. Sauk Village
27. South Chicago Heights
28. Stickney
29. Wheeling
A. Bedford Park*
B. Bridgeview*
C. Des Plaines*
D. Franklin Park*
E. Mount Prospect*

DuPage County
33. Glendale Heights
34. Lisle
35. Oak Brook
36. Oakbrook Terrace
F. Carol Stream*
G. Naperville*
H. St. Charles*
I. Warrenville*
J. Wheaton*

Kane County
30. Aurora
31. Batavia
K. Geneva*

L. Huntley*
M. South Elgin*

Will County
32. Bolingbrook
37. Channahan
38. Joliet

N. Braidwood*
O. Wilmington*

Lake County
39. Lake Forest
40. Fox Lake
41. Antioch

42. Island Lake
43. Lake Villa
P. Highland Park*
Q. Grayslake*

*Note: The numerals on the map indicate Chicago-area suburban cities, towns, and villages where there have been criminal convictions for public or political corruption. The letters with asterisks indicate suburbs where there have been corruption scandals and news reports of corruption but researchers did not find subsequent reports of convictions.

The abundance of suburban corruption contradicts the common perception that the suburbs have clean, open, and effective governments. In fact, corruption affects a large number of local governments throughout the Chicago metropolitan area, and it has persisted for decades.

Figure 7.1 highlights suburbs where officials have been convicted of corruption or involved in scandals. Corruption has been documented in more than sixty suburbs, spanning Cook, DuPage, Kane, Lake, and Will Counties. We have not included corruption in nearby towns in other states like Gary and Hammond, Indiana, or those over the border in Wisconsin. But corruption is rife in those places as well.

Links to Organized Crime

Several high-profile incidents of corruption in suburban Chicago have featured corrupt public officials with connections to organized crime. West suburban Cicero is a prime example. Organized crime took root in Cicero in 1923, when Al Capone settled there. During the following decades, attempts to eradicate corruption proved unsuccessful, as organized crime maintained a strong presence in Cicero with mob bosses such as Frank "the Enforcer" Nitti and Tony "Big Tuna" Accardo. They were involved in liquor, gambling, and strip joints.[1] Corruption was so widespread in the 1950s that Cicero officials considered changing the town's name to improve its image.[2]

Cicero's more recent problems with mobbed-up public officials gained public attention in 1990, when twenty people were indicted for participating in a gambling and extortion scheme. At the time, authorities called it one of the largest-ever crackdowns on Chicago-area organized crime.[3] The investigation centered on the mobster Ernest Rocco Infelise and the Cicero town assessor Frank Maltese.

The Maltese family became the most famous of the Cicero corrupt politicians since Capone moved back to Chicago in 1927. With Infelise's support, Frank Maltese became town assessor and a close associate of town president Henry Klosak. Maltese then helped his wife, Betty Loren-Maltese, become the chief administrative aide to Klosak. Betty and Frank pretty much ran the town. From their government positions, the Malteses helped provide the mob access to city hall and helped shield the mob's criminal activities from police interference.[4] As a result of a federal investigation, Frank Maltese pleaded guilty in 1991 to charges of conspiracy related to gambling. He admitted to serving as a bookmaker for the mob and notifying Infelise of a police raid on a tavern owned by a mobster.[5] Infelise was convicted in 1992 of racketeering and nineteen other charges, including operating an illegal gambling business, intimidation, extortion, and conspiracy to bribe a public official. Prosecutors said that Infelise headed a nine-million-dollar-a-year organized-crime operation that controlled gambling and other illicit activities in Cook and Lake Counties between 1974 and 1989.[6]

Frank Maltese died of cancer in 1991, before beginning his prison sentence. Nonetheless, organized crime's influence in Cicero continued under the leadership of his widow, Betty Loren-Maltese, who became town president in 1993. Betty was a colorful character in her own right.

Betty met Frank when she was twenty-two years old. When they finally got married some years later, they were both working for Cicero. It was Frank who convinced the town board to select Betty as interim town president. She was then elected and reelected on her own after Frank died of cancer.

With the help of former corrupt Chicago Alderman Eddie Vrdolyak, the head of the Cook County Republican party, Betty was able to build a strong Republican party in the town. She was able to incorporate Latinos, who were becoming an ever larger part of the population, into the party organization. "Her wise-cracking, tough-gal persona, flashy clothes, and big hair played well in the bungalow belt and captivated the media."[7] She kept up her mob ties during her reign.

In 2002, she was convicted of racketeering as well as wire and mail fraud for her role in a mob scheme that stole more than twelve million dollars from the city's insurance fund.[8] Prosecutors said that Loren-Maltese and her co-conspirators used the stolen money to invest in a mob-connected luxury golf course in Wisconsin, for loans to family friends, and to lease Cadillacs and other cars for cronies.[9] She was sentenced to eight years in prison and to pay back $3.25 million from her share in the scheme. Michael Spano Sr., an organized-crime boss, and four others in addition to Betty were convicted for their roles in the scheme. The mob-run insurance firm overcharged and falsely billed the town for employees' health-insurance claims.[10]

Corruption associated with organized crime has also surfaced in suburbs such as Rosemont, Northlake, Chicago Heights, Franklin Park, and Stone Park. For example, Seymour Sapoznik, who was police chief in Stone Park from 1980 to 1990 and Northlake police chief from 1990 to 1994, pleaded guilty in 1997 to accepting monthly bribes of five hundred dollars from the mob.[11] He pocketed $24,500 over a four-year period in return for keeping quiet about illegal video-gambling operations in Northlake. Likewise, Stone Park Mayor

Robert Natale pleaded guilty in 2001 to pocketing thirty-five thousand dollars in bribes from Chicago mobsters in return for protecting illegal gambling and allowing an adult bookstore in his suburb.[12]

In Chicago Heights, Finance Commissioner Nick LoBue pleaded guilty in 1991 to accepting fifty thousand dollars in bribes from the south-suburban mob boss Albert Tocco for awarding a garbage-hauling contract to the mobster's firm.[13] Similarly, former Franklin Park police officer Robert Urbinati pleaded guilty in 2002 to taking bribes from the mob in return for ignoring gambling and assisting organized crime.[14]

Federal and state authorities have also accused Rosemont's public officials of having ties to organized crime. In 2005, FBI special agent John Mallul testified that Rosemont Mayor Donald Stephens met with members of organized crime in May 1999.[15] According to Mallul, Stephens and the mob members discussed the control of construction and contracts for the proposed Emerald Casino in Rosemont. In addition, an April 2004 Illinois Gaming Board memo linked the mob to Rosemont.[16] The memo claimed that Mayor Stephens held Tuesday-morning meetings with Nick Boscarino and William Hogan Jr., even after Boscarino was indicted for defrauding the city. Gaming Board officials claimed that Boscarino had connections to organized crime and that Hogan had been ousted from the Teamsters because of his mob ties. The memo also asserted that Mark Stephens, Donald Stephens' son, owned part of a temporary labor company with connections to the mob. Rosemont officials have always maintained that the accusations in the memo were false.[17]

The mob's connections to local suburban officials have been a major source of corruption. Mob leaders traditionally bribed officials and worked with them to steal government funds. Many of their scams involve public officials allowing the mob to run illegal businesses such as gambling in return for bribes or kickbacks.

Nepotism

Nepotism has been a common practice in many Chicago suburbs. The village of Rosemont provides a case study of how public officials can use their power to enrich friends and family. Donald Stephens served as mayor of Rosemont from 1956 to 2003, and he helped transform Rosemont from a small subdivision near O'Hare Airport just west of Chicago into a booming suburb. However, many of the beneficiaries of village contracts under his administration had business or family connections to the mayor.

In the 1980s, firms owned by Stephens's relatives received millions of dollars in city business contracts without competitive bidding.[18] Three firms owned by Stephens's business associates received more than eighteen million dollars worth of contracts to expand the Rosemont Exposition Center.[19] Firms owned by his wife, son, and daughter-in-law also received million-dollar contracts.[20]

Nepotism remains as prevalent under Rosemont Mayor Bradley Stephens as it was before his father died in 2007. In 2010, ten members of the Stephens family received a combined $950,000 in salaries from the village.[21]

In addition to the Stephens family, several other village employees had ties to Rosemont leaders. Harry Pappas, who was married to village trustee Sharon Pappas, was the highest-paid village employee in 2010, with a $230,000 salary for running the Allstate Arena. The Rosemont clerk and village trustees also had family members who worked for the village in 2010.[22]

Nepotism has been visible in other Chicago suburbs, such as Dolton, Orland Hills, Lyons, Cicero, and Waukegan.[23] In Cicero, continuing its corruption tradition, Town President Larry Dominick admitted in 2011 to putting more than twenty current and former family members on the town payroll, including his mother, sister, and wife.[24]

Nepotism undermines the principles of hiring the best-qualified candidates and giving contracts to companies that provide the best government services at the lowest cost. It undermines employee morale, as workers learn that promotions and assignments are not based on merit and qualifications. It hinders accountability within city governments because it is difficult for a supervisor to discipline a family member of a top official. Ultimately, nepotism reduces efficiency, raises the cost of government, leads to higher taxes, and lowers the quality of government services.

Police Corruption

As with the Chicago Police Department and the Cook County Sheriff's Office, corruption has surfaced often within police and law-enforcement agencies throughout the suburbs. Since the 1970s, more than thirty suburban law-enforcement officers have been convicted of crimes related to corruption. Many of the convictions involve officers aiding or extorting criminals.

In one of the largest thefts, the former Country Club Hills police chief Regina Evans was convicted of stealing more than nine hundred thousand dollars in state grants. For her crimes, she was sentenced to five years in prison. Judge Sue Myerscough said in her sentencing, "That's what makes your fall from grace so shocking to me, the fact that you of all people [as a police officer] knew these were crimes."[25]

In Chicago Heights, multiple officers have been convicted of helping or extorting drug dealers. Police officers George Werner and George Sintic were convicted in 1992 for money laundering and drug conspiracy.[26] Prosecutors said that the men were involved in a decades-long conspiracy that began in the 1970s when the police officers provided information to a drug dealer about the activities of police and other competing drug dealers. Werner and Sintic also bought cocaine from a drug trafficker and sold it to a drug dealer in Chicago Heights.[27]

In a similar case, Chicago Heights Deputy Chief Sam Mangialardi was convicted in 1994 of racketeering, narcotics conspiracy, extortion, and theft of government funds.[28] Prosecutors said that the drug kingpin Otis Moore Jr. paid Mangialardi ten thousand dollars a month to allow him to operate a cocaine business. They said that Mangialardi diverted police from Moore's turf in the Wentworth Gardens Housing Project in Chicago, ordered police to pursue Moore's rivals, and kept Moore updated on federal investigations into his drug dealing.[29]

Officers have also been convicted of bribery or extortion in suburbs such as Melrose Park, Harvey, and Lyons. For instance, in 1990 Lyons police officers pleaded guilty to having sex with prostitutes in return for overlooking crimes at a strip joint.[30]

The list of suburban police-corruption cases seems endless. In 1985, the FBI seized records from the Harvey Police Department as part of an investigation into whether officers were stealing cash and drugs during raids.[31] Again in 2008, the FBI raided the Harvey Police Department offices following the federal agency's arrest of four Harvey officers for providing protection for drug dealers.[32]

In Melrose Park, the former police chief Vito Scavo and two other officers were convicted in 2009 of racketeering and extortion. During his ten-year stint as chief, Scavo allegedly pressured bars, restaurants, the Kiddieland amusement park, Our Lady of Mount Carmel church, and other businesses to hire his private security companies.[33]

Dispensing police powers has been a further source of corruption. In 1997, the Village of Dolton began a deputy-marshal program to back up the police department. The mayor of Dolton handed out eighteen badges to private citizens, along with authorization to carry guns, though none of these individuals have ever been called to service.[34] Three of those given badges were later convicted on drug charges, and at least one said that he purchased his badge for thirty to forty thousand dollars.[35] In 2003 in a nearby suburb, Harvey Mayor Eric Kellogg gave out a number of such police badges, resulting in several arrests and convictions when some deputy marshals abused their police powers.[36] Harvey has been under almost constant scrutiny for various instances of police misconduct, abuse, and corruption.

Police corruption is more widespread in the suburbs than is usually recognized. Drugs, prostitution, and other illicit activities provide sources of corruption for too many suburban police forces.

Bribery and Kickbacks

Many elected officials and top government bureaucrats in suburban Chicago have been convicted of using their authority to solicit bribes from businesses and individuals. A corruption scandal in the middle-class suburb of Niles illustrates how suburban elected officials can use their positions to enrich themselves. Nicolas Blasé served as a mayor of Niles for forty-seven years until he resigned in 2008 under the pressure of federal corruption charges. That year, Blasé pleaded guilty for his role in a kickback scheme with his friend's insurance company.[37] Prosecutors said that Blasé pocketed more than $420,000 over three decades in return for pressuring local businesses to use Ralph Weiner and Associates as their insurance broker.[38] And according to a recent investigation, Blasé also handed out about half a million dollars' worth of perks to six retiring or retired village employees. These perks came in the form of bonuses, village cars, and cash payments authorized by Blasé himself and not the Village Board, in violation of Illinois' Open Meetings Act.[39]

Corruption in Niles and the bribing of public officials continued after Mayor Blaisé's conviction. Niles businessmen Jowhar Soultanali and Kabir Kassam, owners of an education company, have been indicted for bribing school officials to spend more than thirty-three million dollars on their substandard tutoring programs. Soutanali and Kassam are awaiting trial in federal court and face up to twenty years on each of five counts of mail fraud and ten years each on three counts of bribery. Among the school systems defrauded across the nation were the Chicago Public Schools.[40]

Altogether, eighteen suburban mayors and town presidents have been convicted of corruption during the last few decades. As a general rule, the longer mayors stay in office and become more secure and powerful, the more likely they are to accept bribes and to use patronage and nepotism to promote family members.

Elected officials also have been convicted for accepting money in return for helping businesses gain approval for development projects in suburbs such as Lyons, Berwyn, and Hoffman Estates. In the 1970s, a former Hoffman Estates mayor and four village officials pleaded guilty to accepting kickbacks from a representative of the homebuilder Kaufman and Broad, Inc., in return for approving its requested zoning changes.[41]

If bribes aren't forthcoming, some officials take advantage of whatever is available. In 1987, Arlington Heights treasurer Lee Poder was arrested for using twenty million dollars in fire-department pension funds to buy and sell securities, keeping profits for himself but passing along the losses to the village.[42]

Bribes from Big Economic Developments

The lure of big developments in suburbs has also been a source not only of potential corruption but massive conflicts of interest, and not only in Rosemont. A recent *Chicago Tribune* exposé on Bridgeview calculates the suburb's total debt as $230 million—a $196.4 million increase from the year 2000. This is by far the largest debt burden of any suburb.[43] A town of only 16,446 residents, this amounts to almost fourteen thousand dollars for every man, woman, and child residing in Bridgeview. This huge debt has also caused Standard and Poor's to downgrade the town's credit rating to near-junk status.[44]

The borrowed money was used mainly to build Toyota Park, home to the Chicago Fire professional men's soccer team, which also serves as a concert venue. But it was the mayor's friends and associates who got contracts to build and maintain the park. Among those receiving contracts were the town's financial advisor, Mayor Stephen Landek's brother, and the mayor's former company, Eco-Chem. The mayor had company ownership transferred to his girlfriend and nephew while the stadium was being built. Also favored was CDK Accounting, which rents office space from a building the mayor owns.[45] To top it off, since the project was proposed, Mayor Landek has received more than $170,000 in political contributions from Toyota Park contractors and vendors.[46]

But it's not only contracts that serve as a source for conflict of interest in Bridgeview. When this book was being written, Landek was mayor, state senator, and chaired the Lyons township political fund. He was previously Lyons township supervisor and highway supervisor.[47] In Illinois parlance, Mayor

Landek is a double- or triple-dipper who has received multiple government salaries simultaneously. His multiple government jobs have allowed him to influence decisions and to provide benefits for family, friends, and contributors.

Schools and Special-Purpose Districts

One of the oldest forms of corruption is straight stealing. There are a number of high-profile suburban cases like the Burnham village clerk Nancy Dobrowski, who stole seven hundred thousand dollars over thirty years from this tiny suburb of 4,500 residents. She used the stolen funds to pay for gambling at Indiana casinos.[48]

Similar cases of corruption have affected a number of suburban school and special-purpose districts. For instance, two major corruption scandals rocked Dixmoor's Park District before it disbanded in 1998. Bobby Jackson, a former Dixmoor Park District trustee, pleaded guilty to stealing one hundred thousand dollars from the agency.[49] The money collected from property taxes was supposed to be used to pay off construction bonds for a recreation center that was never built. Instead, Jackson spent the stolen money on a political campaign and shared it with political allies.[50] Prosecutors said that Jackson and two former Dixmoor Park District trustees stole altogether five hundred thousand dollars of taxpayer funds.[51] All three were convicted. The district never operated recreation programs and only oversaw one tot lot. However, state officials estimate that the park district had amassed more than $1.6 million in bond issues, loans, and tax levies.[52]

Corruption also tainted the Dixmoor Park District Police Department[53] and officials working for special-purpose districts in suburbs such as Batavia, Posen, and Maywood, who have been accused or convicted of corruption-related charges.[54]

Educational leaders from a variety of districts have been convicted of stealing public funds. A senior vice president for business affairs at Triton College pleaded guilty in 1985 to embezzling about $2,500 from the community college in River Grove.[55] A former Bellwood School District 88 superintendent pleaded guilty to embezzlement in 1996. He stole more than two hundred thousand dollars from the district, as checks that were supposed to have been made payable to the district went into his personal bank account.[56]

Similar scandals rocked the Chicago Public Schools. For instance, the schools inspector general reported that Roberto Tirado stole nearly $420,000 from Lake View High School in a fraudulent billing scheme. As the school's technology coordinator, he created fake vendors whose names he forged on checks, which he then deposited into his own account. He also billed $144,000 in reimbursements for expenditures on his personal credit card. He died in Mexico before he could be indicted and tried.[57]

Corruption occurred in other special districts than school districts. In the Palos Heights Fire Protection District in 2013, Michele and Charles Sopko were accused of stealing $352,000. Charles was the deputy fire chief in Oak Forest, and Michele was the former administrative assistant for the Fire Protection District. They manipulated the payroll and accounts-payable systems to divert the money into their own bank account. He also served as vice president of the Oak Forest Park District, and she served on the elected school board. They were seen as model citizens by their neighborhoods until the scandal was uncovered. As one reporter wrote, "Yesterday, the Sopkos were community leaders. Today, their mugshots are in the newspapers."[58]

Because school and special-purpose districts often receive less public scrutiny than city governments, public corruption can go undetected for years. There is often little oversight because there are few employees at such agencies.

Ending Suburban Corruption

There needs to be a comprehensive approach to fix the culture of corruption evident in many of Chicago's suburbs. Voters, prosecutors, state leaders, suburban public officials, good-government groups, and educational institutions can all take steps to reduce corruption.

One of the most obvious and effective methods for dealing with corrupt officeholders would be electing new public officials dedicated to ethical and governmental reform. Reform candidates, if elected, can help change the culture of corruption.

Next, the state legislature should create a suburban inspector general who could report issues of corruption to the attorney general to be prosecuted if warranted. As an interim step, some suburbs have agreed to use Cook County Sheriff Tom Dart's office as their town's inspector general. Dart sent a letter to all 130 suburban cities and towns in Cook County inviting them to use this service. Dart and his staff are currently serving as the inspector general in three Cook County suburbs; already his office has issued reports of conflicts of interest in several of them. The sheriff correctly argues, "When you have [corruption] on larger levels of government, there are multiple ways where you have people watching it. In smaller jurisdictions . . . there is this cloistered little universe where corruption goes on for the longest time and you never know about it."[59]

A suburban inspector general covering all suburbs would help deter public officials from taking corrupt actions and could help publicize the problems of corruption. Until there is such an official, citizens who want to report corruption have no one to turn to. Currently, the only deterrent to suburban corruption seems to be prosecution by the U.S. Attorney's office, which has limited resources and can only investigate possible violations of federal law. Since there are more than 1,200 separate units of government in the Chicago metropolitan region, there are too many jurisdictions and officials for the U.S. Attorney adequately to police.

Suburban governments also need to increase transparency to hold officials accountable for the decisions they make. Greater transparency can deter police misconduct and can discourage officials from only awarding contracts to the politically connected firms. It can give a sense of clean and efficient government to their respected towns.

One form of transparency is for local governments to provide information on decisions, expenditures, and contracts on official Web sites. Local governments (or a suburban inspector general, if one is created) should also set up phone hotlines and Internet sites so constituents can report suspected waste or corrupt acts.

Suburbs can also take swift and decisive action to mitigate the effects of corruption when confronted with problems. For example, leaders of suburban Des Plaines took a number of steps to stem corruption in the last decade as the city pursued a casino license.[60] Concerns about corruption arose after it was discovered that former Assistant City Manager William Schneider might have had an illicit relationship with Jim Dvorak—a convicted felon accused of having connections to the mob—who was associated with two firms doing business with Des Plaines.[61] After the relationship between Schneider and Dvorak attracted public attention in 2004, Schneider resigned from his city post. Des Plaines also spent $215,000 to terminate a contract with a marketing firm linked to Dvorak because Schneider had renewed the contract without the necessary approval from the city council.[62] The city cut all ties to Dvorak, and city leaders, including Mayor Anthony Arredia, voluntarily met with federal investigators to provide information about the possible illegal relationship between Schneider and Dvorak.[63] Following the incident with Schneider and Dvorak, Des Plaines bolstered its ethics laws to attempt to prevent corruption.[64] In 2007, the city created a new ethics officer to serve as an ombudsman for citizen complaints, and the council passed a law that created a fine for aldermen who do not turn in their economic disclosure forms on time.[65] Des Plaines' responses illustrate a few of the ways suburbs can mitigate corruption on their own initiative.

Unfortunately, suburban corruption is so endemic that there is no magical or quick solution. One starting point is to recognize that corruption is not only a Chicago problem; the culture of corruption is an Illinois problem. While some individual suburbs may be exempt from this epidemic, many are not. Suburbanites must demand reforms by local and state government.

If more than sixty suburbs have corruption and conflicts of interest, then it is necessary to take additional steps to eliminate this corruption. In a time of economic recession and government cutbacks in services, it would seem essential to eliminate all forms of waste and corruption. What is needed is the will to act.

Chicago Police Lieutenant Jon Burge and officers under his command were implicated in more than one hundred cases of forcing confessions by torturing African American suspects on the city's far South Side. By the end of 2013, the city paid out more than ninety-six million dollars to settle wrongful conviction cases. In 2010, Burge was found guilty of obstructing justice and perjury for lying about the torture. *Photo courtesy of Sun-Times Media.*

CHAPTER 8

Police Abuse and Corruption

BY HIS ACTIONS AT JESSE'S SHORTSTOP INN on the night of February 19, 2007, the twelve-year veteran police officer Anthony Abbate demonstrated that he strongly believed, as many police officers do, that he could break the law with impunity. He believed that victims and onlookers would be afraid to report his actions. And if they did, his fellow officers would intimidate witnesses, hide the evidence, and cover up his crimes. Every police officer knew by this time about the cover-up of torture in a South Side police station, about cops working together to shake down taverns, and how police sometimes stole from drug dealers. They also knew about officers losing files and failing to adequately investigate the mayor's nephew for manslaughter. Such police abuses mostly went unpunished.

Fortified with his belief in his own invincibility and with too much alcohol, the drunk, 250-pound off-duty Abbate went behind the bar at Jesse's and repeatedly punched and kicked a 115-pound female bartender for refusing to serve him any more drinks.[1] The bartender, Karolina Obrycka, called 911 for help, but Abbate fled before other police arrived. The responding officers left Abbate's name off their report and failed to note that he was a police officer. They also didn't indicate that the tavern had surveillance video showing the brutal beating.[2] An unidentified person came into the bar before it closed and offered the bartender money to forget about the attack.[3] Before he was arrested, Abbate checked himself into a substance-abuse program.[4] When he came out nearly a month later, he was arrested and charged with a misdemeanor, not a felony.[5]

Fearing that Abbate's attack would be covered up and unpunished, the bartender's lawyers released the videotape to WFLD-TV Fox 32.[6] It was aired on March 21, picked up by other TV stations, and shown on national newscasts. Subsequently it was posted on YouTube, enabling millions of people throughout the world to see the hulking Abbate pummeling the petite bartender. Although police officials and prosecutors viewed the videotape a few days after the attack, it wasn't until a month later, after the TV airings sparked a huge public uproar, that the state's attorney's office upgraded the charges against Abbate to a felony.[7]

Following a bench trial, Abbate was found guilty of aggravated battery by Circuit Court Judge John Fleming, who dismissed Abbate's claim that he was acting in self-defense when he punched and kicked the bartender. Abbate was acquitted on official misconduct charges because, according to the judge, there wasn't evidence that he said he was a police officer.[8] Despite the damning videotape evidence and testimony from the bartender that she was still suffering from the aftereffects of the beating, Abbate got away with no jail time. Instead, Judge Fleming sentenced him to two years probation and ordered the rogue cop to perform 130 hours of community service and to observe an 8:00 P.M. to 6:00 A.M. curfew.[9]

Police superintendent Jody Weis told the *Sun-Times* that as a citizen, he was surprised that Abbate received probation for a "horrific" incident that embarrassed the department but that he respected the judge's decision.[10] Six months later, Abbate was fired from the police department. More than five years after the notorious beating, a federal jury awarded Karolina Obrycka $850,000 in damages in a civil lawsuit, which Chicago's taxpayers had to pay. The jury also established that a police culture of impunity protects cops who commit crimes.

"We proved a code of silence at every level in the Chicago Police Department," said Obrycka's attorney, Terry Ekl. He pointed to the jury's finding that there was a "widespread and persistent code of silence," resulting in a policy of inadequately investigating police misconduct.[11]

In a move that only reinforced the common, well-founded belief that Chicago hides, denies, or minimizes police crime, the city's attorneys offered to forgo an appeal and quickly pay the bartender and her attorneys if they and the judge agreed to strike the jury's finding. The city wanted to erase the jury's assertion that the city had a widespread practice of failing to investigate and discipline its officers. Mayor Rahm Emanuel declared that this would protect the city in future lawsuits.[12]

Fortunately, U.S. Circuit Court Judge Amy St. Eve rejected the city's request. She said that the city had a chance to settle the case but decided to pursue a jury trial, calling it a matter of principle. After it lost at trial, the city agreed to pay the $850,000.[13]

Officer Abbate is only one of the embarrassing examples of serious police misconduct that has plagued Chicago. The extent of the problem can be grasped by looking at the statistics. Since 1960, more than three hundred Chicago police officers have been convicted of serious crimes, such as drug dealing, beating civilians, destroying evidence, protecting mobsters, theft, and murder.[14] However, this doesn't include all the illegal and unethical activities that have gone undetected or were covered up internally by the police department.

Chicago is not the only municipality to struggle with this problem. Many suburban police departments have had similar experiences. But Chicago's failure to rein in its errant officers, the department's lax discipline, and its active involvement in cover-ups have led Chicago's twelve thousand police officers to believe that they can break the law with near-total impunity.

Lieutenant Jon Burge's House of Screams

Beginning as far back as 1972, Chicago police detective Jon Burge was implicated in the torture and abuse of suspects at Area 2 Police Headquarters. By 2010 Burge was an overweight, Florida retiree living the good life. But in the last decades of the twentieth century, the burly, white police commander was a terror to be reckoned with in this South Side, predominantly African American police district.

Since 1989, numerous courts have determined that a crew of Chicago police officers under Burge's command kicked, burned, suffocated, administered electric shock, and employed other dehumanizing torture techniques to force suspects to confess to crimes. Dozens of defendants have had their convictions set aside or overturned because judges or juries believed that evidence of torture was sufficient to invalidate the convictions. The cost to the city to settle wrongful-conviction lawsuits in Burge's cases had reached ninety-six million dollars by the end of 2013.[15] It will continue to grow by ten million dollars or more a year for some time to come.

From 1972 through 1991, numerous African American suspects charged that they were tortured with electric shock and suffocation by Burge and his "Midnight Crew."[16] From 1981 to 1988, when Richard M. Daley was Cook

County state's attorney, a total of fifty-five separate victims alleged that they were tortured.[17] Prosecutors on the state's attorney's staff, according to the People's Law Office, were aware of the allegations and nonetheless used the coerced evidence in hearings and criminal trials to convict victims and send them to prison.[18]

In 1985, the Chicago Police Department's Office of Professional Standards (OPS) dismissed complaints from a convicted cop killer, Andrew Wilson, that he had been tortured. Wilson had been convicted in 1983 and then was retried and convicted a second time. He then filed a federal civil-rights case. The city defended Burge, and in 1989, the jury found that there was a pattern and practice of police torture and said that Wilson's constitutional rights had been violated. Wilson won a new trial, but he was not awarded monetary damages. Despite the evidence presented in court, the city took no action against Burge or the other police officers. OPS, however, reopened its investigation into Wilson's complaints.

On January 25, 1990, the *Chicago Reader* weekly newspaper published "The House of Screams," John Conroy's twenty-thousand-word article describing horrific torture sessions at Burge's interview room in Area 2. The article presented details about specific torture techniques used by Burge and several other officers. It also included denials from Burge and others that any torture occurred.[19]

Nine months later, OPS completed its investigation, but its two reports were sealed. The first report recommended that the superintendent fire Burge and two other officers for torturing Wilson. The second found that abuse at Area 2 under Burge was "systematic, methodical, and included psychological techniques and planned torture."[20]

In February 1992, a federal judge ordered the OPS reports unsealed and made available in an unrelated brutality case. An angry police superintendent LeRoy Martin, who had commanded Area 2 detectives for nine months, during which some of the abuse occurred, said it was an "outright lie" that he or other commanders knew about or condoned torture. Martin said that he took no action for a year after receiving the report because he believed the allegations were unsubstantiated. Former State's Attorney Richard M. Daley, who by that time was mayor, reiterated Martin's assessment of the OPS report. "These are only allegations," he said. "These are not substantiated cases."[21]

After delays and legal wrangling, the Chicago Police Board on February 1993 fired Jon Burge for physically abusing Andrew Wilson. It also suspended two of Burge's detectives for fifteen months.[22]

The firing of Burge, however, was not the end of the story, nor was it the end of the city's efforts to suppress evidence that the police department, state's attorney, or mayor knew about the torture. Burge retired to his home in Florida, worked occasionally for a security firm, and continued to receive his pension. In 2002, the chief judge of the Cook County criminal courts appointed a special prosecutor to investigate if Burge and other Area 2 officers committed crimes while interrogating suspects. In 2003, Governor George Ryan pardoned four death-row inmates after he determined that their convictions were obtained by torture. In later civil lawsuits, Burge and more than thirty other detectives refused on constitutional grounds to answer questions about torture.

In July 2006, the special prosecutor said that he found credible evidence in about half of the 148 cases of alleged torture and abuse by police, but he didn't issue indictments because the statute of limitations prevented prosecutions.[23] Two years later, Patrick Fitzgerald, U.S. Attorney for the Northern District of Illinois, arrested Jon Burge after a special grand jury indicted him for obstruction of justice and perjury for allegedly lying about whether he and officers under his command tortured and abused suspects. The indictment alleged that Burge lied on two occasions in discovery in the lawsuit *Hobley v. Jon Burge et al.* in U.S. District Court.[24] The five-year statute of limitations on torture had expired. But the alleged perjury occurred in 2003, and the indictment for that was brought before its five-year statute of limitations ran out. "There is no place for torture and abuse in a police station, and no place for perjury and false statements in federal lawsuits. No person is above the law, and nobody—even a suspected murderer—is beneath its protections," Fitzgerald said.[25]

In June 2010, almost thirty years after Burge and his "midnight crew" were first accused of torturing African American suspects, the ex–police commander was found guilty of obstruction of justice and perjury for lying about the torture.[26]

Federal Judge Joan Lefkow, who sentenced Burge to four and a half years in prison, said that neither she nor the jury believed Burge's denial of "any knowledge of torture." Commenting on his perjury, the judge told Burge, "It demonstrates at the very least a serious lack of respect for the due process of law and your unwillingness to acknowledge the truth in the face of all of this evidence." She then focused on the significance of the torture Burge covered up. "When a confession is coerced, the truth of the confession is called into question. When this becomes widespread, as one can infer from the accounts that have been presented here in this court, the administration of justice is undermined irreparably. How can one trust that justice will be served when the justice system has been so defiled."[27]

After many years of the city denying torture at the hands of Burge, Mayor Rahm Emanuel offered an apology. He called the Burge era "a dark chapter in the city's history."[28] Emanuel commented after the city council approved another $12.3 million settlement for two African American men who were tortured before making false confessions: "So yes, there has been a settlement, and I do believe this is a way of saying all of us are sorry about what happened here." He called it "a stain on the city's reputation" and said, "That is not who we are."[29] The mayor suggested that we should all move on. However, that will be difficult, because in 2014 there were still numerous uncompensated alleged victims and several lawsuits in the pipeline.

Mob Connections

Since the days of Scarface Al Capone and Mayor "Big Bill" Thompson, there have been sporadic rumors that the Chicago Outfit's tentacles reached into the upper echelons of the Chicago Police Department. Often observers of the police suggested that certain powerful ward organizations could determine who would be selected as commanders of their local police districts.

In 1980, about a year after Jane Byrne was elected mayor, acting Police Superintendent Joseph DiLeonardi charged that two of Byrne's top aides told him to remove Deputy Superintendent William Duffy from his position as head of the organized-crime unit. According to DiLeonardi, one of Byrne's aides said that the removal was requested by John D'Arco, Democratic committeeman for the mob-dominated First Ward. DiLeonardi said that he refused and was passed over for promotion to superintendent. Two months later, both DiLeonardi and Duffy were demoted to the rank of captain. Duffy retired.[30] A grand jury investigated, but no one was charged. Mayor Byrne fired the aides and named Richard Brzeczek as her new superintendent.

In 1997, the *Chicago Tribune* revealed that Police Superintendent Matt Rodriguez was a close friend of Frank Milito, a convicted felon. Milito had been questioned in the unsolved murder of the Amoco Oil Company executive Robert Merriam. The department's Rule 47 prohibits police officers from fraternizing with convicted felons, but it is rarely enforced.[31] The next day, Rodriguez announced his retirement and said that the disclosure of his thirty-year relationship with Milito had "pained" Mayor Richard M. Daley.[32]

Milito was a politically connected North Side businessman who owned several Amoco gas stations; Orso's, a popular Italian restaurant; two travel agencies; and real estate worth more than one million dollars.[33] Although it wasn't known until he retired, Rodriguez's relationship with Milito was deeper than friendly chats at the restaurant. Milito took Rodriguez on trips to Italy and Israel and arranged for Rodriguez to obtain discount travel fares. He also hired Rodriguez's son-in-law to work at Orso's.[34]

Milito had bipartisan political connections and ties to members of the Chicago Outfit. In the 1980s, he was a part-time investigator for the city council Committee on Traffic and Public Safety. He was also a Cook County holiday-court bailiff with a badge and the right to carry a gun. In 1986, he pleaded guilty to mail fraud and tax evasion after failing to report the sale of $4.6 million worth of gas from four stations. Milito's car wash had a city contract, worth ninety thousand dollars a year in 1990. The business was in his wife's name so that it could qualify as a woman-owned business. His wife, Nicolina, also had several Park District contracts to run food concessions on the lakefront.[35] Milito donated an office below his travel agency to the Forty-third Ward Democratic organization. For an ex-con, Milito was indeed a well-connected guy.

Following Milito's 1986 tax conviction, Amoco executive Robert Merriam tried to strip Milito of his ownership of the gas stations. Milito was forced to sell several at fire-sale prices but was allowed to transfer ownership of one station to his sons. Milito had a motive to get back at Merriam.

The investigation of Merriam's murder was overseen by sheriff's police Captain George Nicosia, who was also a friend of Superintendent Rodriguez. The investigation fizzled and was quietly shelved. Milito was questioned, but there was never a report that he was a suspect. No one was charged with the murder, which is still unsolved.

In October 2001, former chief of detectives William Hanhardt pleaded guilty to running a mob-connected jewelry-theft ring. He used police information and contacts that he had nurtured while on the department's payroll. The ring robbed more than one hundred jewelry salesmen and stole more than five million dollars in watches, diamonds, and other gems over a fifteen-year period, including some years when Hanhardt was still on the force.[36] After he retired in 1986, Hanhardt relied on two Chicago police officers to tap into police databases to get information on jewelry salesmen.[37] Four of Hanhardt's codefendants also pleaded guilty. They include: Paul Schiro, a mob hitman who was found guilty of murder and racketeering in the notorious Family Secrets trial; Joseph Basinski; Guy Altobello, a reputed associate of a mob boss; and Sam DeStefano, nephew of the mob killer "Mad Man" DeStefano.

Hanhardt's mob connections were first exposed shortly before he retired, when he was a witness in a Las Vegas trial. His testimony discredited a key witness against the mobster Anthony Spilotro, who coincidentally was accused of operating a jewelry-burglary ring.[38] According to a prosecution document presented at Hanhardt's trial, the mobster and government informant Ken Eto told the FBI that he paid Hanhardt for favorable treatment of his gambling business.[39] After Hanhardt was convicted, First Assistant U.S. Attorney Gary Shapiro said, "It's our evidence that Bill Hanhardt for decades has been a corrupt policeman."[40] The city continues to pay Hanhardt an annual pension of $68,088, although the federal government seizes 25 percent of it to help pay the $5.1 million restitution he owes. Hanhardt began working for the police department in 1953, two years before a new law went into effect stripping pensions from government employees convicted of job-related felonies.[41]

The Family Secrets trial also exposed connections between members of the Chicago Outfit and police officers, former officers, and the son of a convicted cop. Officer Anthony "Twan" Doyle was hired by the city after doing political work in the Eleventh Ward. He worked in the Streets and Sanitation Department and then ran a parking lot at police headquarters before becoming a patrolman. He was assigned to the CPD evidence room in 1999, when he told his pals in the Chicago Outfit about the FBI retrieving a bloody glove that connected Nick and Frank Calabrese Sr. to the murder of the mobster John Fecarotta.[42] At the conclusion of the Family Secrets trial, Anthony Doyle was found guilty of racketeering conspiracy.[43] The former Chicago police officer Michael Ricci was indicted in the case as well. He joined Anthony Doyle on prison visits to Frank Calabrese Sr. and delivered information about the bloody glove. Before the trial, Ricci died from complications following heart surgery.[44]

In a related case, John Ambrose, a deputy U.S. marshal, guarded the mob hit man Nicholas Calabrese, who was hiding in the witness-protection program while cooperating with Family Secrets prosecutors. Ambrose relayed to Bill Guide, a longtime family friend, details that Nick Calabrese told investigators about his brother Frank and numerous mob murders.[45] Guide, a corrupt ex-cop, passed the information on to other mobsters. In 1982, Guide was convicted along with Ambrose's father, Thomas, in the Marquette Ten case.[46] John Ambrose was convicted in April 2009 and sentenced to four years in prison for leaking the information to the mob.[47]

Buccaneers in Blue

For nearly a century, Chicago's political machines provided police protection for gambling and prostitution under vice lords like Michael McDonald and "Big Jim" Colisimo. In the 1920s, Prohibition led to beer-war violence and an alliance between Capone's mob and Republican Mayor "Big Bill" Thompson. The 1930s New Deal saw the Democratic party taking power, while the alliance between city hall and Frank Nitti's Outfit continued.

Since 1958, however, there has been a fundamental change in the principal pattern of police abuse and corruption. Historically, various crime outfits have paid off top cops, who shared the money with other police officers to protect various rackets like prostitution, gambling, and illegal saloons. Over the years we have seen police officers also participating in burglaries, extorting criminals, partnering with drug dealers, and operating drug rings. The later pattern has seen the proliferation of street gangs and drug sales and direct payoffs of the beat cops and special gang and drug police units.

Summerdale Police Burglary Ring

Before he became a professional burglar, Richard Morrison went to grade school with several boys who grew up to become police officers. Several worked out of the Summerdale Police District in the Edgewater neighborhood on the North Side of Chicago. In the late 1950s, Morrison would occasionally have dinner with officers and their wives. Sometimes he would bring gifts of merchandise that he picked up on his after-hours forced entry into neighborhood retail stores. Eventually, one of the officers suggested that Morrison cut them in on the loot. The cops provided cover and served as lookouts for other police not privy to the deal. Soon the cops were specifying the merchandise they wanted, such as golf clubs and motor-boat engines.[48]

The nightly operations went smoothly for months. Then Morrison was arrested by honest detectives unaware of his special arrangement. He was jailed and faced a long prison sentence. He contacted Cook County State's Attorney Ben Adamowski, a Republican, who was gearing up his reelection campaign. Adamowski cut a deal with Morrison for a reduced sentence in exchange for information about the ring of police thieves. Adamowski was eager to use the scandal to embarrass Democratic Mayor Richard J. Daley. Morrison obliged and spilled the beans. Eight cops were arrested, and four truckloads of stolen merchandise were taken from their homes.[49] In 1961, the eight Summerdale patrolmen were convicted and imprisoned. Two others were found guilty but escaped with five-hundred-dollar fines.[50]

Police Commissioner Tim O'Connor resigned after thirty-one years on the force. Mayor Richard J. Daley was shaken and visibly mortified by the scandal. He appointed a three-person committee to find a new police commissioner. The committee included O. W. Wilson, dean of criminology and professor of police administration at the University of California. The committee recommended and Daley appointed Wilson as the new police commissioner to help him fend off an upcoming 1963 election challenge from Adamowski.[51]

Tavern Shakedowns

In 1971, U.S. Attorney James Thompson indicted District Commander Clarence Braasch and twenty-three officers who worked under him for shaking down numerous taverns in the Chicago Avenue Police District. The district included the Rush Street and Old Town nightclub strips and the North Michigan Avenue Gold Coast. The indicted officers were charged with extortion for threatening at least fifty tavern owners with loss of their liquor licenses if they refused to pay bribes.[52] In federal court, Braasch and eighteen of the officers were found guilty of conspiring to extort the tavern owners. Braasch and ten vice cops were also convicted for perjury. Only four officers were found not guilty.

On the city's West Side, a ring of Austin District police officers, led by Commander Mark Thanasouras, was indicted for shaking down tavern owners for $275,000. Thanasouras pleaded guilty in federal court and was sentenced to three and a half years in prison.[53] A total of fifteen officers involved in the ring were convicted. Thanasouras was sent to prison but was released after eighteen months when he agreed to testify against other police captains whom he said were involved in shakedown schemes.[54] At 5:00 A.M. one Friday in 1977, when he was returning from a bartending gig, he was murdered outside his girlfriend's apartment.[55] Joseph DiLeonardi, citywide homicide commander, said that it was a "professional" job.[56] Samuel Skinner, a former U.S. Attorney in Chicago, said that Thanasouras was an associate of crime-syndicate figures. "Anytime you associate with people in organized crime, you take the risk that your former friends may become your enemies," Skinner said.[57]

Gangs, Cops, and Drugs

Drug trafficking in Chicago today is a multi-million-dollar operation run at the street level by gangs. Gang members are often willing to pay for protection, either to the local beat cops or to special gang or narcotics units. Gang control of drug sales has led to increased shootings and murders in neighborhoods on the city's South and West Sides. It also led to a large number of police officers participating in the drug trade.

"In the Al Capone era, beat cops and commanders were bribed by beer haulers, bootleggers, and speakeasy operators. Today numerous police officers steal and sell drugs, protect drug dealers, and do business with gang leaders," said Professor John Hagedorn of the University of Illinois at Chicago. In 2012, Hagedorn and a graduate researcher, Bart Kmiecik, analyzed three hundred police-corruption convictions since the 1960s. They discovered that ninety-five convictions, or 32 percent of the total, involved gang-related illegal drug dealings, weapon sales, and gang activity.[58]

Marquette Ten: Payoffs for Protection

Shortly after he was sworn in as acting U.S. Attorney in 1981, Dan K. Webb indicted ten undercover police officers from the Marquette District on Chicago's West Side.[59] The indictment charged that nine tactical-unit officers and one gang-crimes officer accepted money, sexual favors, jewelry, and other gifts from drug dealers, in exchange for protecting the dealers from arrest and providing advance warning of raids. They also were charged with returning seized drugs to the dealers they were shielding. Officers William Guide and William Haas allegedly received more than one hundred thousand dollars from two drug rings. Thomas Ambrose and another officer were charged with receiving weekly payments totaling nearly seven thousand dollars.[60] The jury convicted all ten of the defendants.

Officers Sell Drugs

In 1982, Chicago police officers were selling drugs while on duty. They sometimes made drug sales directly from their squad cars.[61] A nine-month investigation culminated in the indictment of thirteen police officers and one former officer. Two of the officers were drivers for Commissioner Lenora

Cartright, head of the city's Department of Human Services. They sold drugs from her official car without her knowledge.[62] At trial, twelve police officers were convicted or pleaded guilty.

Wentworth Corrupt Cops

In the Grand Boulevard and Washington Park neighborhoods, many residents complained for years about the out-in-the-open gambling and drug dealing on their blocks. They told the police, but nothing ever happened. In 1987, after two officers complained that a suspect they arrested said he was paying police for protection, the Wentworth district police commander and his secretary decided to pose as corrupt cops while secretly working with the FBI. Commander Mardren Johnson let it be known that he wanted his share of the bribes and that his secretary, Sargeant Cynthia White, would collect the money.[63]

After a twenty-month investigation, twelve police officers were indicted by the U.S. attorney in October 1988, charged with accepting payoffs from gamblers, pimps, and drug dealers.[64] Bribe-taking officers steered narcotics dealers and gamblers to Cynthia White and drove her to meetings to collect protection money.[65]

The jury convicted seven police officers for racketeering conspiracy and accepting thousands of dollars in bribes. A former police officer, three gamblers, and a woman dope dealer were also convicted. Later, three additional officers and six additional drug pushers and gamblers were convicted.[66]

In September 2006, four Chicago police officers, members of the now-disbanded Special Operations Section (SOS), were arrested and charged with home invasion, kidnapping, auto theft, filing false reports, and other crimes. The four officers—Jerome Finnigan, Keith Herrera, Thomas Sherry, and Carl Suchocki—were arrested following an investigation by the CPD's Internal Affairs Division and the Cook County state's attorney.[67] Police Sergeant James McGovern and two additional officers were charged with home invasion, armed violence, and official misconduct. Finnigan, Herrera, and Suchocki were charged with crimes in three additional incidents.[68]

The investigators discovered that SOS cops were failing to appear in court for numerous drug cases, leading them to suspect that the arrests were bogus or tainted. Before any of these officers were brought to trial, Finnigan was arrested by the FBI and charged with trying to hire a hit man to murder another officer who was a potential witness against him.[69]

In September 2009, four SOS cops pleaded guilty after they admitted that they shook down drug dealers and others.[70] SOS officers stole nearly half a million dollars after targeting a Hispanic man driving an expensive car. They also withheld needed medicine from another man until he told them where he hid cocaine and cash.[71]

In April 2011, Finnigan pleaded guilty to plotting to hire a hit man to kill a fellow officer whom he suspected of cooperating with investigators. At his sentencing hearing, Finnigan told the judge, "My bosses knew what I was doing out there; it went on and on. And this wasn't the exception to the rule. It was the rule."[72]

Police Drug Rings

Joseph Miedzianowski, often described as the most corrupt cop in Chicago history, made a fortune robbing drug dealers, providing protection, arresting rival gang members, and then taking over a drug-selling operation for himself and his girlfriend. Miedzianowski was a decorated member of the gang-crimes unit when he was indicted for running a Miami-to-Chicago cocaine operation.[73] Also indicted were eleven gang members and drug dealers, who, along with Miedzianowski, allegedly distributed two hundred pounds of powder and crack cocaine on the streets of Chicago from 1995 through 1998.[74] Before the case against Miedzianowski was closed, a total of twenty-four members of his drug ring were convicted.

At trial, prosecutors presented evidence that Miedzianowski met drug couriers at airports and took them to drug stash houses. He was present when members of the drug ring cooked crack cocaine at his girlfriend's apartment.[75] They also alleged that beginning in 1985, Miedzianowski operated a criminal enterprise that involved bribery, ripping off rival drug dealers, kidnapping clients who owed drug debts, and money laundering. He also falsified search warrants in order to raid dealers' homes and steal their drugs. Miedzianowski was found guilty of drug conspiracy and racketeering.[76] The jury found that he operated drug rings with leaders of four street gangs.[77] He was sentenced to life in prison without the possibility of parole, while his girlfriend, Alina Lis, was found guilty of perjury and sentenced to thirty years in prison.[78] The federal investigation led to the conviction of twenty-two others, mostly drug dealers and informants.[79]

In December 1996, seven members of the Austin District tactical unit were arrested by the FBI for extorting and robbing undercover agents posing as drug dealers. The police officers, led by Edward Lee Jackson Jr., were charged with conspiracy to commit robbery and extortion.[80] Charles Vaughn, a civilian who did not work for the police department, was charged with attempted extortion. Jackson, known as "Pacman," was a member of the Conservative Vice Lords street gang.[81] Prosecutors said the officers "brazenly ripped off drug dealers for cash and narcotics, confident their victims would be too fearful to report the crimes."[82] Edward "Pacman" Jackson and three other of the "Austin Seven" went to trial and were found guilty. Three other officers pleaded guilty before the trial.[83]

Police Towing and Phony Repairs

Booze, gambling, and prostitution have traditionally provided the leading temptations luring some cops into a life of corruption. Narcotics and other illegal drugs were added to the list in the 1970s. Vehicle towing also attracts ethically deficient police officers. Corrupt police involved in towing scams often escape detection because the car owners are not on the scene when the crimes occur. The cops get their bribes from tow-truck drivers or chop-shop owners. These transactions aren't observed, and none of the corrupt participants dare rat on their cohorts. Usually, the only way to catch such criminals is when someone goes undercover to gather evidence against them.

Beginning in 2007, the FBI and the CPD's Office of Internal Affairs conducted Operation Tow Scam, which resulted in the indictment of eleven Chicago police officers with seven convictions by January 2013. Three civilians, including two truck drivers, were also convicted.[84] Officer Ali Haleem, an informal liaison between the CPD and the Southwest Side Arab community, was caught in 2008 trying to extort a bribe from a tow-truck owner for steering towing business his way.[85] He was not charged at the time because he agreed to help authorities arrest others involved in the towing referral racket. He wore a wire—a concealed recording device—to document evidence against seven individuals who paid kickbacks to receive state grants. One of the individuals snared by the secret recording was the campaign treasurer of State Senator Ricky Hendon (D-Chicago).[86] The treasurer was involved in a kickback scheme to rig thousands of dollars in federal grants. He pleaded guilty to conspiracy to bribe a public official and received a sentence of probation and community service.[87] Senator Hendon resigned in 2011 but had not been charged with a crime as of May 2014. As Operation Tow Scam was winding down in April 2013, Haleem pleaded guilty to extorting bribes from a tow-truck driver and for selling firearms to a felon.[88]

In July 2012, a twelve-year veteran of the Chicago police force, Juan Prado, pleaded guilty to taking payoffs from a tow-truck driver who was working with the FBI. Prado admitted accepting a total of $3,790 in bribes for steering business to tow-truck operators.[89] Another officer pleaded guilty to attempted extortion for collecting more than fifty-five thousand dollars in bribes over a seven-year period.[90]

While he was still a Chicago police officer but also running a towing business, Kenneth Quinn was charged in a fifty-seven-count indictment by the Cook County state's attorney for his connection with nine stolen cars, including one found at his wife's home. In 1985, he pleaded guilty to obstruction of justice and was sentenced to two and a half years probation.[91] From 1999 to 2003, Quinn was vice president of Northside Towing, which had a subcontract with a politically connected company, Environmental Auto Removal (EAR).[92] Earlier in 1989, Mayor Richard M. Daley turned the city's towing over to EAR, which had ties to Daley's close friend and advisor, former State Senator Jeremiah Joyce. In 2004, the *Chicago Sun-Times* published a multipart series exposing how the city sold about seventy thousand towed cars a year to the company for scrap-metal prices. Many of the cars were then resold at much higher prices, while the car owners received nothing but still had to pay parking fines and towing fees.[93]

In an unrelated scam, two police officers, five civilian motor-pool employees, and a Southwest Side auto-repair shop were charged in January 1981 with operating a phony billing scheme with kickbacks that cost taxpayers six hundred thousand dollars. Bruno Roti, the son of convicted First Ward Alderman Fred Roti, pleaded guilty to approving ten thousand dollars in phony work orders for the repair shop. Bruno Roti at the time was a foreman in the Chicago Police Department's motor-maintenance division.[94] Seven motor-pool employees were convicted of mail fraud and extortion for submitting bills totaling six hundred thousand dollars for work that wasn't done. Much of the money was kicked back to the employees.[95] In March 1983, Fred Roti arranged for Bruno to be hired as a thirty-five-thousand-dollar-a-year foreman in the Chicago Water Department, despite his previous felony conviction.[96]

Chicago's Response to Police Corruption

In the past half century, an embarrassingly large number of police officers have violated citizens' rights, engaged in corruption, and committed crimes while escaping detection and avoiding discipline or prosecution. In numerous cases, the code of silence prevented supervisors and civilian authorities from identifying bad police officers and holding them accountable. However, in other cases, honest police officers have found ways anonymously to report corrupt behavior.

Police superintendents and mayors typically denounce each new case of serious police misconduct as the work of a "bad apple." They dismiss suggestions of any widespread or systematic problem. They have failed to establish meaningful internal reforms or effective oversight. The Fraternal Order of Police and members of the city council repeatedly opposed establishing a powerful independent police-review board.

Instead, time and again, the city has responded to police scandals by appointing a committee, reorganizing, or renaming the internal department responsible for policing the police. This response has been a public-relations ploy rather than a serious attempt to end corruption.

In 1960, after the Summerdale police scandal led to the resignation of the Police Commissioner Timothy O'Connor, Mayor Richard J. Daley named O. W. Wilson as the new superintendent. In addition, Daley appointed a five-member "nonpartisan" police board to hear police-disciplinary cases previously handled by the Civil Service Commission.[97]

In 1966, the American Civil Liberties Union called for the Chicago Bar Association to review citizen complaints against the police. O. W. Wilson and a past president of the Chicago Bar Association concluded that there was no need for an independent review of complaints against police. At the same time, a committee created by Mayor Daley determined that there were no faults with the Internal Investigation Division's operations.[98]

In 1967, Police Superintendent James Conlisk Jr. merged the Inspections and Investigations Divisions and charged the new division with detecting corruption without waiting for it to be reported by others.[99]

In 1972, Mayor Richard J. Daley responded to increased public dissatisfaction with police oversight by calling a conference of civic leaders. At the conference Superintendent Conlisk said that the Chicago Commission of Human Relations would review misconduct files and if necessary reinvestigate certain cases. This was the first time a civilian entity was given the opportunity to investigate Chicago police. However, the commission was not given disciplinary authority, only the power to recommend discipline.

In 1973, the Chicago Law Enforcement Study Group analyzed the Police Board and how it was performing its main functions of adopting a budget, adopting rules and regulations, nominating superintendent candidates, and police-officer discipline. The report said that the board only effectively handled discipline and that its other duties were listed mostly for show.[100]

In 1974, Superintendent James Rochford wanted police misconduct cases directly under his command. He created the Office of Professional Standards, but it did not have subpoena power, did not hold public hearings, and was not asked to make policy recommendations.[101] Tellingly, the Office of Professional Standards failed for two decades to bring charges against Jon Burge, although multiple victims and civil-rights groups had demanded action.

In 1992, in response to citizens' complaints about Burge and his team of torturers, the Illinois legislature passed a law not to aid victims but to shield perpetrators. The legislation established a five-year statute of limitations on administrative proceedings for police brutality. Commander Burge was brought up on disciplinary charges nine years after he tortured Andrew Wilson, and the supporters of the bill felt that was unfair.[102]

In 2006, University of Chicago Law School professor Craig B. Futterman and two colleagues published a report analyzing 10,149 complaints of excessive force, illegal searches, racial and sexual abuse, and false arrest filed by civilians from 2002 to 2004.[103] Futterman found that:

- only nineteen of the 10,149 complaints led to a suspension of a week or more;
- the chance of meaningful discipline for a police brutality complaint was less than .3 percent;
- only one of 3,837 charges of illegal searches led to meaningful discipline; and
- over a three-year period, not a single charge of false arrest or planting of drugs or guns led to meaningful discipline.

In 2007, Mayor Richard M. Daley created a new Independent Police Review Authority (IPRA) to replace the Office of Professional Standards. IPRA was assigned to investigate allegations against police officers and was given intake responsibility for all complaints from the department and the community.[104]

In 2009, the nonprofit Chicago Justice Project studied Police Board decisions in 310 cases in which the superintendent sought to fire sworn officers or civilian employees. They found that the Police Board upheld the recommended discipline by the superintendent in only 37 percent of the cases of sworn officers. They also found that in 20 percent of the cases, officers were returned to work without any discipline at all. The authors questioned why police discipline is still the Police Board's responsibility: "Looking at the numbers, it is hard to see how the board serves the public interest by retaining two-thirds of the officers the Superintendent is trying to fire."[105]

The High Cost of Corruption

In a six-year period from 2006 to 2011, the city paid out more than $282 million, or forty-seven million dollars per year, to settle lawsuits and judgments involving Chicago police officers.[106] Since part of the total included traffic accidents, it's difficult to estimate how much was the result of abuse, brutality, crime, and other misconduct committed by Chicago cops. Since then, the cost of these lawsuits has increased. In the first half of 2008, the city paid out more than sixty-two million dollars in police-related lawsuits.[107]

Wrongful-conviction and torture cases against Burge and his crew played out over a longer time period. From 1988 to 2013, Burge-related cases cost the city more than ninety-seven million dollars, including settlements and payments to victims, payments of $15,288,388 to outside law firms to defend Burge and other cops, and the cost of representing the city before the special prosecutor.[108]

Burge was not the only police officer whose negligent or illegal behavior resulted in lawsuits, judgments, settlements, court costs, and legal fees. For example, in January 2013 the city agreed to pay $22.5 million to a woman suffering from a bipolar breakdown who was arrested and then released by the police into a high-crime neighborhood, where she was raped and beaten, resulting in severe brain injuries.[109] A month earlier, Karolina Obrycka, who was severely beaten by Officer Abbate, was awarded $850,000 in damages.[110] In February 2013, the city council approved the payment of $4.1 million to the family of an unarmed twenty-nine-year-old man who was lying on the ground when he was fatally shot by a police officer.[111] And in March 2013, Chicago settled a case for $4.5 million to the family of a woman who was fatally shot by an off-duty police officer.[112]

For more than a decade, the city's taxpayers have been paying about fifty million dollars per year to settle cases involving police abuse, neglect, and corruption. Since the early 1960s, the city and the police department have often turned a blind eye to police abuse and have fought lawsuits in court, even if the police officer's defense was weak.

In addition, the department has frequently trampled on citizen rights. In 1981, the city paid $306,250 to groups and individuals who were illegally spied on and infiltrated by the police department's Red Squad. In 1986, a federal judge ordered the city to pay fifty-one thousand dollars to two organizations and a civil-rights activist who were spied upon illegally by the secret police Red Squad, which has since been disbanded.[113]

Thus, for practical reasons and to regain citizens' faith in their government, it is imperative that police abuse and corruption be curbed. For law and order to exist, citizens must be able to trust the police.

In 1994, Circuit Court Judge Thomas Maloney was convicted of accepting a ten-thousand-dollar bribe to fix the murder trials of two El Rukn gang leaders. He was also found guilty of sharing in a one-hundred-thousand-dollar bribe to acquit three New York gang members for a murder of a rival in Chicago's Chinatown. *Photo courtesy of Sun-Times Media.*

CHAPTER 9

Jailbird Judges and Crooked Courts

RICHARD LEFEVOUR WAS A LOYAL, hard-working member of the Cook County Democratic machine before he was appointed an associate judge in 1969. As a reward for his work with the party, he was slated for election to a full judgeship in 1974. He and his wife, Virginia, worked in the mayoral elections of Richard J. Daley and helped Richard M. Daley win election as Cook County state's attorney. Virginia was chair of Women for Daley in the campaign, and Judge LeFevour was given the honor of swearing in State's Attorney Daley when he took office.

No wonder Judge LeFevour was furious when he learned that State's Attorney Daley knew about the undercover Operation Greylord investigation of LeFevour and other judges. Daley knew about it for three years before it became public but never gave him a warning. James LeFevour, Judge LeFevour's cousin and "bagman," said that the judge called Richie Daley "a little bastard" and removed pictures of Daley from his office.[1]

Richard LeFevour was the son of a Chicago police captain. He graduated from Loyola University Law School and became a well-respected chief judge of the traffic court. He was then made presiding judge of the First Municipal District. Before his criminal activity was exposed, he built a reputation as an innovative court administrator and an amusing storyteller.[2]

Traffic court under Judge LeFevour encouraged a group of hustling lawyers, known as the "miracle workers," to fix drunk-driving cases for one hundred dollars each.[3] The judge's cousin, police officer James LeFevour, worked every day in the courtrooms and hallways of traffic court. As the designated bagman, he would collect cash bribes from the lawyers and deliver them to the judge with a list of the cases to be fixed. When the indictments came down, Jimmy LeFevour pleaded guilty to a tax-evasion charge and testified against his cousin to receive a lesser sentence. At trial, he admitted that he fixed at least one drunk-driving case each day for seven years.[4]

Jimmy also disclosed that Judge LeFevour only assigned corrupt judges to the major courts where drunk-driving and leaving-an-accident-scene cases were heard. These were the courtrooms where corrupt lawyers and crooked judges could make easy money. Honest judges were assigned to hear lesser traffic offenses.[5]

In 1981, when Judge LeFevour became head of the Municipal District, he created a "hustler's bribery club" in branch courts. The club's five lawyers paid five hundred dollars a month to Jimmy LeFevour for the privilege of working the hallways. Jimmy kept five hundred for himself and gave two thousand dollars to his cousin. Jimmy also passed bribe money from the hustling lawyers to other corrupt judges. They were allowed to keep all they could make from the lawyers, but they had to fix cases for Judge LeFevour for no charge.[6]

Judge LeFevour and seven others were indicted in 1984. He was charged with committing nearly one hundred specific criminal acts over a fourteen-year period. He allegedly received at least twenty-five thousand dollars for dismissing parking tickets and fixing drunk-driving cases. Jimmy LeFevour, two other Chicago policemen, and four attorneys were charged with racketeering, mail fraud, and income-tax violations.[7]

The indictment also charged that Judge LeFevour was given free use of a new Cadillac every year for seven years by Hanley Dawson Leasing Company and its predecessor.[8] During LeFevour's trial, Hanley Dawson Jr. testified that the cars, other gifts, and loans were given in exchange for the judge agreeing to drop thousands of parking tickets for which the leasing company was potentially liable. Dawson said that he leased a new Pontiac Grand Prix to Judge LeFevour's wife for two years at the rate of $205 per month and loaned sixteen thousand dollars to the judge so he could pay private-school tuition for his sons. Dawson testified that LeFevour never made any payments on the Pontiac lease and failed to repay the sixteen-thousand-dollar loan.

Prosecutors said that Judge LeFevour paid cash for his wife's hairdresser, jeweler, housekeeper, grocer, milkman, and pharmacist. The government documented that Judge LeFevour from 1978 to 1982 made cash expenditures totaling $125,000, more than the amount of money available to him through legitimate sources of income.[9]

Judge LeFevour, of course, denied fixing cases. His lawyers argued that he could not have been taking bribes like the government said because he was more than one hundred thousand dollars in debt. They argued that the cars were a form of free advertising, and the practice was normal in the car-leasing business. They also said that his cousin, Jimmy LeFevour, and the other witnesses against him were liars motivated to receive lenient plea deals and to save their pensions.

The defense argument was vigorously rebutted by special U.S. Attorney Dan Webb, who declared that Judge LeFevour's career was "unequaled in the annals of corruption."[10] Webb said that from the day he took office, LeFevour "sold—day in and day out, week in and week out, month after month and year after year—he sold and peddled justice like it was apples."[11] The jury concurred and found LeFevour guilty of mail fraud, income-tax fraud, and racketeering.[12] In 1985, Judge LeFevour, the highest-ranking judge charged in the Greylord investigations, was sentenced to twelve years in federal prison.[13] Prosecutors wanted a long sentence to encourage LeFevour to provide evidence against divorce court Judge John Reynolds. LeFevour eventually agreed to cooperate, which then caused Reynolds to plead guilty.[14] After serving six years in prison, LeFevour worked as an insurance-claims consultant. He was sixty-five years old when he died.[15]

Bugs, Moles, and Phony Cases

LeFevour was one of the three most important judges to be convicted by the intensive, decade-long Operation Greylord investigation. The other two Greylord headliners were Judges Wayne Olson and Reginald Holzer. To get convictions against judges who were held in high esteem by the general public, federal prosecutors believed it was necessary to amass an overwhelming amount of evidence. To do this, they used hidden tape recorders, moles, informants, court data, and financial records.

To avoid interfering with real cases already in the court system, federal investigators created phony arrests and bogus indictments. They directed government agents to pretend, like actors, that they were crime victims. The feds even wrote fictitious testimony for them. Through the astute use of plea bargaining and grants of immunity, the prosecutors were often able to get lawyers, bailiffs, policemen, and judges to testify against each other.

In the early stages of the Greylord probe, investigators became suspicious of Judge Wayne Olson, who was assigned to narcotics court. Information that

Olson was fixing cases was picked up by Terrence Hake, an undercover FBI mole who was posing as a corrupt assistant state's attorney. After getting Justice Department permission, the FBI for the first time ever placed an electronic "bug" in a judge's chambers.[16]

The device transmitted conversations to a secret listening post in the Dirksen Federal Building, where FBI agents recorded hundreds of hours of conversations. They listened as Olson told attorney Bruce Roth, "I love people who take dough because you know exactly where you stand." Roth, a bagman and briber, responded, "Sure, that's the way to do business."[17] The feds also heard Olson talking with attorney James Costello as they conspired to split bond refunds from defendants. Costello represented defendants he hustled in Olson's courtroom. Olson would dismiss the cases or make favorable rulings for Costello's clients, who in turn would sign over the bond money to Costello.[18] Once, after counting his share, Olson was heard telling Costello, "We can make one thousand dollars a week."[19]

Warbling Wayne Olson was indicted in December 1983. Olson's moniker referred to his penchant for singing in bars and once singing "Happy Birthday" to a defendant in his courtroom. After confronting the tape-recorded evidence and information supplied by undercover agents, Olson confessed and became the first judge in Illinois history to plead guilty to judicial corruption. Costello pleaded guilty to paying cash bribes to Hake, the undercover FBI mole, to influence the outcomes of narcotics cases.[20] Later, the bagman, Bruce Roth, was convicted of sharing forty thousand dollars in bribes with Olson and other judges.[21]

Judge Reginald Holzer, like Olson and LeFevour, was addicted to bribery. But his modus operandi was different. Instead of splitting bond refunds with corrupt lawyers or accepting bribes for dismissing drunk-driving cases, Judge Holzer solicited loans. These loans amounted to as much ten thousand dollars at a time from lawyers who had cases before him. Judge Holzer sat in the Law Division and then in chancery court, which had jurisdiction over business, financial matters, foreclosures, and appointing of receivers of property. Lawyers practicing in chancery court had reason to stay on the good side of Judge Holzer.

In 1979, Holzer asked former Illinois State Senator Bernie Neistein for a ten-thousand-dollar loan.[22] Neistein was the Twenty-ninth Ward Democratic committeeman, even though he hadn't lived in the ward for years. He was also a partner in the law firm of Bilandic, Neistein, Richman, Hauslinger, and Young. Partner Michael A. Bilandic had been mayor of Chicago from 1976 to 1979.

Wanting to stay on the judge's good side, Neistein and Richman arranged for the quick ten-thousand-dollar bank loan, which Holzer was to repay at the rate of one thousand dollars per month. Six months later, when they discovered that Holzer failed to make any of the required payments, Neistein and Richman made the payments for him.[23]

Holzer also put the arm on Fred Lane, a personal-injury lawyer who had many cases in front of Holzer. He borrowed $2,500 from Lane that he never paid back. When it was revealed in court documents, the existence of the loan became a big problem for Lane, who was president of the Illinois State Bar Association.[24] Even in Illinois it is unethical for a lawyer to loan money to a judge who rules for or against the attorney's clients.

When Holzer moved to chancery court, he met with Earnest Worsek, a real-estate businessman who had been given receiverships from Holzer's predecessor. Holzer over the years awarded him seventy more receiverships. Holzer suggested that Worsek buy a million-dollar life-insurance policy from Holzer's wife, Estelle, who was in the insurance business. Instead, Worsek bought a five-hundred-thousand-dollar policy. Then Holzer asked for and received a fifteen-thousand-dollar loan and later, two additional ten-thousand-dollar loans from Worsek.[25]

In 1985, a grand jury indicted Judge Holzer and charged him with obtaining $195,000 in loans and payoffs from lawyers who had cases before him. He was also charged with attempting to defraud the Internal Revenue Service by getting others to pay bills for him and by dealing in cash and cashier's checks. It was the largest case of judicial corruption in Cook County history in dollar terms.[26] In 1986, a federal jury found Holzer guilty of mail fraud, extortion, and racketeering, and he was sentenced to eighteen years in prison, the longest sentence imposed on any Greylord defendant.[27]

After the trial, Assistant U.S. Attorney Scott Turow said, "Corruption of this kind . . . robs all citizens of confidence in the belief that they can go into a courtroom and seek justice where there are no secret influences and no secret alliances."[28] Turow would go on to become a well-known author of many books of popular fiction, including *Presumed Innocent,* his 1987 best-selling legal thriller that subsequently was made into a movie.

In 1988, after the U.S. Supreme Court narrowed the scope of the mail-fraud statute, the U.S. Court of Appeals vacated the mail-fraud and racketeering convictions against Holzer but let stand the conviction for extortion.[29] Holzer was resentenced to thirteen years in prison.[30]

In addition to Judges Olson, LeFevour, and Holzer, twelve other judges and associate judges were tried and convicted or pleaded guilty as a result of Operation Greylord.[31] Only two judges were acquitted.

The Greylord probe also produced two star-quality good guys: Terrence Hake and Judge Brocton Lockwood. They both worked undercover for the feds. Hake was an assistant Cook County state's attorney when he became disgusted with the corruption he witnessed. He went to the FBI and volunteered to wear a wire, which he used to gather evidence against scheming lawyers and dirty judges in narcotics court. He later posed as a corrupt defense attorney in private practice eager to fix his cases. Every client Hake represented over two and a half years was a fake defendant, an FBI agent charged with a phony crime. Hake bribed judges, passed money to the judges or their clerks, and recorded conversations confirming the deals. During Greylord, Hake was secretly sworn in as an FBI agent. When Greylord wound down, the FBI transferred Hake to Philadelphia. After a few years, he resigned to become inspector general for the Regional Transportation Authority of Northeastern Illinois.[32]

Brocton Lockwood, an associate judge from downstate Williamson County, spent a couple of weeks each year in Cook County's traffic court, helping to reduce huge backlogs of cases. One year, while at a party with traffic-court clerks, he was told how the clerks, deputies, and police officers all made money doing favors for defendants and their lawyers. He also befriended an attorney who told him that Judge Richard LeFevour was "the first judge to extract a million dollars from traffic court."[33] At first Lockwood took no action, because he was worried about retaliation and his possible removal from the bench. He overcame his fears, but went to the Justice Department in Washington, D.C., rather than risk talking to the authorities in Chicago. He observed that you could buy a judge in Chicago cheaper than you could hire a lawyer in his home town of Marion, Illinois.[34] He was recruited by the FBI director and equipped with a microphone wired to a tape recorder in his cowboy boots that he always wore. His work helped the FBI prepare criminal cases against judges, court officials, lawyers, and others.[35]

By 1989, when the Operation Greylord curtain came down, seventeen judges had been indicted and fifteen convicted. Also convicted were sixty-nine other court denizens, including lawyers, clerks, police officers, and sheriff's deputies.[36] Six years earlier, when the first nine indictments were announced, U.S. Attorney Dan Webb predicted, "When this project is over and all of the cases have been tried, I believe this will be viewed as one of the most comprehensive, intricate, and difficult undercover operations ever undertaken by a law enforcement agency."[37] While this claim may contain some hyperbole, the indictments of these judges and the details of their illegal behavior illustrate the extent of their crimes and the brazenness of their actions.

Operation Gambat

Well before Operation Greylord was completed, federal prosecutors launched Operation Gambat, named after a corrupt gambling attorney, Robert Cooley. In 1986, Cooley walked into the Federal Strike Force Chicago office and offered to wear a wire to prove that First Ward politicians and mobsters were fixing murder trials and other cases.

Cooley was a former cop whose father, two grandfathers, and six siblings were Chicago police officers. While working for the police department, he went to Chicago Kent Law School at night. After passing the bar in 1970, he began working as a criminal defense attorney representing bookies and prostitutes. Although he often won cases on the merits, he was also adept at bribing judges and fixing cases. Word of his court successes reached the ears of John D'Arco Sr., Democratic committeeman and former alderman of the mob-controlled First Ward. D'Arco asked him to teach his son, attorney and State Senator John D'Arco Jr., how to try cases. Cooley accepted the mentoring assignment in exchange for all of the Outfit's criminal defense work.[38] Cooley testified that during his years practicing law, he bribed twenty-nine different judges and made payoffs to assistant state's attorneys, public defenders, sheriff's deputies, police officers, court clerks, assistant corporation counsels, and aldermen.[39]

After more than a decade representing sleazebags, Cooley was feeling guilty about his participation in corruption. He was also struggling to pay his gambling debts and was aware of news about the many Greylord convictions. He was then asked by Pat Marcy to represent a weightlifter, Michael Colella, who was charged with beating up a woman police officer. Colella's uncle had connections with the mob and politicians.

Marcy's official title was secretary for the First Ward Democratic organization, but this relatively humble title hid important facts. Marcy was a "made" member of the mob, and he, not Committeeman John D'Arco Sr., was the real power in the First Ward. Marcy was the main conduit between the Outfit and politicians, judges, and the police.

Cooley took the Colella case. He thought that he could win or limit the conviction to lesser charges.[40] While the pretrial maneuvering was going on, Marcy called Cooley and told him not to ask for a jury but to take a bench trial. Cooley said Marcy told him not to worry, "the fix was in." The judge found

Colella not guilty.[41] There was a huge uproar in the news media, which caused the judge's defeat in the next retention election. But Colella walked free.

For Cooley, the Colella case was the last straw. Years later, Cooley said that this case and growing pangs of conscience triggered his decision to help federal prosecutors.[42] For three and a half years, Cooley wore a wire as he continued bribing judges and fixing cases. Often he would check in with Marcy, who lunched at the Counselor's Row restaurant directly across the street from city hall. The restaurant was a popular hangout for lawyers, judges, and politicians. It was on the ground floor of the building that also housed Cooley's and young D'Arco's law offices. The First Ward Democratic headquarters and the Anco insurance agency were also in the building. John D'Arco Sr. had an interest in Anco, and First Ward Alderman Fred Roti was listed as one of its executives.[43] U.S. Congressman Frank Annunzio, who is discussed in chapter 10, was at one time a co-owner of Anco with John D'Arco Sr.

The undercover phase of Cooley's life ended in 1989, when news organizations were told that a Counselor's Row busboy discovered a hidden FBI camera pointed at the table in the front corner that was always reserved for Pat Marcy and his First Ward honchos, including Alderman Fred Roti. Frequent lunchtime compatriots included Aldermen Bernard Stone (Fiftieth Ward), Dick Mell (Thirty-third), John Madrzyk (Thirteenth), Burton Natarus (Forty-second), Patrick Levar (Forty-fifth), Robert Shaw (Ninth), and William Beavers (Seventh); County Commissioners Frank Damato and Marco D'Amico;[44] and Chicago Police Deputy Chief of Detectives William Hanhardt.[45] The FBI also bugged the phone on a pedestal beside Marcy's table. After the bugs were discovered, Cooley immediately went into hiding.

Eighteen months later, the fruits of Cooley's undercover work began to appear. A week before Christmas in 1990, U.S. Attorney Fred Foreman indicted Pat Marcy, Alderman Fred Roti, and State Senator John D'Arco Jr. Also indicted were Judge David Shields and Pasquale "Pat" De Leo, D'Arco Jr.'s brother-in-law.[46] Marcy was charged with taking money to fix the trial of the weightlifter Michael Colella and with giving ten thousand dollars to Cooley to bribe the highly respected Judge Frank Wilson. Judge Wilson then acquitted the mob hitman Harry Aleman of the notorious 1972 murder of William Logan, a Teamsters union steward.[47]

The evidence against Aleman was strong, including two eyewitnesses. Yet in a bench trial, Judge Wilson found Aleman not guilty, which immediately caused a firestorm of media criticism. When Cooley delivered the payoff, Judge Wilson told Cooley, "You ruined me." Wilson retired to Arizona but in

1989 committed suicide after the FBI served him with a subpoena to appear before a grand jury.

Soon after Harry Aleman escaped the murder rap, he was convicted on charges of conspiracy, racketeering, and interstate transportation of stolen property for operating a home-invasion ring in Indiana and Illinois. He was sentenced to thirty years in federal prison.[48]

In comments to the *Chicago Sun-Times,* the retired FBI agent William F. Roemer Jr. said, "When we talk about the 1st Ward—that's a generic term. We're talking about the corruption in the entire Chicago metropolitan area, which is spearheaded for the mob by Pat Marcy. . . . The 1st Ward is like the center of a web where the big spider sits."[49]

Cooley testified for the prosecution in seven Gambat trials; all seven resulted in convictions. First to fall were Judge David Shields and attorney Pat De Leo, a former corporation counsel for the city of Chicago. A jury found both guilty of conspiracy, extortion, and causing interstate travel to promote bribery. Testimony at the trial alleged that De Leo accepted eleven thousand dollars from Cooley and gave six thousand dollars to Judge Shields to fix a case for Cooley.[50]

Next, State Senator John D'Arco was convicted for accepting a $7,500 bribe from Cooley to introduce the insurance bill and for failing to report another five-thousand-dollar bribe on his tax return.[51] Then a jury convicted Alderman Roti of accepting $7,500 from Cooley to rig a zoning change and for receiving ten thousand dollars for fixing a civil trial. Cooley's recorder picked up Roti's voice accepting the cash bribes in the back of Counselor's Row and in Roti's city-hall office.[52] Roti was found not guilty for allegedly sharing in a $72,500 bribe to help fix the Chinatown murder trial.[53] Nonetheless, based on his other convictions, Roti was sentenced to four years in prison. He got out in 1999, two years before dying at age seventy-eight.[54] Pat Marcy, who had been indicted along with Roti, suffered a heart attack before his trial and was severed from the case. He died in 1993.[55]

Also as a part of Operation Gambat, Circuit Court Judge Thomas Maloney was found guilty of accepting ten thousand dollars to fix the double-murder trial of two El Rukn gang leaders in 1986. Judge Maloney, who had the nerve to attempt the fix even while the Greylord trials were still under way, subsequently became the first Cook County judge to be convicted of rigging murder cases for money.[56] In the El Rukn case Maloney suspected he was under surveillance, so he returned the money, called off the fix, and convicted the gang members. However, in 1993 Maloney was convicted for sharing in the hundred-thousand-dollar bribe for acquitting three New York gangsters in a 1981 Chinatown murder, and he was convicted of accepting a bribe in the earlier El Rukn case. He also was found guilty of accepting bribes to reduce charges against another accused murderer and to give probation and work release to a thief with five felony convictions.[57] Before being appointed judge, Maloney had been a private attorney for twenty-five years. For a time he shared office space with the alderman and later convicted corrupt power broker Edward Vrdolyak. Maloney was eighty-three when he died in 2008.[58]

By the time the Gambat trials were completed in 1997, a total of twenty-six individuals, including judges, mobsters, politicians, and police officers, were convicted or pleaded guilty.[59] In addition, Cooley and federal prosecutors convinced the Cook County state's attorney to re-indict Harry Aleman for the murder of William Logan. They argued successfully that double jeopardy did not apply because Aleman was not in jeopardy when Judge Wilson agreed to fix the case. Aleman was found guilty of the Logan murder twenty years after the initial trial and was sentenced to one hundred years in prison.[60] He was seventy-one when he died at the state-run Hill Correction Center in downstate Galesburg, Illinois.[61]

Prosecutors were quoted in the *Chicago Tribune* in 2004 on the publication of Cooley's book, *When Corruption Was King*. They praised Cooley's effectiveness and said that because of him we live in a different city today. They further declared that the Outfit is only a vestige of its former strength. The average citizen can walk into a courtroom or ballot booth without presuming the fix is in. Mob hits are a rarity. "I don't think Cooley ever got the credit he deserved," said former U.S. Attorney Scott Mendeloff.[62]

Judges Depend on Money, Friends, and Clout

While the Greylord and Gambat scandals are extreme examples of how the Cook County courts operated in previous decades, a large percentage of the public believes that there are still some judges who are corruptly influenced by money and politics—that there are still judges engaged in illegal or unethical behavior. This perception is fostered by the way we appoint, elect, and retain judges. Since money and political clout are required for attorneys to be selected for judgeships, many believe that money and political clout influence judicial decisions.

There are four ways that judicial-selection procedures thrust judges into the political arena:

1. Slating: Every two years, the Cook County Democratic Central Committee meets to choose which candidates it will back for election in the Democratic primary. (The Republican Central Committee also selects judicial candidates, but they almost always lose Cook County judicial elections.) In much of Cook County, being slated as a party-backed judicial candidate is a huge advantage. Qualifications are of some importance, but not as important as political backing, past work for the party, and ethnic or gender appeal to the voters. At slating sessions, candidates who want to become judges say what they know is important to the party leaders. Here are some examples of what numerous judicial candidates recently told the Democratic Party slating committee:

> "I was born and raised in the Eleventh Ward." (The Eleventh is the home ward of the Daley family and the political domain of ward committeeman and County Commissioner John Daley.)
> "I was adopted by the Fourteenth Ward, by a wonderful man, Edward Burke." (Burke is alderman and committeeman of the Fourteenth Ward and one of the most important slate makers.)
> "I am a lifelong Democrat."
> "I'm a good Democrat, and I promise to make the party proud."
> "I really believe in loyalty and being a team member."
> "My name is Jessica O'Brien. I am the Asian American with the Irish last name."
> "I voted in each of the Democratic primaries in the last twenty years. . . . When the Democratic party wanted somebody to go down to Springfield to testify, I did that. When they needed help writing legislation, I did that."[63]

The promise and expectation is that after the election, these Democratic party-backed judges will continue to be loyal and aid the party when any political cases come before them.

2. Competitive political elections: Candidates in judicial elections must raise political donations to pay for campaign literature, ads, phone banking, and to pay party workers to collect petition signatures. Candidates must contribute up to thirty thousand dollars to the Cook County Democratic party to cover these costs.[64] The party's support is very important because voters have a difficult time acquiring information about who is running for judge. There are long bedsheet ballots with many candidates unfamiliar to the voters running for numerous judicial seats. This makes it nearly impossible for voters to know for whom to vote. If a candidate is on the party slate, party workers will mention his or her name and tout their qualifications. The party label will help insure

their election, especially if they are lucky enough to be listed on the "palm cards" given to voters on election day, telling them for whom they should vote.

Most judicial candidates can't pay the thirty thousand dollars required of slated judicial candidates out of their own pockets. And many have to raise additional funds to pay for their own campaign costs of flyers, buttons, and mailings. They have to raise these funds primarily from law firms and attorneys who might appear before them after they are elected. Often they need to rely on more powerful politicians to host fund-raising events, chair their fund-raising committees, and supply mailing lists of potential donors. If they are successful and win their elections, these judges start their terms indebted to those who provide the funds as well as to the party that supplied the votes.

3. Retention elections: A few years after their first successful election, sitting judges must run in retention elections. They must win the support of 60 percent of the voters who cast ballots. Even though nearly all judges win these elections, they can't risk seriously offending their political supporters or a large number of voters. While organized campaigns have succeeded in defeating judges in only a few retention elections, sitting judges must maintain the support of powerful political leaders to retain their office.

4. Appointments: When judicial vacancies occur between elections, the Supreme Court makes temporary appointments. The justices, who have to run for election themselves, consider whom to appoint after listening to the wishes of political leaders. The process keeps them immersed in partisan politics. In 2012, the *Chicago Tribune* reported that on numerous occasions the Supreme Court justices kept politically connected judges on the bench after they were defeated by the voters. The justices simply appointed the losers to other vacancies.[65]

The Supreme Court's appointment process came under fire in 2013, when it appointed Justice Charles Freeman's law clerk, Jean Cocozza, to fill a vacancy on the Cook County bench. She had no courtroom experience, she did not have to appear before any screening committee, and no bar association evaluated her work to determine if she was qualified. She had worked for Freeman for fifteen years with duties including drafting opinions and orders, and she had general supervisory authority over Freeman's staff. But many questioned whether she was qualified to become a judge.[66]

Associate judges in Cook County are selected by a secret-ballot election by the full circuit-court judges. This process too is influenced by internal court politics and by the wishes of the political sponsors of those who want to be chosen. Most of the full circuit judges who vote on these appointments were themselves slated by the judicial slating committee and elected by the Democratic party. For many years, the judicial slating committee has been run by Fourteenth Ward Alderman Edward Burke. Similarly, the Illinois Democratic party is controlled by Speaker of the House Michael Madigan, who is the elected state-party chairman. He is also the father of Illinois Attorney General Lisa Madigan, who has the power to hire attorneys to serve as assistant attorneys general to handle cases when there is an excessive backlog of work or when the attorney general has a conflict of interest.

The power and effectiveness of Speaker Madigan also has influenced who gets elected as associate judge. Attorneys seeking election must work hard for the party, and many of them make political donations hoping to get on the "Madigan List." In 2011, the *Chicago Tribune* reported that "since 2003, Madigan has recommended 37 lawyers to become associate judges and 25 were selected outright." Several more Madigan candidates eventually made it to the bench through appointments.[67]

Curing Corrupted Courts

Since the days of Greylord and Gambat, some court reforms have been adopted. This is most notable in the jury-selection process, in which voters are selected by lot to serve on juries. There is also now random assignment of court cases to judges. Despite this, suspicions remain that some court cases in Illinois are affected by clout or influenced by money. Illegal and unethical behavior by judges and other court personnel causes voters to doubt that the law is applied equally.

Money certainly played a huge role in one of the most spectacular cases of judicial conflict of interest in recent Illinois history. In 2004, Judge Lloyd Karmeier from downstate Washington County was elected to a seat on the Illinois Supreme Court after spending $4.5 million on his campaign. Campaign donations included $350,000 from lawyers and executives with ties to State Farm Insurance.[68] After winning the election, Justice Karmeier cast the deciding vote to overturn a $1.2 billion judgment against State Farm. Despite the obvious conflict of interest and apparent bias, the U.S. Supreme Court refused to consider the appeal.[69] Party clout and money in judicial campaigns remain a problem in judicial elections throughout Illinois.

Judges face tremendous pressure to amass large amounts of money to secure appointment to the bench or to win competitive political elections. According to prosecutors, this pressure led Cook County Circuit Court Judge George

Smith to break several federal laws by raising more than twenty thousand dollars to give to an unnamed individual to influence the Illinois Supreme Court to appoint him to the bench in 1995.[70] Smith, a former Chicago police officer, was appointed on the recommendation of Justice Charles Freeman. In federal court in March 2002, Smith pleaded guilty to tax evasion and currency violations.[71]

Sometimes political connections are the basis for a conflict of interest that can taint civil and criminal cases. In 2012–13, two different judges were asked to step aside from hearing an involuntary manslaughter case against Richard Vanecko, the nephew of former Mayor Richard M. Daley and grandson of the late Mayor Richard J. Daley. Associate Judge Arthur Hill, the first judge who was randomly selected to hear the case, stepped aside after the media raised questions about his political connections. Hill worked with Richard M. Daley when Daley was Cook County state's attorney. After Daley became mayor, he appointed Hill to the Chicago Transit Authority Board.[72] Hill also helped elect State's Attorney Richard Devine and then held high staff positions in Devine's office. In 2004, Devine and his staff said that there was insufficient evidence to bring charges against Vanecko. Devine's successor, State's Attorney Anita Alvarez, who had served on Daley's and then Devine's staffs, declined to bring charges against Vanecko in 2011.[73] After Judge Hill stepped aside from the politically explosive case, the special prosecutor Dan Webb said that the case should be assigned to a judge from outside the county. Stephen Senderowitz, an attorney with the special prosecutor's office, said it would be difficult to find a judge in Cook County without ties to Daley or the two state's attorneys who declined to charge Vanecko.[74]

Cook County's chief judge asked the Illinois Supreme Court to assign a non–Cook County judge to the case. The court appointed McHenry County Judge Maureen P. McIntyre. At the first hearing in the case, she announced, "I don't know anyone involved, and my family does not know anyone involved."[75] She tried to put the conflict questions to rest—but it was not so simple. In May 2013, Judge McIntyre was under investigation by the Judicial Inquiry Board because of her questionable divorce from her ex-husband and former law partner Raymond Henehan. Although their home and most other assets were placed in the judge's name, McIntyre and Henehan were still living together in the same Barrington Hills house when she took over the Vanecko case. One of Henehan's former clients suggested that it was a "divorce of convenience" to protect their assets from his creditors and to avoid repayment of hundreds of thousands of dollars in debts.[76]

As it turns out, the judge's live-in ex-husband, Raymond Henehan, had extensive connections to the Cook County Democratic machine, which was dominated for more than fifty years by Vanecko's grandfather and his uncle, Mayors Richard J. and Richard M. Daley. Over the years, Henehan and his parents held various patronage jobs. His father worked for twenty-two years as an engineer for the Cook County Highway Department. In 1974, Henehan's mother, a Democrat, ran unsuccessfully for Illinois state representative. She was then hired to work in the Cook County assessor's office.[77]

In the early 1970s, Raymond Henehan worked for two years for the City Council Traffic Committee under its chairman, Forty-ninth Ward Alderman Paul Wigoda, who was convicted for income-tax evasion in a zoning scheme.[78] Henehan left three weeks before Wigoda was indicted. Next he was hired for a job with the Illinois Department of Transportation.[79]

In two editorials, the *Chicago Sun-Times* called for Judge McIntyre to step aside. In one, the editorial writers described "a manslaughter case soaked in suspicions of lapsed legal ethics."[80] In the other, they said, "Political and family connections are at the heart of the Vanecko case. Any questions about the judge's impartiality are potentially damaging. . . . The appearance of a potential conflict is there. Every person involved with this case, including Judge McIntyre, will be better off without that."[81] Judge McIntyre refused to step aside and set a trial date in February 2014. Before the trial, Richard Vanecko pleaded guilty to involuntary manslaughter.

Conflicts like Judge McIntyre's remain too common in our courts. Eliminating the corrupting influence of money and political clout in the way we select judges and in how our courts operate remains a daunting challenge. As the investigations chronicled in this chapter demonstrate, crooked courtrooms are not the way to achieve justice nor to gain citizens' faith in their government.

In 1958, U.S. Representative Dan Rostenkowski was selected by Mayor Richard J. Daley to run for Congress from Chicago's Northwest Side. With the machine's help he was reelected seventeen times and rose to become chairman of the powerful House Ways and Means Committee. In 1966, Rostenkowski pleaded guilty to two counts of felony mail fraud and was sent to federal prison. *Photo by Paul Merideth.*

CHAPTER 10

Congressional Corruption

UNTIL 1992, U.S. REPRESENTATIVE Dan Rostenkowski (D-Illinois) lived a charmed life. He got an early start in politics; he had family and political connections; he breezed up the ladder of success and became one of the most powerful politicians in Washington. He was at the top of his game and had become a friend and confidant of three successive presidents before his political life began to unravel.

Rostenkowski was born into a family that had more money and resources than most of its working-class neighbors. Young Dan was sent to a private boarding school in Wisconsin, away from the temptations of the big city. His father, Joseph, known as "Big Joe Rusty," was a powerful Polish politician who was the Democratic committeeman and alderman of Chicago's Thirty-second Ward. His mother, Priscilla, owned the saloon on the ground floor of the family's three-story building at 1347 North Nobel Street in the heart of Chicago's Polonia neighborhood on the city's near Northwest Side. The building also housed the family's insurance business and was headquarters for the Thirty-second Ward Democratic organization, led by Dan's father.

Even before going to boarding school, Dan worked in the family business—politics. He quickly learned one of the basic tenets of machine politics: that a governmental position can be leveraged for personal gain. After graduating from high school and serving two years in the army, Dan landed a patronage job as an investigator for the Chicago Corporation Counsel's office, the city's legal department. As the son of a powerful committeeman, Dan had a leg up over other candidates for this "little-work" or "no-show" gig.

In 1952, with help from his father, Dan Rostenkowski, then only twenty-four years old, won the Democratic party's nomination for state representative. He was easily elected and became the youngest member of the Illinois state legislature. Two years later, the Cook County Democratic Committee pushed aside an incumbent state senator to make way for the election of Dan Rostenkowski. While in the state senate, he became a "double dipper" when he was given a second job as a public-information officer for the Chicago Park District.

After less than four years in the state's upper house, Dan sought the blessing of Mayor Richard J. Daley to get elected to Congress in 1958. The mayor was indebted to Joe Rusty for his courageous support at a 1954 slating session, when Daley was selected as the party's mayoral candidate. He was also grateful to Joe, Dan, and the Thirty-second Ward organization for mobilizing voters in 1955 for his first mayoral election. As chairman of the slating committee for the 1959 primary, Daley arranged for Dan Rostenkowski to run for Congress without opposition. With the mayor's solid support, Rostenkowski won the general election, racking up 75 percent of the vote. Even at thirty, as the youngest member of the Eighty-sixth session of Congress, he was given a choice assignment to the powerful Commerce Committee.

The savvy Dan Rostenkowski quickly became Richard J. Daley's point man in the Chicago delegation as well as his eyes and ears in Washington. Rostenkowski would usually meet with Daley on Friday mornings after driving home from Washington all night Thursday with a bipartisan carload of friendly Illinois congressmen.

In 1965, Rostenkowski was placed on the House Ways and Means Committee, and three years later he was elected chairman of the Democratic Caucus. "Rosty" ascended to chair of Ways and Means in 1981 and ruled this powerful committee for thirteen years. The committee's purview was broad and deep. It controlled all legislation on taxes, social security, unemployment compensation, health policy, international trade, and almost every aspect of our country's economic life. Its control of the federal tax code was especially significant.

As chairman, Rosty used his deal-making skills and his knowledge of the political and private interests of other committee members to pass legislation acceptable to Democrats and Republicans alike. He left little to chance. Among his counterparts, he was seen as a tough but honest negotiator. He could twist arms and play rough, but he kept his word.

In Congress, Rostenkowski was Mayor Daley's guy and Chicago's muscle.

He was reelected seventeen times as he rose steadily up through the House Democratic leadership into the small circle of the ruling elite in Washington.

Most of Rostenkowski's legislative accomplishments occurred in a twelve-year period from 1981 to 1992, when Republicans Ronald Reagan and George H. W. Bush occupied the White House. With Democrats in control of the House of Representatives and Rosty chairing the Ways and Means Committee, he was able to make deals with Democratic members to pass the Republican administration's bills. A high point came in 1986, when Rostenkowski received praise for his leadership in rewriting the federal tax code for the first time in thirty years.

Mr. Chairman, as Rostenkowski preferred to be addressed, met frequently with the president and then made sure the gossip columnists were told. Magazines and newspapers gushed about his legislative exploits, but rarely if ever did Rosty hold news conferences or sit for interviews to answer questions about the substance of bills or what was traded to get agreements.

In the fall of 1991 and the first quarter of 1992, Dan Rostenkowski for the first time was campaigning hard in the Democratic primary. Since 1958, when he was first handpicked by Richard J. Daley to run for Congress, Rostenkowski had little or no opposition in his primary battles. And, since winning the primary in his heavily Democratic district was tantamount to winning the general election, he usually faced Republican opponents who had little public appeal and no chance to win.

However, in the 1992 March primary, Rostenkowski would face an experienced, combative opponent: Dick Simpson, a former two-term Chicago alderman who from 1971 to 1979 was the leader of the small independent bloc in the city council. Simpson, co-author of this book, was also a political science professor at the University of Illinois at Chicago. His campaign's communications director was Tom Gradel, the other co-author.

Even though he faced an experienced and qualified challenger in a redrawn, partially new congressional district, Rosty had a massive war chest. He enjoyed support from political leaders of both parties, and he was endorsed by Chicago's two major daily newspapers. Unless something went terribly awry, Rostenkowski was on course to win election to Congress for the eighteenth time.

It was at this point, just after the beginning of 1992, that Rosty's charmed life began to come apart. It would take more than three years to unravel completely. But by the end, Rostenkowski would be a convicted corrupt politician on his way to federal prison.

On January 22 of that year, the *Washington Times* reported that U.S. Attorney Jay Stephens, the chief federal prosecutor for the District of Columbia, was investigating the theft or misappropriation of nearly $250,000 in cash and stamps at the House post office.

Although the article said that no members of Congress were being investigated, and Rostenkowski's name wasn't mentioned, he had reason to be concerned. Two decades earlier, House Postmaster Robert Rota got his job with Rostenkowski's help. Like many patronage workers, Rota often complained that his position involved doing personal favors for Rosty.[1] Rostenkowski knew—but the prosecutor, the media, and the public did not discover until much later—that over the years Rota had allowed the Chicago congressman to requisition stamps worth thousands of dollars. They were purportedly for official use but were returned for cash, which Rostenkowski used personally.

The public had no hint of Rostenkowski's involvement in the House post-office scandal when they voted in the Democratic primary on March 17. Rostenkowski won the primary with 57 percent of the vote, while Dick Simpson received 43 percent. Rostenkowski spent $1,400,000 in the 1991–92 election cycle and outspent Simpson's campaign total of $215,000 by more than a six-to-one margin.[2]

Two days after Rostenkowski won the primary, House Postmaster Robert Rota resigned. The next day, Rostenkowski met with Rota and promised to pay his legal fees. Rostenkowski also told Rota how to testify, saying, "Remember, I always got my stamps."[3]

For more than a month as the scandal developed, there was still no indication that Rostenkowski was involved. This ended on May 6, 1992, when a federal grand jury subpoenaed the financial records of Rostenkowski and two congressmen from other states.

The *Washington Post* reported that James Smith, a longtime House post-office employee, had been given immunity from prosecution and was cooperating with federal prosecutors.[4] Smith was a friend of Virginia Fletcher, Rostenkowski's administrative assistant who ran his congressional office. Smith held his patronage job at the post office through Rostenkowski's sponsorship.[5]

The *Chicago Sun-Times* wrote that public documents showed that since 1986 Rostenkowski had submitted vouchers for stamps worth more than $17,500.[6] Its report noted that members of Congress can use the franking privilege to mail letters and asked why Rostenkowski would need so many postage stamps. Then a *Chicago Tribune* article reported that the Justice Department was also investigating allegations that campaign funds were converted to personal cash.[7]

Throughout the summer and fall, Rostenkowski denied that he ever received cash for stamps. He explained his extremely high usage of stamps with a cryptic retort, "I mail a lot."[8] His staff said that stamps rather than franking were needed for overseas letters, for certified mail, and for return envelopes for constituents.

As the November 1992 general election approached, the federal grand jury investigation of the House post office was still under way, and Dan Rostenkowski had a cloud over his head. Nonetheless, Rosty was endorsed by the *Chicago Sun-Times* and the *Chicago Tribune*. The editorial boards reasoned that his clout on the House Ways and Means Committee outweighed concern about his unproven ethical shortcomings. The presidential candidate Bill Clinton campaigned for Rostenkowski, as did Mayor Richard M. Daley. Political leaders from both parties expressed their support.

On election day, despite the scandal and the threat of indictment, Rostenkowski easily beat Republican Elias "Non-Incumbent" Zenkich and was elected to Congress for the eighteenth time. Many Rostenkowski supporters took comfort in the fact that the nation's voters elected Democrat Bill Clinton over the sitting Republican President, George H. W. Bush. Traditionally a new president appoints a new attorney general and new U.S. Attorneys for Washington, D.C., and the fifty states. It seemed highly likely that Clinton would soon name a new U.S. Attorney to replace Jay Stephens, a Republican appointee who was leading the investigating into the House post-office scandal. Stephens, according to Rostenkowski, was engaged in "a political witch hunt."[9]

Although Stephens eventually would be replaced, Clinton wasn't sworn in until January 20, 1993. After that, it would take some time for a new attorney general to be nominated and confirmed and for the president to appoint new U.S. Attorneys. Jay Stephens wasn't about to sit quietly while waiting for his replacement. Neither were the journalist Chuck Neubauer and other investigative reporters at the *Chicago Sun-Times*. *Sun-Times* news articles informed Stephens's investigators, and apparently sources close to the U.S. Attorney's office fed information to the *Sun-Times* and other news outlets. Less than a month after the election, Jay Stephens indicted an aide to Congressman Joseph Kolter (D-Pennsylvania), and a federal grand jury subpoenaed Rostenkowski's campaign records. Next the *Sun-Times* reported that Rostenkowski's campaign committee had paid more than seventy-three thousand dollars in campaign funds to rent a "phantom" campaign office in a building owned by Rosty and his sisters.[10]

Another *Sun-Times* investigation revealed that Rostenkowski spent $68,250 of taxpayers' money to lease three vehicles that later became his personal property. The newspaper also reported that the Rostenkowski for Congress Committee paid $19,717 to Wil-Shore Motor Sales of Wilmette for cars for his daughters, Gale and Stacy. And the *Sun-Times* reported that Rostenkowski's campaign committee paid $24,822 for auto insurance over a four-year period, even though the campaign did not own or lease any cars.[11]

Early in March 1993, Janet Reno, President Clinton's nominee for U.S. attorney general, was confirmed by the Senate. Two weeks later, she asked for the resignation of the country's ninety-three U.S. Attorneys, including Jay Stephens, who was leading the Rostenkowski investigation. Even though it is fairly common for a new president to appoint his own team of federal prosecutors, some of the congressman's friends hoped that the replacement of Stephens was a sign that the Rostenkowski investigation would be dropped. Instead, Reno named J. Ramsey Johnson, a sixteen-year veteran of the U.S. Attorney's D.C. office, as its top prosecutor and told him to proceed "full steam ahead" with the investigation.[12] Two weeks later, the *Washington Times* reported that "prosecutors appear to have broadened the investigation. They issued additional subpoenas to Rostenkowski, his reelection committee, his political action committee, and to his protege, 32nd Ward Alderman Terry Gabinski."[13]

In 1993, D.C. Superior Court Judge Eric Holder Jr. was appointed as U.S. Attorney for the District of Columbia. In July, former House Postmaster Robert Rota pleaded guilty to helping two unnamed congressmen embezzle more than thirty thousand dollars from the House post office. The *Washington Post* reported that the amounts, dates, and descriptions mentioned in the court documents corresponded to stamp "purchases" by Congressmen Rostenkowski and Kolter.[14] In March 1994, Rostenkowski again won his primary election. Although he no longer won a majority, he received 47 percent of the vote, more than the vote of any of the other four candidates.[15] When the indictment of Rostenkowski finally was announced on May 31, 1994, it wasn't just a couple of charges of misappropriation of postage stamps or failing to pay income taxes on stamps converted to personal use; it was a sweeping indictment of seventeen felony counts that described Rostenkowski's "elaborate scheme to steal more than $685,000 in taxpayer and campaign funds."[16]

When U.S. Attorney Eric Holder announced the federal grand jury indictment of Congressman Rostenkowski, he stressed the broad scope of the charges:

He regularly put people on his congressional payroll who did little or no official work, but who instead performed a variety of personal services for him, his family, his family insurance business, and his campaign organizations. Payments to these people exceeded one-half million dollars.

He obtained at least $50,000 in cash from the House Post Office by disguising his transactions as stamp purchases.

He charged to Congress and the taxpayers more than $40,000 for the purchase of valuable merchandise—including hand-painted chairs, crystal sculptures, and fine china—which he handed out as gifts to friends.

He caused Congress to pay over $70,000 in taxpayer money for personal vehicles used by himself and his family.

Finally, he obstructed justice by instructing a witness to withhold evidence from the grand jury.[17]

Four days after the indictment, Rostenkowski fired his attorney, Robert Bennett, who, according to the *Chicago Sun-Times,* had urged Rostenkowski to plead guilty to a felony charge, quit Congress, and spend six months in prison.[18] The next day, Rostenkowski announced that he had hired the former federal prosecutor Daniel Webb, a leading defense attorney and the chief prosecutor of the Operation Greylord cases. "There will be no deals," Rostenkowski promised. Webb declared, "We are going to fight this case. We're going to go to trial."[19]

As required by the rules of the House of Representatives, Rostenkowski had to step down as chairman of Ways and Means, but he remained on the committee. President Clinton praised his work and said that he needed Rostenkowski to win congressional support for his health-care and trade bills. Rostenkowski increased his efforts to get credit for steering federal funds to a community college, a hospital project, and repairs to Chicago's lake shore.

In the fall, with the general election looming, Webb tried unsuccessfully to get the charges dismissed, claiming that Rostenkowski violated House rules, not criminal statutes. Webb argued that the Constitution authorizes the House, not the courts, to prosecute such violations.[20]

Despite the indictment and more than two years of negative publicity, many politicians, including Mayor Daley and President Clinton, continued to support Rostenkowski and to insist that he would win the 1994 election. A few weeks before the election, top management of the *Chicago Sun-Times* turned its back on more than two years of solid work by its investigative reporters and minimized the significance of the federal indictment against Rostenkowski. In its editorial, the *Sun-Times* wrote,

> In the general election, we endorse Dan Rostenkowski. Rostenkowski's legal prob-
> lems . . . continue to hang over his head. . . . We remain appalled by his apparent
> belief that being a congressman brings with it generous personal entitlements. . . .
> However, there is no denying that Rostenkowski has been a real leader in Congress.
> As chairman of the House Ways and Means Committee he shepherded President
> Clinton's successful deficit-reduction bill and the North American Free Trade Agree-
> ment through Congress. . . . And, yes, he has delivered federal dollars to Chicago.[21]

On other occasions, journalists, commentators, and editorial writers won-
dered why Illinois voters are so tolerant of the state's rampant political corruption. These newspaper endorsements of known corrupt politicians may
be one of the reasons voters tolerate corruption and the culture of corruption
persists.

Ironically, the *Chicago Tribune,* which usually treated Rostenkowski much
better than the *Sun-Times,* declined to endorse either him or his Republican
opponent, Michael Flanagan. The *Tribune* editorial noted that "[a]fter reading
the detailed indictment and listening to Rostenkowski's defense, a voter can
fairly draw the conclusion that Rostenkowski abused the privilege of his office
and merits repudiation." However, the *Tribune* said that Flanagan "has yet to
establish either a substantial law practice or a noteworthy civic record."[22]

In the end, the voters apparently gave greater weight to the indictment
and the negative news articles than they did to politicians' praises and the
predictions of victory. On November 8, 1994, Michael Patrick Flanagan won
by a healthy margin of 55 to 45 percent and handed Rostenkowski his first
election defeat in his forty-two-year political career.

After the election, the U.S. Attorney continued to build the case against
Rostenkowski. By October 1995, federal prosecutors had convicted nine persons involved in the House post-office scandal. They also hauled many of
Rostenkowski's Chicago assistants before the federal grand jury and indicted
several of his cronies on ghost-payrolling charges. Robert Russo, a Chicago
Water Department employee and a tenant of Rostenkowski's family-owned
building, was found guilty of perjury and obstructing justice. Over a ten-year
period, Russo received ninety thousand dollars from Rosty's congressional
payroll for doing little or no work. James Nedza, the son of the State Senator
Edward Nedza, pleaded guilty to obstructing justice by lying to the grand jury
about his "ghost" job on Rostenkowski's congressional staff.[23]

Despite many assertions that he would never cop a plea, on April 9, 1996,
Rostenkowski pleaded guilty to two counts of felony mail fraud. Judge Norma
Holloway Johnson sentenced the former congressman to seventeen months in

prison and castigated him for abusing his position and disgracing the institution he served.

Outside the courtroom Rostenkowski was unrepentant. He claimed that he was singled out by prosecutors and was subjected to an "unprecedented government investigation." He told news reporters that he only committed "technical violations" and that he did nothing different "than the vast majority of members of Congress and their staffs, who have experienced enormous difficulty in determining whether particular services by congressional employees should be classified as congressional, political or personal."[24]

Rostenkowski, like Governor Blagojevich and many other convicted politicians, continued to argue that he was only guilty of normal politics. His friends and apologists argued that Rostenkowski was an old-time pol doing what politicians always did. The rules changed, but sadly, he didn't.

But Rostenkowski knew where the lines were. Throughout his long career he used his office to help himself. He benefitted personally and politically from numerous conflicts of interest, and he often engaged in unethical behavior. An early example was a major scandal that erupted in 1971 following reports that IRS investigators found that various racetrack interests had given profitable stock deals to more than a dozen Illinois politicians. After the head of the Illinois Racing Board demanded that all racing associations disclose their stock holders, the *Chicago Sun-Times* and other publications reported that Rostenkowski secretly held 2,500 shares of Egyptian Trotting Association stock. Rostenkowski made his initial investment in 1957 when he was a state senator. He paid only five hundred dollars for his shares and later invested an additional $1,300 in redeemable bonds. By 1970, he had received more than forty-two thousand dollars in dividends on his shares. There were never allegations that Rostenkowski took any official action to help the racing association, so he was not indicted. Federal prosecutors were after bigger fish. In 1973, former governor Otto Kerner and former state revenue director Theodore J. Issacs were convicted of a scheme to secretly purchase racetrack stock at bargain prices in exchange for favors such as signing racing bills and approving racing dates. Kerner was convicted of bribery, conspiracy, income-tax evasion, and perjury, for which he was sentenced to three years in prison. But Rosty got away with the sweetheart racetrack deal early in his political career. It was not surprising that he would be involved in other corruption schemes later, as his power grew.

In 1986, as chairman of the tax-writing House Ways and Means Committee, Dan Rostenkowski approved 650 special tax breaks, called transition rules, for thousands of wealthy individuals and hundreds of corporations. The *Philadelphia Inquirer* called the tax-law changes "licenses not to pay taxes" and "the largest tax giveaway in the 75-year history of the U.S. income tax." The *Inquirer* estimated that the cost to the U.S. taxpayers could run as high as thirty billion dollars.[25]

In the same tax bill, Rostenkowski placed a secret provision that gave $119 million in tax breaks to fifteen insurance companies. The names of the insurance companies were still secret when the U.S. Senate considered the bill. Senator Howard Metzenbaum (D-Ohio) raised a stink about being asked to vote on the bill when the names of the insurance companies were secret.

Only then did Senator Bob Packwood (R-Ore.) release the names. Packwood said that it was Rostenkowski's idea to help the insurance companies, but Packwood confessed that he made a mistake agreeing to it.[26] The fifteen companies were among the largest insurance companies in the world, with assets worth hundreds of billions of dollars and with billions of dollars in profits. A subsequent analysis of campaign donations indicated that eleven of the fifteen insurance companies contributed more than thirty-two thousand dollars to Rostenkowski's campaign committee in the five years following the passage of the tax bill. In the same five-year period, Rostenkowski's campaign received $101,000 from insurance-industry political action committees and $125,000 from insurance executives and insurance brokers.

Congressman Mel Reynolds Convicted in Two Courts

Numerous Illinois congresspersons besides Rostenkowski have been involved in corrupt, unethical activities, or just plain bad behavior. Besides being one of only two Illinois congressmen other than Rostenkowski to be convicted of a crime in the past fifty years, Mel Reynolds, like Rostenkowski, was also nurtured by a Mayor Daley. Mayor Richard M. Daley supported Mel Reynolds in his three challenges to incumbent Congressman Gus Savage. Reynolds lost his first two tries but won the 1992 Democratic primary and the general election to become U.S. Representative for the Second District of Illinois. Daley gave his wife, Marisol Reynolds, a job as a secretary in the mayor's scheduling office.[27] Daley and Rostenkowski approved the appointment of Reynolds to the powerful House Ways and Means Committee. He was the first and only freshman congressman to be named to that committee during Rostenkowski's tenure.[28]

Mel Reynolds has a rare distinction in the chronicle of Illinois corruption: he was convicted in both state and federal courts in the United States and overseas in Zimbabwe. In 1992 he was convicted in Cook County Criminal Court of criminal sexual assault, child pornography, and obstruction of justice for having sex with a volunteer campaign worker when she was only sixteen.[29] Reynolds had served less than three years in Congress when he was convicted. Facing a move by his congressional colleagues to oust him, he resigned his seat. But it wasn't the end of his troubles, and it wasn't the last time a congressman from the Second District would be accused of campaign and sexual misconduct. Democrat Jesse L. Jackson Jr., who later would be convicted of a felony and resign from Congress, won a special general election in 1995 to serve out the remaining thirteen months of Reynolds's second term.

While Reynolds was serving the first year of his five-year prison sentence for sexual crimes, he and his wife Marisol were charged in federal court with fraud in obtaining a $279,000 mortgage for their home in Dolton, Illinois. They were also charged with misusing campaign funds and filing false campaign reports.[30]

After testifying that Reynolds beat her repeatedly during their eleven-year marriage, Marisol pleaded guilty to fraud. She said that fear of her husband led her to lie on loan applications and campaign documents.[31] The case of Marisol Reynolds is a rarity in the story of Illinois corruption. She and Alderman Sandi Jackson, the wife of Reynolds's successor, are the only politicians' wives to be convicted of public corruption.

Following a trial in federal court, a jury found Reynolds guilty of defrauding banks and lying to the Federal Election Commission.[32] He was sentenced to serve six and a half years in federal prison on top of thirty months in the state penitentiary. His wife was sentenced to three years probation.

After nearly eight years of investigations, indictments, and convictions, and five years of incarceration, Mel Reynolds caught a break. On his last day in office, President Clinton commuted his sentence, allowing the former congressman to serve the remaining time at a halfway house in Chicago.[33] In March 2004, after he served his time, Mel Reynolds ran in the Democratic primary against Jesse Jackson Jr. for his old Second Congressional District seat. Even with support from Dolton Mayor Bill Shaw, he received only 6 percent of the vote.[34]

A decade later, in February 2014, Mel Reynolds pleaded guilty to overstaying his visa after more serious pornography charges were dropped in Zimbabwe.[35] In his newest career, Reynolds was a business consultant and American liaison for African businessmen. He praised Zimbabwe's unpopular dictator as "one of the last lions of Africa that brought freedom to the people of this great continent."[36] At the time of his arrest and conviction, Reynolds was involved in a failed deal to build a multi-million-dollar Hilton Hotel in Zimbabwe. Although his business career, like his congressional career, has ended badly, he was freed from jail in Zimbabwe and has returned to the United States to start over once again.

Congressmen with Mob Ties and Conflicts of Interest

Like other politicians, some congressmen had mob ties. A politician's connections to the Chicago Outfit are always an indicator that political corruption is lurking nearby.

Two prominent Italian-American politicians from Chicago's notorious First Ward served a combined twenty-six years in Congress, even though they had mob connections. U.S. Representative Roland "Libby" Libonati, who served in Congress from 1958 to 1965, began his political career as a low-level attorney-politician who frequently bragged about his friendships with mobsters and occasionally defended organized-crime figures in court.

Libonati graduated from Northwestern University Law School in 1924 and began practicing law in Chicago.[37] He met Al Capone in Philadelphia while defending a Capone underling. Libonati gave legal advice to Capone, and Libonati's attorney brother, Eliador, also frequently represented Capone.[38]

With Capone's help, Roland Libonati won a special election at the end of 1929 to become an Illinois state representative.[39] He had the backing and support of Chicago's mob-controlled First Ward Democratic organization. He became a leader of the notorious bipartisan West Side Bloc and the Democratic minority whip in the House.[40] He was elected to the Illinois Senate in 1942.[41] During his thirteen years in the Illinois legislature, Libonati worked to scuttle anticrime legislation and to do the bidding of the Outfit.[42]

In Congress, he was an ardent critic of FBI tactics, and he used his position on the House Judiciary Committee to attack U.S. Attorney General Robert Kennedy and other officials when they attempted to investigate or prosecute organized-crime figures.[43] Congressman Libonati frequently visited the gangster Paul "The Waiter" Ricca in prison.

According to the author Gus Russo, the Outfit's legal mastermind, Curly Humphreys, worked with Congressman Libonati to introduce legislation that would outlaw Kennedy's surveillance techniques. In a conversation overheard by the government with Pat Marcy at the First Ward headquarters, Libonati bragged about his warfare with the attorney general: "I killed six of his bills—that wiretapping, the intimidating informers bill."[44]

Libonati attracted unwanted attention in 1963, when it became known that he employed Anthony Tisci, the son-in-law of the well-known gangster Momo Salvatore Giancana, as a nine-hundred-dollar-a-month secretary in his congressional office. Tisci continued to be paid his government salary in July 1963, even though he spent most of that month in Chicago helping Giancana in a legal battle with the FBI. Tisci didn't see any conflict of interest, and neither did Libonati.[45]

In President John F. Kennedy's last year in office, he called on Chicago Mayor Richard J. Daley to lean on Libonati to support preliminary action on the Civil Rights Act. "He'll vote for it," Daley told the president. "He'll vote for any goddamn thing you want."[46] According to sources, Daley instructed Libonati: "This is the way we want it, and that's the way it's gonna be."[47]

Despite the mayor's assurances, Libonati voted against Kennedy.

Embarrassed and angered by Libonati's insubordination, Daley dumped Libonati for renomination six months later, but the mayor didn't cross the mob's political team.[48] Daley replaced Libonati with Frank Annunzio, First Ward Democratic committeeman and business partner with John D'Arco Sr., First Ward alderman and reputed mob associate. Annunzio co-owned Anco Insurance with D'Arco.[49] After Libonati left Congress, he served as a trustee of the Illinois General Assembly Retirement System when it granted convicted Illinois Attorney General William Scott an annual pension of $26,600, despite a law prohibiting pensions for officials convicted of felonies.[50] Roland Libonati was ninety when he died on May 27, 1991, at his West Side home.[51]

His replacement, Frank Annunzio, was born in 1915 in Chicago. He graduated from Crane Technical High School and earned a B.S. degree from DePaul University before teaching for seven years in the Chicago Public Schools. He was an educational director and lobbyist for the United Steelworkers of America and First Ward committeeman when he was appointed Illinois Director of Labor by Governor Adlai Stevenson.[52]

Annunzio was fired by Stevenson after newspapers reported that he was a partner in the Anco insurance sales agency with First Ward Alderman and Committeeman John D'Arco Sr. and with Buddy Jacobson, a former cop who was once convicted of vote fraud. Jacobson was also an enforcer and bodyguard for the bootlegger and organized-crime figure Hymie Weiss.[53]

Nonetheless, Frank Annunzio was elected to Congress in 1964 after being slated by Mayor Richard J. Daley to replace Libonati. Annunzio inherited Libonati's Seventh Congressional District on Chicago's West Side, which included the infamous First Ward. He also inherited Libonati's chief assistant, attorney Anthony Tisci. In 1965, the Better Government Association asked the Chicago Bar Association to seek Tisci's disbarment after he cited his Fifth Amendment rights and refused to testify in a federal investigation of organized crime.[54] After redistricting in 1971, Annunzio accepted Mayor Daley's order to move to the Eleventh Congressional District on the Northwest Side of Chicago to open up a spot for an African American, George Collins, to run for Congress.

In 1984, two executives of the Board of Trade Clearing Company pleaded guilty to funneling more than twenty thousand dollars in illegal campaign contributions, including five thousand dollars to Congressman Frank Annunzio. No evidence was presented that Annunzio knew the donations were illegal.[55]

In the 1980s and 1990s, Frank Annunzio was a high-ranking Democrat on the House Banking Committee and chairman of a subcommittee on regulation. He had a long, friendly relationship with the nation's savings-and-loan industry. Some critics said that he helped cause the savings-and-loan crisis that cost the American taxpayers more than ninety billion dollars.[56] Of course, many other congresspeople, elected officials, and banking executives were largely culpable, while Annunzio's role was comparatively minor. Nonetheless, as he was running for his fourteenth term in Congress, Annunzio was sharply criticized by Steve Neal, a *Sun-Times* political columnist. Neal argued that Annunzio, as chairman of the subcommittee on regulation, was partially to blame for the savings-and-loan fiasco. "Annunzio sought to delay the Federal Home Loan Bank Board's 1985 attempt to ban S&Ls from making questionable investments," Neal wrote. "Two years later Fearless Frank fought the Reagan administration's $15 billion bailout plan that would have cut taxpayers' losses to a fraction of the eventual final bill."[57]

Annunzio also came under heavy political fire for accepting fifty thousand dollars in campaign donations from the principal S&L political action committee over a ten-year period and another $4,500 of S&L money in 1990.[58] Reporter Greg Hinz disclosed in the Pulitzer-Lerner newspapers that Annunzio's sons-in-law Kevin Tynan and Sal Lato held top posts with Skokie Federal Savings and Loan before it was taken over by federal regulators at a cost of $168 million to taxpayers. Both Tynan and Lato also worked for the U.S. Savings and Loan League, a major lobbying group.[59] Despite the apparent conflicts of interest, there was no reported evidence that Annunzio committed any crimes.

After reapportionment put him in the same district as Rostenkowski, Annunzio declined to run against Rosty in 1992. Mayor Richard M. Daley quickly appointed the retired congressman to the Illinois International Port District. Annunzio died from Parkison's disease in 2001 when he was eighty-six.

Another Congressman with S&L Conflicts of Interest

U.S. Representative Henry Hyde was another Illinois congressman with conflicts of interest and close ties to the savings-and-loan industry. Hyde, a Republican from Bensenville, represented the Sixth Congressional District in the suburbs west of Chicago for thirty-two years (1975–2007). Before that, he served in the Illinois legislature from 1967 to 1974.

In 1975, when he began his first term in Congress, Hyde joined the House Banking Committee. Although he initially said that he wouldn't, Hyde accepted campaign contributions from bank and S&L political action committees. He dropped off the Banking Committee in 1981 and became a director of Clyde Federal Savings and Loan Association in North Riverside. He served on that board until 1984 and was paid four thousand dollars per year as a director. From 1981 to 1992, Hyde accepted more than $111,000 in campaign contributions and fourteen thousand dollars in speaking fees and honoraria from the savings-and-loan and banking industry.

Throughout the 1980s, while on the Banking Committee and then as a director of Clyde Savings and Loan, Hyde voted to support the industry on seven major pieces of legislation to deregulate S&Ls and to enrich their directors and officers. In 1989, Hyde introduced an industry-sought amendment to give 241 savings-and-loans a mechanism to escape the need to raise six billion dollars in new capital as reserves against potential loan losses. A *Washington Post* editorial called Hyde's device "a fig leaf invented to hide the financial nakedness of many S&Ls." Hyde promoted the measure on the House floor and wore a large campaign button supporting the industry. Although the measure failed, his fight for it illustrated how hard he was willing to work for his benefactors.[60]

Meanwhile, Hyde's Clyde Federal's financial situation deteriorated. In 1990, the Resolution Trust Corporation, an arm of the federal government, bailed out Clyde at a cost to U.S. taxpayers of at least $148 million.

Conflicts of interest and politicians using their official actions to financially benefit campaign contributors often are not prosecuted. Either they aren't illegal, or there isn't sufficient evidence that a crime was committed. As with Annunzio, that was true for Henry Hyde.

Hyde's relationship with the grossly mismanaged Clyde Federal Savings and Loan and his role in the ninety-five-billion-dollar savings-and-loan crisis is little known by the general public. He is, however, famous for passing the Hyde Amendment that prohibited any federal funding for abortions.[61] He also attracted national attention when he spearheaded the unsuccessful prosecution of President Bill Clinton's impeachment. The U.S. House voted to impeach the president for lying under oath about a sexual relationship, but the Senate failed to convict him. In 1998, while the impeachment process was under way, *Salon* reported that Hyde had a five-year affair with a younger married woman. It occurred in the 1960s when the forty-one-year-old Hyde, who was married at the time, was a member of the Illinois House. Many news organizations picked up the story, which Hyde then admitted, describing the relationship as a "youthful indiscretion."[62] Henry Hyde did not run for reelection in 2006 and retired in January 2007. He was eighty-three when he died of heart failure in November 2007.

Sexual Indiscretions

Sexual indiscretions, youthful or not, have entangled a handful of other Illinois congressmen. Sometimes the misbehavior became public and embarrassed the elected official. Sometimes it resulted in the congressmen being voted out of office.

In 1981, the *Wilmington News Journal* reported that an attractive woman lobbyist shared a cottage during a Florida golfing vacation with Congressman Thomas Railsback, a Republican from Moline, Illinois, and two other GOP congressmen. All were married and vacationing without their spouses. News stories indicated that the lobbyist, thirty-year-old Paula Parkinson, was a fetching, good-time party girl and lobbyist. Parkinson was working to defeat legislation that would have extended federal control over crop insurance. The bill passed in the House by a wide margin, but the three congressmen voted against it. Some articles suggested that she may have exchanged sexual favors for the congressmen's "No" votes. After the vacation but before the stories broke, Paula Parkinson posed nude for the November 1980 *Playboy* magazine feature on the "The Women of Washington."

During a Justice Department investigation, Parkinson told prosecutors that she had affairs with "fewer than a dozen" Republican House members but that "none of them had done anything illegal."[63] Railsback admitted sharing the vacation house with Parkinson and the other congressmen but said that he was never involved with Parkinson and that she didn't affect his vote. "I never touched that woman. I wouldn't have a thing to do with her," Railsback said in a news conference.[64] A different relationship was suggested by Parkinson when she told the *Washington Post* columnist Rudy Maxa that Railsback was her entree to power and politics. She claimed that she and Railsback met a couple times a week after work in October 1979, sometimes at his suburban Virginia apartment. A spokesman for Railsback said that the congressman refused to elaborate on his press-conference comments.[65]

In the end, it didn't matter whether voters believed Railsback's denials or if they found Parkinson's tale more credible. The bad publicity took its toll. Railsback's troubles were compounded by redistricting, which gave him many new constituents who were unfamiliar with his record of service. In the next primary election, the twelve-year incumbent lost to a more conservative Republican challenger, who then lost to a Democrat in November 1982.

In 1983, Republican Congressman Daniel Crane from Danville was censured by the U.S. House of Representatives for having sex with a seventeen-year-old female congressional page. A report by the House Ethics Committee said that the sexual relationship, which took place two or three times in 1980 at Crane's apartment in Arlington, Virginia, was consensual. There was no criminal action against Crane because the age of consent in Virginia was sixteen.[66]

Crane, a married father of six, was only the twenty-second member of Congress in history to be censured by his colleagues. The Ethics Committee had proposed a reprimand, a lesser penalty, but the House voted 288–136 to increase the penalty to censure. Among those voting for a lesser penalty were a bipartisan group of Illinois congressmen, including Democrats Dan Rostenkowski, Frank Annunzio, and Gus Savage, and Republican Henry Hyde.[67] Crane did not resign his seat, but he was defeated in the next general election by a Democrat.

Gus Savage, who preceded Mel Reynolds as U.S. Representative for the Second District, had a reputation as an outspoken and strident advocate for African American causes and contracts for minority businesses. He also was known for having a foul mouth and for incendiary anti-Jewish verbal attacks. In 1989, during his fourth term in office, the *Washington Post* reported that a twenty-eight-year-old Peace Corps volunteer complained that Savage fondled her, urged her to have sex with him, and ignored her repeated attempts to make him stop. The woman said that the assault occurred on March 19, in a chauffeur-driven U.S. embassy car in Kinshasa, Zaire. Savage, a sixty-three-year-old widower, was on an official fact-finding trip.[68] At a news conference,

Savage denied the accusation and said, "This lie was leaked by the State Department for political reasons." The next day, three Democratic members of Congress officially requested an investigation by the House Committee on Standards and Official Conduct. The panel, commonly known as the Ethics Committee, decided to conduct a preliminary inquiry.[69]

In February, prior to a March 20 primary election, the Ethics Committee issued a report stating that Savage "did, in fact, make sexual advances to the Peace Corps volunteer," but the committee recommended no formal House punishment partly because Savage, in a letter to the woman, "acknowledged that he may have acted inappropriately."[70] In a three-way Democratic primary, Gus Savage received 51.5 percent of the vote and defeated challenger Mel Reynolds, who received 43 percent.

In April, Savage received another blessing when the Justice Department closed a criminal investigation into the hiring of Thomas J. Savage, the congressman's son, by Walter E. Fauntroy, the nonvoting Washington, D.C., delegate to Congress. House rules require congressional employees to work in Washington or in the member's district, which for Fauntroy was Washington. At the time, Thomas Savage was running for the Illinois General Assembly when he was supposed to be working in Washington. The investigation also looked into the possibility that Thomas Savage didn't do any work for the two thousand dollars per month that he was paid. Thomas Savage lost his election bid but was hired by the Metropolitan Water Reclamation District in Chicago. The investigation was dropped because of "insufficient evidence."[71] Gus Savage went on to handily win the 1990 general election. However, two years later he lost to Mel Reynolds, whom he had twice previously defeated.

The Jesse Jackson Jr. Case

Jesse Jackson Jr. followed Gus Savage and Mel Reynolds as the U.S. Representative for the Second Congressional District. He, too, ran into trouble with the law.

Jackson, a Democrat from Chicago, was first elected in a special election in 1995 to replace Congressman Reynolds, who resigned after being convicted of sexual misconduct. Jackson is the son of Rev. Jesse Jackson Sr., the well-known civil-rights leader and former candidate for the Democratic nomination for president. He is also the husband of Sandi Jackson, an alderman and committeeman of Chicago's Seventh Ward.

In 2006, after a decade in office, Jackson flirted with the possibility of running for mayor against the incumbent, Richard M. Daley. In the end, he couldn't raise the resources, so he didn't run. But in 2008, after U.S. Senator Barack Obama was elected president, Jackson campaigned vigorously and publicly to be appointed to Obama's unfinished Senate term.

In the early morning on December 9, 2008, Governor Rod Blagojevich was arrested by the FBI and was taken from his home in handcuffs. He was charged with several crimes, including trying to sell the Senate seat to several prospects, including Jackson. Blagojevich was recorded by the FBI saying that he was approached by an emissary offering to raise $1.5 million if he appointed Jackson to the Senate seat.[72] Jackson denied the accusation.

According to the *Chicago Sun-Times*, Raghuveer Nayak, an Indian-American businessman, also told investigators that he paid for two airline trips for Giovana Huidobro, a Washington martini-bar hostess, to visit Representative Jackson in Chicago. When questioned about the woman, Jackson said that she was a "social acquaintance." He and his wife Sandi Jackson said that they had dealt with the matter before it became public and asked that their privacy be respected.[73]

Three weeks prior to the general election, the *Chicago Sun-Times* reported that federal investigators had launched a probe into the congressman's finances.[74] The news did not alter the outcome. Jesse Jackson Jr. easily won reelection, since the congressional district was drawn to make it safe for any Democrat. A few weeks after his election victory, Jackson sent a letter of resignation to House Speaker John Boehner, putting an end his seventeen-year congressional career.[75]

Three months later, the U.S. Attorney filed criminal charges against Jackson for misusing more than $750,000 in campaign funds. His wife was charged with filing false tax returns. Federal authorities alleged that Jackson used campaign funds to make numerous luxury purchases for Rolex watches, flat-screen TVs, fur coats and capes, celebrity memorabilia, children's furniture, and many other items. Jackson was also charged with making false statements to the House of Representatives and with failing to report $28,500 in loans and gifts he received.[76]

Within a week, Jackson appeared before a U.S. District Court Judge in Washington, D.C. "I am guilty, your honor," Jackson said, entering his plea. "Sir, for years I lived off my campaign. I used monies that should have been used for campaign purposes, and I used them for myself personally, to benefit me personally."[77] He also acknowledged the accuracy of the government's twenty-two-page statement detailing his criminal behavior.[78]

Alderman Sandi Jackson pleaded guilty to failing to report on the couple's income-tax returns nearly $570,000 in taxable income, primarily from the illegally used campaign funds. In her case, she failed to report at least fifteen thousand dollars in taxable income earned through her political consulting firm J. Donatella and Associates. Her husband's campaign reported paying $452,500 to her firm over ten years.[79]

In 2013, Jesse Jackson Jr. was sentenced to thirty months in federal prison and ordered to perform five hundred hours of community service and to pay a forfeiture of $750,000.[80] Sandi Jackson was sentenced to a full year in prison, but the judge allowed her to remain free until the completion of her husband's term. She was also ordered to pay twenty-two thousand dollars in restitution.[81]

Not Telling the Whole Truth

Jackson was not the only politician who coveted Obama's Senate seat. Former Illinois Attorney General Roland Burris actively sought the "golden" position. But unlike Jackson, Burris got the appointment and served out the remaining two years of the term.

Roland Burris was experienced in the rough and tumble of Illinois politics. In 1977, he won election as Illinois comptroller, making him the first African American to be elected to statewide office. Before that, he was an attorney who worked for the state and federal governments. He was reelected twice as state comptroller, and in 1990 he was elected Illinois attorney general. After that, he ran unsuccessfully for higher office numerous times. When not in public office, he was an attorney in private practice, a lobbyist, a political consultant, and a fund-raiser. Throughout most of his career Burris avoided negative publicity and was not known to be involved in criminal or unethical behavior.

Things change. When they do, ambitious politicians look for opportunities to move up. In the fall of 2008, when it became likely that Senator Obama would be elected president, Burris began maneuvering to be appointed to serve for the remaining two years of the term. Governor Blagojevich, who had the sole authority to select Obama's replacement, was arrested and charged with several crimes, including attempting to sell the Senate seat. Despite his arrest and pending indictment, Blagojevich appointed Burris to the spot.[82] There was an immediate uproar, followed by speculation that Burris and Blagojevich may have made a secret, nefarious deal. Burris denied any pay-to-play arrangement. He claimed he spoke to no "representatives" of the governor prior to December 26, 2008. Then, in later testimony, Burris said that he told the governor's former chief of staff, Lon Monk, that he was interested in the seat.[83]

In 2009, Roland Burris was sworn in as a U.S. senator from Illinois. Then he changed his story again. According to the *Chicago Sun-Times,* Burris had expressed interest in the Senate seat to five people in the Blagojevich camp. The newspaper also said that Burris filed a second affidavit admitting that Rob Blagojevich, the governor's brother, had asked him for a ten-thousand-dollar campaign donation before the appointment was made.[84] The following month, Burris announced that he would not run for election to a full term in the Senate in 2010 but that he would serve until his term expired in January 2011.

In November 2009, almost a full year after Blagojevich was arrested, the U.S. Senate Ethics Committee admonished Burris and said that his behavior "reflected unfavorably on the Senate," but found no "actionable violations of the law." The committee said that Burris "should have known" he was providing "incorrect, inconsistent, misleading, or incomplete information" to the Senate and those conducting legitimate inquiries. They wrote that Burris's "phone conversation with Rob Blagojevich, while not rising to the level of an explicit quid pro quo, was inappropriate." They noted that in the same phone call, Burris "appeared to agree to write a check and even potentially raise money for Blagojevich" and "repeatedly brought up his desire to seek the Senate seat." Burris retained the seat and did not suffer any reduction in pay or benefits.[85] A *Chicago Sun-Times* editorial concluded: "Burris lied, then he lied about lying."[86]

Other Congressional Scandals

Over the last several decades, there have been many other congressional scandals. While none of these congressmen have gone to jail, several have lost reelection bids.

The former Republican congressman from Yorkville and former Speaker of the House Dennis Hastert made a profit of two million dollars in 2006 when he sold a portion of farmland he owned. The land was close to a proposed highway, the Prairie Parkway, in Kendall County, west of Chicago. A year earlier, he had used his power in the House to deliver $207 million in federal transportation dollars for the Parkway.[87]

Republican Congressman Jerry Weller from Morris married Zury Rios Sosa, a Guatemalan senator and daughter of the notorious Guatemalan dictator Gen. Efrain Rios Montt. The *Chicago Tribune* reported that Weller didn't declare the extent of his real-estate holdings in Nicaragua on his congressional disclosures and that he reported different purchase prices on American and Nicaraguan records "to lessen the bite of local taxes."[88] Citizens for Responsibility and Ethics, a Washington watchdog group, labeled Weller one of the twenty-two most corrupt members of Congress. Just two weeks after the *Tribune* exposé, Weller announced that he would not seek reelection in 2008. He retired from Congress when his term ended.

U.S. Representative Luis Gutierrez, a former Chicago alderman, was first elected to Congress in 1992 in a new Fourth Congressional District that was politically drawn to favor the election of a Hispanic candidate. He had become a savvy real-estate investor and property flipper. In 1998, the *Chicago Tribune* columnist John Kass reported that Congressman Gutierrez only paid $274 a year in property taxes on his $340,000 home, while others were paying about five thousand dollars annually for similar properties.[89] Gutierrez said that it wasn't his fault and that he paid the tax bills he received. Gutierrez built the home on a previously vacant plot. Between the Building Department, which should have reported the permits, and the assessor's office, which apparently didn't notice a huge, new occupied home on the lot, someone made a big "mistake" in Gutierrez's favor. By the end of the year, he paid $13,775 in back taxes and penalties.[90]

A decade later, Gutierrez was entangled in another questionable real-estate deal. Alderman Isaac Carothers (Twenty-ninth Ward) was indicted for accepting free home-remodeling work in exchange for helping a builder, Calvin Boender, obtain a zoning change to allow a commercial and residential development called Galewood Yards on Chicago's West Side.[91] Both Carothers and Boender were convicted. According to testimony in the trials, Congressman Gutierrez wrote a letter to city planners supporting the development after receiving a two-hundred-thousand-dollar loan from Boender. In addition, according to reports, Gutierrez personally lobbied Mayor Richard M. Daley to urge zoning approval, and Gutierrez received forty-one thousand dollars in campaign contributions from Boender and his associates. Gutierrez was not charged with any crime in this case.

The deals kept coming. Over a five-year period, Gutierrez bought six properties in and near his congressional district from campaign contributors and later sold them for a profit of more than four hundred thousand dollars, according to the *Chicago Tribune*. Several of the developers, including Krzysztov Karbowski, who did real-estate deals with Gutierrez, obtained zoning changes from Alderman Manuel Flores, Gutierrez's former aide and political ally.[92]

Gutierrez also did a real-estate deal with Antoin "Tony" Rezko, a political fixer and major fund-raiser for former Governor Blagojevich. In 2003, before federal investigations of Rezko or Blagojevich were launched, Gutierrez purchased a condo from Rezko for $434,900 and paid less than other investors. After just three years, he sold it for $610,000.[93]

In a very different case, Carol Moseley-Braun, daughter of a Chicago policeman and a medical technician, in 1993 became the first African American woman senator in the nation's history. Before that, she served for ten years in the Illinois House of Representatives and four years as Cook County recorder of deeds. Her path to the Senate included a surprising Democratic primary victory over Alan Dixon, a well-liked two-term incumbent, and a third credible candidate, Al Hofeld.

Less than six weeks before the November general election, NBC TV Channel 5 reported that Moseley-Braun received a check for $28,750 for her seventy-one-year-old mother's share of inherited timber rights. Her mother was in a nursing home and on Medicaid. Moseley-Braun's Republican opponent, Rich Williamson, jumped on the issue and suggested that the Illinois Department of Public Aid should have received the money and that the IRS should investigate.[94] A week before the election, Moseley-Braun reimbursed the state with a $15,239 check to resolve the investigations.[95] She weathered the storm and defeated Williamson.

Shortly after she was elected and before she was sworn in, Moseley-Braun and her campaign manager, Kgosie Matthews, took a month-long vacation to Africa. At the time, Matthews was her fiancé and co-owner of her Hyde Park apartment. Later, for a few months in mid-1994, Matthews was a registered foreign agent and lobbyist for the Federal Republic of Nigeria. In May 1996, Senator Moseley-Braun testified before a Senate subcommittee against legislation that would have imposed economic sanctions against Nigeria's military dictatorship.[96] In August of that year, she and Kgosie Matthews secretly visited Nigerian dictator General Sani Abachi without advising the State Department. It was not known if Matthews was working for the Nigerian government. At the time, Matthews was living in his native South Africa and was not subject to U.S. lobbying disclosure laws.[97]

Campaign records show that for her first senatorial campaign, Moseley-Braun spent more than seven million dollars and ended with a debt of

$447,000.[98] After the election, there were numerous allegations that Moseley-Braun and Matthews had spent $281,000 in campaign funds on vacations, designer outfits, jewelry, and Jeeps. The Chicago journalist Carol Marin reported that three times the IRS tried to bring evidence of Moseley-Braun's campaign-spending infractions to a grand jury, but the Justice Department declined further action due to "insufficient evidence."[99] An audit by the Federal Election Commission in 1997 found no evidence that the senator had personally used campaign funds.[100]

After only one term, Moseley-Braun was defeated for reelection by Republican Peter Fitzgerald. The trips to Nigeria, the campaign-spending investigation, and other negative publicity contributed to her defeat. Although she later ran for president of the United States and mayor of Chicago, she lost both of those elections.

In 2013, the *Chicago Sun-Times* published a Better Government Association investigation of U.S. Representative Bobby Rush. The articles raised serious questions about the Chicago Democrat's numerous unethical and possibly illegal entanglements.

The investigation by reporters Chuck Neubauer and Sandy Bergo revealed that AT&T and its predecessor company gave a one-million-dollar grant to Rebirth of Englewood Community Development, a nonprofit corporation founded by Congressman Rush while he sat on the House Telecommunications, Trade, and Consumer Protection Committee. The grant was for a technology center in the Englewood neighborhood of Chicago that was never built. Other than asserting that the funds paid for programs, Rush has not disclosed what happened to the grant money. Rebirth of Englewood, Beloved Community Christian church, and two other charities founded by Rush received an additional $737,500 from AT&T, Comcast, and ComEd. Rush is the founder and pastor of Beloved church.[101]

According to articles in the *Sun-Times,* AT&T spent another three hundred thousand dollars on special "receptions" in Rush's honor. Since 1992, ComEd/Exelon's employees and political action committee gave Citizens for Rush a total of $113,000. ComEd also gave a surplus substation worth seventy-five thousand dollars and additional thousands of dollars to Beloved church and its social-service arms.[102]

While neither the *Sun-Times* nor the Better Government Association alleged that Rush traded his votes for donations, they pointed out that "Rush often took positions in Congress that were aligned with his corporate benefactors." Both the *Sun-Times* and the BGA called for investigations of Rush and his campaign committee by the House Ethics Committee, Federal Elections Commission, and IRS.[103]

Also in 2013, the *Chicago Tribune* reported that Carolyn Rush, the congressman's wife, was paid three hundred thousand dollars over a five-year period for working on his campaign committee.[104] Other members of the Illinois congressional delegation practiced this form of "family values" by using campaign funds to pay relatives to do political work. According to the *Tribune,* Congressman Gutierrez's campaign paid his wife, Soraida, more than $176,000, and Congressman Michael Quigley's wife, Barbara, was paid seventy-three thousand dollars over four years for office work.[105] Also, Congressman Aaron Schock's campaign employed his sister.

The *Tribune* also reported that many of the state's congressmen used campaign cash as slush funds. In an editorial, the *Tribune* said that Schock, a Republican from Peoria, spent $139,000 on lodging, airfare, and meals through his leadership political action committee and that in 2012 he had to repay $1,136 to his campaign for a stay at a luxury hotel in Greece, which was not a campaign expense.[106]

Scandals Fade

Incumbent congressmen, like many other public officials, usually avoid suffering significant consequences when they exploit conflicts of interest, unfairly reap personal benefits from their public positions, or engage in unethical behavior. Numerous congressmen have survived news reports of a scandal, as well as Ethics Committee slaps on the wrist. When they seek reelection, contributors donate, colleagues provide support, and editorial writers give them a pass. And, unless they were already politically vulnerable or are forced to run in a new district, the voters will often return them to office. One major exception to this rule is criminal indictment. That usually ends a congressman's career.

Based on all these cases of congressional corruption and conflicts of interest, it seems clear that without major, sustained public pressure we cannot count on Congress either to police itself or to pass major legislation to curb corruption.

Between 1991 and 2012, Rita Crundwell stole $53.7 million from the city of Dixon, Illinois, where she was the comptroller/treasurer. She used the money to purchase dozens of vehicles, a house in Florida, and more than four hundred expensive horses for her horse farm. *Photo provided by Sauk Valley Media.*

CHAPTER 11

Ending the Culture of Corruption

CORRUPTION HAS BEEN WOVEN into the fabric of government from Chicago's city hall to Illinois' governor's mansion. It extends from downstate towns to sacred courtrooms. It morphs from simple bribes for building inspectors to multimillion-dollar crooked contracts. It is stitched onto nearly every aspect of our government ever since Illinois was a territory. It blossomed into full bloom after the Chicago Fire, when political-party machines systematized the "Chicago way" of corruption. Machine and machine-like political parties then spread throughout the state. Over the last century, they have institutionalized corruption and created the culture of corruption. This has made Illinois the third most corrupt state in the nation.[1]

The history of Illinois is filled with legendary crooks like Al Capone, who bought a Chicago mayor, "Big Bill" Thompson. Numerous colorful rogue aldermen like "Bathhouse" John Coughlin, "Hinky Dink" Kenna, Johnny "da Pow," and Paddy Bauler "stuck to the small stuff" and weren't convicted. Paddy went on to famously proclaim that "Chicago ain't ready for reform." He could have said the same thing about Illinois as a whole.

Our corruption history is also filled with simply bizarre events like the eight hundred thousand dollars in small bribes hidden in shoeboxes in Secretary of State Paul Powell's hotel room closet. Or Dixon, Illinois, comptroller Rita Crundwell, who financed her rich lifestyle by stealing fifty-three million dollars from her town. Not to be outdone, Governor Rod Blagojevich gave his famous outcry on tape, "I have this thing and it's fucking golden." Selling U.S.

Senate seats is now an unfortunate Illinois tradition dating back to William Lorimer, the "Blond Boss" of Chicago's West Side Republican party, bribing members of the state senate in 1909 to win the post.

Some claim that Illinois' culture of corruption is not that big a deal. Cynics argue that it is only human nature and can't be changed. There are many excuses for our scoundrels and their excesses.

James Merriner concluded in his book, *Grafters and Goo Goos: Corruption and Reform in Chicago, 1833–2003,* that corruption on such a scale "would not have endured through so many whirlwinds of change unless it served some societal function and value."[2] He quotes the political scientist Samuel J. Huntington: "[C]orruption provides immediate, specific, and concrete benefits to groups [like new immigrants] which might otherwise be thoroughly alienated from society."[3]

Whatever functions corruption might have served in the past—to cut through bureaucratic red tape and to make it easier for new immigrant groups to assimilate—it is no longer useful in the twenty-first century. Our odd civic pride in being the most corrupt city and almost the most corrupt state in the country is no longer a cute parochialism. In a time of economic recession and cutbacks, the "corruption tax" and companies unwilling to move to Illinois because of our corrupt reputation are a high price to pay. Jokes about the "Chicago way" have long since gone stale.

But can Illinois corruption be cured?

Cost of Corruption

There are numerous costs of corruption. The most extreme are death and bodily harm. At least nine people, including children, died as a result of selling driver's licenses to unqualified truck drivers. Secretary of State George Ryan's employees took bribes for licenses, and the resulting accidents by unqualified truck drivers killed innocent motorists.

A porch in Chicago's Lincoln Park neighborhood collapsed, killing celebrating college students on graduation day because of faulty building inspections. Thirteen people died and fifty people were injured in that one accident.[4]

Drug sales, shootings, and murders by street gangs in Chicago and suburban neighborhoods have continued because of police payoffs. Additionally, police officers have been convicted of stealing and selling drugs. Corrupt police have engaged in criminal activity rather than capturing the criminals.

Even our judicial system has been subverted, as the FBI investigations Operations Greylord and Gambat have proven. Court cases, including murder cases, were fixed by bribes to judges, court personnel, and attorneys. Unjust verdicts and unfair trials have undermined citizens' faith in our judicial system. There have been some reforms, but the taint on the courts remains, as judges get elected and appointed by political parties.

The financial cost of corruption is at least five hundred million dollars a year—enough to help solve, or at least lessen, the insolvency of state and local governments in Illinois. Andy Shaw, the executive director of the Better Government Association and a former television reporter, asserts that the cost is in billions, not millions, of dollars a year. Either way, as former U.S. Senator Everett Dirksen used to say, "A billion here and a billion there and pretty soon you're talking about real money."[5] Whatever the exact amount, corruption costs more than we can afford.

One simple example of the cost of corruption is our state's borrowing costs. Immediately after Governor Blagojevich's impeachment, the state's bond rating was lowered, and it cost the state twenty-two million dollars more to borrow on the next bond issue than it would have before his impeachment. No one has yet calculated the total cost of corruption caused by a lowered bond rating, when rating agencies became convinced that corrupt government officials weren't likely to be able to solve our state or local budget problems.

There is the additional cost of the inflation of crooked contracts, which may be 5 percent or more of the total cost of government contracts. Moreover, the latest research calculates that the most corrupt states, like Illinois, had greater expenditures over the spending in noncorrupt states of $1,308 per capita per year, or $25,210 per person over the decade from 1997 to 2008.[6] This is because the spending in corrupt states is greater than that needed to meet the needs of the public and spending is further exacerbated by stealing by the public officials involved.

There are many documented direct costs of corruption as well. We have listed many examples, such as paying to lease trucks in Chicago in the Hired Truck scandal that cost the city an extra ten to fifteen million dollars a year for ten years.[7] The scandals of Governor Blagojevich cost at least $22.1 million, and those of Governor Ryan at least another five million. The payments for Commander Jon Burge's forced confessions of black men who didn't do the crimes have cost taxpayers nearly one hundred million dollars. The cost of investigations and trials of corruption by the federal government in Illinois have reached hundreds of millions of dollars to convict nearly two thousand crooks involved in dozens of corrupt schemes over the last forty years.

At a time of severe cutbacks, the loss of the dollars paid for corruption has resulted in closed schools, laid-off teachers, overcrowded jails, fewer dollars to support higher education, and delayed infrastructure improvements to streets, highways, and bridges. We cannot afford these continuing costs of corruption.

In addition, Jim Nowlan's research shows that corruption and the state's reputation for corruption causes companies to avoid locating to Illinois. In his 2011 survey of economic-development professionals who work to attract business to Illinois, "three out of four surveyed said corruption in Illinois had a negative impact on their business recruiting."[8] Some of the written responses included: "Unfortunately and especially in manufacturing and international circles there is an understanding that Illinois corruption that once occurred at an individual level has moved to systemic corruption." And, "that is what Illinois is becoming known for—pay to play."[9]

Yet, the greatest cost of corruption is loss of faith in our government. If citizens believe "the fix is in" and all politicians are crooked, they won't report corruption. They may stop voting or participating in elections. Because citizens distrust the police and refuse to report crimes, Chicago continues to be the murder capital as well as the corruption capital of the country. The latest public-opinion polls show that only 28 percent of Illinoisans trust their state government.[10]

Without trust in the government to spend their taxes wisely, citizens feel free to cheat and to avoid government taxes whenever possible. They conclude that the politicians and their cronies simply steal the money, so why pay any more than they absolutely have to pay to corrupt governments?

Because corrupt political machines continue to rule in Illinois, young people are discouraged from working in government or running for office. They are warned not to work in government because "politics is dirty."

Patterns of Corruption

Corruption does not come in one size or one flavor. Corrupt officials and businesspeople have been infinitely creative in stealing from government. As we have shown in the previous chapters, each unit and branch of government tends to specialize in a dominant form of corruption.

Chicago aldermen tend to be caught taking bribes for zoning and building permits. In earlier years, many of them were convicted for taking modest bribes, as little as five hundred dollars, to arrange for necessary zoning for developers to build what they wanted in order to achieve the greatest profit possible. Admittedly crafty aldermen like Tom Keane were able to use their law firms to take much larger bribes. He sold off alleys and streets for huge projects like the Sears Tower. But smaller bribes from developers and campaign contributions from vulnerable businesses like taverns were the most common patterns of aldermanic corruption.

The less dramatic aldermanic corruption stands in contrast with grander gubernatorial corruption. Governors Blagojevich and Ryan, along with other high-ranking state officials, created pay-to-play schemes that raked in millions of dollars. Blagojevich would have sold the U.S. Senate seat to the highest bidder, but he had a more effective way to collect bribes and campaign contributions. As governor, he appointed cronies and contributors to state boards and commissions that granted crooked contracts in return for payoffs for his buddies and campaign contributions for himself.

Other state officials also profited from corruption schemes. Early Governor Joel Matteson issued nearly a quarter of a million dollars in false script (worth millions in today's dollars). At the turn of the twentieth century, William Lorimer's supporters paid one hundred thousand dollars to bribe state legislators to select him for the U.S. Senate. In the 1950s, State Auditor Orville Hodge outright stole $1.5 million, while Governor William Stratton used nearly one hundred thousand dollars in campaign contributions for personal expenses including a lodge, expensive clothes for his family, and painted portraits of himself and his wife. Corrupt state politicians, unlike most aldermen, often go for the big score.

Outside the council chambers, corruption at Chicago city hall is more systematic and revolves around the famous Chicago political machine. Machine politics depends on and begets patronage, nepotism, favoritism, and crooked contracts at inflated prices. We all pay for this corruption through higher-than-necessary taxes and diminished government services. Since the 1970s, patronage has been partially curtailed by the Shakman, Sorich, and Sanchez court cases. Court decrees, appointed monitors, funding cutbacks, and jail time for those convicted of patronage hiring and firing all combined to reduce the number of Chicago patronage jobs from thirty-five thousand during the Richard J. Daley years to five thousand or fewer during the Richard M. Daley and Rahm Emanuel administrations.

While court-appointed hiring monitors are being removed from Chicago city government and the Cook County Forest Preserve District for coming into compliance in limiting patronage, new patronage court cases are still being filed against other units of government, such as the Illinois Department of Transportation. Patronage may be declining, but it is too soon to declare it dead in Illinois.

However, fewer patronage jobs has meant that the number of "ghost pay-rollers"—political-party and family members who do no government work for their government paychecks—have similarly been reduced. But based upon recent convictions, they haven't yet been eliminated either.

Despite the decrease in patronage and ghost payrollers, corrupt contracts have continued. A classic example of contracts obtained by bribes and clout is the Hired Truck scandal. That single program over ten years of hiring trucks from trucking companies cost the city well more than one hundred million in taxpayer dollars wasted hiring unneeded trucks. This is the way that former State Senator Roger Keats described the program in his fictionalized but ac-curate account in *Chicago Confidential*:

> As [*Chicago Sun-Times*] reporter Mason [Hunter] walks to the "L" train he passes a gas station. In the parking lot are two trucks just idling. Mason wouldn't have thought anything of it except both had signs saying they were part of the City of Chicago Hired Truck Program. Sitting in the trucks were two sleeping drivers with doughnut bags on the dash boards. Two hours later Mason realizes this might be an all day job [covering the unused trucks for the story]. . . . [T]he program was set up to save Chicago money by not having to buy so many trucks that would just sit around. The[se leased] trucks are paid over $50 an hour at a minimum. That might be reasonable if they are actually doing something [but they are not].[11]

Such crooked contracts today include the current "red light" contract to catch speeding motorists on cameras. It was obtained by illegal bribes and continued despite purchasing reforms and more transparency in the Daley and Emanuel administrations.

Specific forms of police corruption occur as well. Since 1960, more than three hundred Chicago police officers have been arrested and convicted for abuse of civilians, torture, violating civil rights, theft, and accepting bribes to overlook crimes.

Police abuse of African Americans, including middle- and upper-class blacks, led to a political revolt in the 1970s, led by Congressman Ralph Met-calfe. Yet, police torture of black suspects in Area 2 under Commander Jon Burge continued for several more decades. These cases of police abuse stem from the police department's inability or unwillingness to effectively train, monitor, and discipline its officers' use of violence to preserve order. This is distinctly different from the other forms of corruption that we record.

There has been a major change in the form of police corruption over time. In the past, in the days of Al Capone, the Outfit would bribe top-level police officers or politicians such as superintendents, deputy superintendents, and commanders, who would then share the bribes with underlings to ignore gambling and other crimes. Today, it is more common for street gangs involved in drug deals to give bribes to the police directly charged with policing their turf. Police also deal in drugs and stolen goods directly with their gang allies. This form of police corruption contributes to the spike in murders and violence, especially on the South and West Sides of Chicago.

Of course, all these forms of corruption are not confined to Chicago government and the Chicago Police Department. Cook County corruption has followed the same basic pattern of patronage, "ghost payrollers," nepotism, favoritism, and crooked contracts since the nineteenth century. Not only do county assessors like Joe Berrios employ many of their relatives on their payrolls, but there have been bribes for lowering property-tax assessments since before the time of P. J. "Parky" Cullerton in the 1950s. And when corruption is beaten back in one county office, it pops up in another, like in Republican Sheriff O'Grady's. In his day, ghost payrolling, patronage, mob protection, and bribes from bookmakers for gambling protection all held sway. In another example, former Cook County Board Presidents George Dunne and John and Todd Stroger engaged in "crony contracting."

Chicago's suburbs are not to be outdone in the corruption game. In our research we found more than 130 suburban officials convicted since the 1970s. They followed five familiar patterns: (1) ties to organized crime, (2) nepotism, (3) suburban police aiding or extorting criminals, (4) kickbacks and bribes, especially for large development projects, and (5) stealing funds from school and special-purpose districts. This corruption occurred across more than sixty suburbs throughout the Chicago metropolitan region—in rich and poor as well as black, white, and Latino areas. Some suburbs like Cicero are best known for mob ties, while others like Rosemont are known for nepotism. Officials in suburbs such as Chicago Heights, Melrose Park, Harvey, and Lyons have aided and extorted criminals. Long-serving mayors, like Nick Blaise of Niles, succumb to bribes and kickbacks. In another example, suburban Bridgeview is drowning in debt from building Toyota Park stadium while Mayor Landek and his friends and family profit.

Of course, with this much corruption at the local level, it reaches loftier government positions as well. The poster child for congressional corruption was Dan Rostenkowski, who was indicted for an elaborate scheme to steal more than $685,000 in taxpayer' money and campaign funds. He also hired ghost payrollers, stole stamp funds from the House post office, used campaign funds to pay for vehicles for personal and family use, and instructed a witness to withhold evidence from a grand jury. Not to be outdone, Congressman Mel Reynolds was convicted of criminal sexual assault, child pornography, and obstruction of justice for having sex with a sixteen-year-old campaign worker. He was later arrested in Zimbabwe for pornography and visa violations. In an earlier period, congressmen like Roland Libonati and Frank Annunzio had mob connections. Henry Hyde had a conflict of interest over the Savings and Loan scandal. Tom Railsback was forced to resign after a sex scandal, and Dan Crane was censored for the same reason and defeated in the next election. Gus Savage, Reynolds's predecessor, lost his reelection for making unwanted sexual advances to a Peace Corps volunteer. The most recent congressional corruption conviction was of Jesse Jackson Jr. for misusing campaign funds.

The contributing factor in all this congressional corruption is too much unchecked power leading to the mindset that powerful congressmen can get away with almost anything. They believe that they can abuse minors and women without getting caught; that conflicts of interest are perfectly all right; and that government and campaign funds are freely available for personal use.

Running like a red thread through all patterns of corruption is machine politics, in which controlled and stolen elections lead to absolute control of the government. This allows jobs, government services, and contracts to be used to benefit family, friends, supporters, and oneself. It encourages connections to regulated businesses, illegal activities, criminals, illicit businesspeople, and drug-selling street gangs.

Future Studies of Corruption

In our book, we provide a case study of corruption in a single state. Yet, this survey of Chicago and Illinois corruption can teach us much because they are what social scientists call extreme cases—among the most corrupt cities and states in the country. Moreover, theories about corruption and reform practices from around the world can guide our thinking about how to cure corruption.

However, given the level of corruption in many parts of the world, future studies will need to organize the analysis of corruption as has been done with the staging of cancer or kidney disease.

Stage 1 might be individual cases of corruption, as suggested by the "rotten apple" theory. The cure for intermittent individual public theft might well require only the prosecution of individual offenders along with new laws or regulations to make particular forms of corruption more difficult to undertake.

Stage 2 might be bureaucratic corruption, which is so widespread that a bribe—or "dash," as they call it in West Africa—is required to obtain permits or official government action. This will be much more difficult to contain than isolated Stage 1 corruption. It will require new managers, personnel, codes of ethics, and rules to strengthen enforcement of anticorruption laws. It will require encouragement to citizens and government officials to report those who accept bribes or perform other illegal acts.

Stage 3 is likely to be corruption that is institutionalized and so entrenched that a culture of corruption pervades the system. In the case of Illinois, our more advanced stage of corruption can be eliminated only if we change the political machines and machine-like political parties that have dominated the state for 150 years.

Stage 4 is likely to occur mostly in totalitarian systems in which the entire government has been taken over and has become both repressive and completely corrupt. Only a change of the entire political system to a more democratic government and society will be sufficient to transform this advanced stage of corruption. In Stage 4 cancer or Stage 4 kidney disease, the patient will usually die. But a corrupt society can be transformed over time into a new social system.

Surely Illinois is at least at Stage 3 in any such scheme that future scholars may devise. Our cure will require serious and sustained reforms over decades. While we await a social-science consensus about political corruption and its cures, we must act based upon existing theory and experience.

Reforms

So what is to be done to curb corruption in Illinois?

Rasma Karklins, in her study of corruption in post-Soviet countries, believes that to fix the problem of so many people participating and accepting a low level of corruption because "everyone else does it" requires three steps:

1. We must recognize that corruption is a serious problem.
2. We must create legal and institutional mechanisms of accountability.
3. We must fine-tune the anticorruption mechanisms so that they become a normal functioning part of a developed democracy.[12]

In Illinois, we seem finally to have recognized that corruption is a serious problem. This particularly followed the Blagojevich scandal and documented proof that Chicago is the most corrupt city and Illinois is one of the most corrupt states.[13] The Illinois Ethics Commission and the Mayor's Ethics Reform Task Force have since laid out blueprints for necessary legal reforms. While more reforms have been adopted at the city than at the state level, some important state ethics and limited campaign-finance-reform laws have been passed. Some members of the former Illinois Ethics Commission are still meeting informally to plan next steps, and other good-government groups are still attempting to implement more proposed reforms that have not yet been adopted.[14]

Karklins's theory suggests that we in Illinois have now had sufficient experience—with these new laws, recent inspectors general, ethics training of government employees, and more government transparency—that we can fine tune our laws and regulations and make them part of an ongoing democratic practice.

Robert Klitgaard in his book, *Controlling Corruption,* argues that corruption occurs when government has a monopoly of power while officials have too much discretion in exercising their authority and too little accountability. He recommends collecting information about corruption, as we have done in this book, in order to determine which forms and patterns are most severe. He further recommends that we establish clear rewards and incentives for ethical behavior, along with clear punishments for corrupt actions. According to Klitgaard, there is a need to punish high-ranking officials so that all government officials realize that their corrupt actions will be penalized. Most of all, in keeping with our overall theory of a culture of corruption, the public's attitudes toward corruption must be altered. It has to be agreed that corruption will no longer be tolerated.[15] Specific laws, regulations, and officials like inspectors general need to focus on preventing the documented forms of corruption in the future, where officials with a monopoly of power have too much discretion.

Following the belief that the fundamental problem is that we have a culture of corruption, Transparency International provides a model "Integrity System." Such a system must be built on a foundation of societal values and public support. If public values strongly support honest government, and public awareness of the level of corruption is high, the necessary governmental and civil-society institutions can be built to provide good government.[16] The issue in Illinois has always been how to develop societal values and public support for good government.

Attempts to Reform Corruption in Illinois

In Illinois, the most common effort to end corruption has been to prosecute and convict individuals practicing it. It has been "Job One" for the U.S. Attorneys, and occasionally an important priority for the state's attorneys, to battle corruption. This approach stems from the prevailing theory that corruption is a matter of the "rotten apple in the barrel." Getting rid of a few bad guys and gals will set an example. Prosecutors believe that if they convict some individuals and make them serve significant prison sentences, other potential offenders will decide that corruption is too dangerous. After 1,913 federal convictions in Illinois from 1976–2012, those theories seem inadequate. Prosecuting corruption is a necessary, but not sufficient, step to cure corruption.

Nonetheless, some corruption scandals have brought legislative changes; the media coverage and public outcry have forced them. After buying the U.S. Senate seat in 1909, the resulting Lorimer scandal helped to pass a constitutional amendment to require the direct election of senators. Unfortunately, this did not prevent the planned sale of the U.S. Senate seat by Governor Blagojevich a century later.

Scandals in federal-government hiring, especially under presidents like Andrew Jackson, led to the Civil Service Reform Act of 1883 and the Hatch Act of 1939. They helped end patronage in the federal government and to prevent federal employees from engaging in partisan activities. However, civil service has been slower to take root in Illinois.

In general, all major legislation curbing corruption came much later to Illinois than to the rest of the country. The first Chicago Ethics Ordinance wasn't passed until 1987, during the final days of the Harold Washington administration and a hundred years after the Civil Service Reform Act. And that ordinance has had to be amended a number of times to close loopholes revealed by various ethics scandals and corruption convictions.

After Rahm Emanuel was elected mayor in 2011, he appointed an Ethics Reform Task Force headed by distinguished Chicagoans, including the late comptroller Dawn Clark Netsch. But the mayor's task force fell short of getting aldermen and their staff members covered under the Chicago inspector general. And despite the ethics ordinance and its many amendments, Chicago corruption persists.

Serious campaign-finance-reform legislation wasn't passed at the state level until after Governor Blagojevich's impeachment and eventual conviction. Until then, Illinois was the "Wild West" of campaign-finance regulations, with almost no limits on who could contribute and how much they could give. After Governor Pat Quinn replaced Blagojevich in 2009, he created the Illinois Ethics Commission, which proposed fundamental reforms to state laws, but only a few of those were adopted. A new law that limits individual and group contributions to five thousand dollars per campaign and requires more stringent contribution disclosures did pass. However, Illinois has not adopted public funding of campaigns, like New York City or states like Maine and Arizona. And the *Citizens United* decision by the Supreme Court allows Super PACS (501c4 and 501c6 organizations under the national tax code) to spend unlimited amounts on political ads. And they don't have to disclose their donors, as long as their activities are not coordinated with candidates' campaigns. So there have been only partial gains in curbing corrupting campaign contributions.

In general, legislative reforms in Illinois have tried to narrow the opportunities for graft and corruption by governmental officials and to increase the penalties for offenses. As Cynthia Canary and Kent Redfield have written, "[L]aws do matter and new laws can make a difference. Laws define what is legal and illegal. They set the tone for what society considers acceptable behavior and allow us to draw a line in the sand." Canary and Redfield maintain that additional key "changes in the laws that govern Illinois politics would significantly reduce both actual corruption and the appearance of corruption."[17] The problem is to generate sufficient public support and the necessary legislative votes to pass new restrictions and to provide new resources, such as public funding of elections.

Pat Collins, the head of the Illinois Ethics Commission, in his book *Challenging the Culture of Corruption,* concludes that more needs to be done.[18] Since only a few of his commission's proposals had become law, he proposes an additional four-point program:

1. True campaign reform.
2. Creating a fair remap of legislative districts.
3. Allowing state's attorneys to authorize wiretaps.
4. Increasing citizen participation by:
   a. Moving the February primary to warmer-weather months.
   b. Mail-in voting.
   c. Permit bills with support to get to the floor of the legislature.
   d. Better access to government information through the Freedom of Information Act and Internet technology.

The logic of the Illinois campaign finance reforms adopted in 2009 was that by requiring better information on campaign donors and by restricting contributions to five thousand dollars per candidate, voters would know which interest groups and individuals were funding candidates. More critically, the contribution limit would keep any one individual or group from "buying the election."[19]

A solution to the campaign-funding problem would be to provide public funding for campaigns. States like Maine and Arizona and cities like New York already do so. The ability of Super PACs to spend unlimited amounts and not disclose their donors would remain, but opposing candidates would have sufficient funds (provided by the taxpayer) to get their message to the voters. The 2012 elections proved, especially in congressional campaigns, that candidates with the most money don't always win, as long as their opponents have sufficient funds to get their messages out. Without public funding, the money necessary for campaigns is difficult to raise. Contested Illinois legislative races were estimated to cost from one to two million dollars in 2014, while the gubernatorial race is likely to cost major candidates more than twenty million dollars. No wonder candidates for higher office often succumb to knowingly taking corrupt campaign contributions.

Pat Collins's other reform proposals have yet to be adopted. The legislative remap after the 2010 census was entirely partisan. This allowed the Democratic party to gain overwhelming control of both houses of the state legislature, the governorship, and additional congressional seats. In 2013, the League of Women Voters and other plaintiffs filed a lawsuit asserting that the Chicago ward remap was likewise gerrymandered. Yet the effort to get a state constitutional amendment on the ballot and passed has thus far failed.

Collins's third suggestion is that the attorney general and the county state's attorneys in Illinois be given the power to wiretap. Currently, 90 percent or more of the prosecution of political corruption is done by U.S. Attorneys. Even with two anticorruption teams, the U.S. Attorney in the Northern District in Illinois can prosecute only the most salient offenses. While Republican state's attorneys in Democratically controlled Cook County have been able to try some corruption cases successfully, this usually happens only when there is a political advantage to do so. The attorney general and county state's attorneys argue that they don't have wiretap authority or the U.S. Attorney's investigative resources of the FBI and IRS. Easier ability for state and county prosecutors to use wiretaps could threaten the civil liberties of some innocent citizens. But

Collins argues that it is more important to be able to prosecute those who are currently getting away with corruption.

The goal of Collins's final proposals is to increase citizen participation as the very best antidote to corruption. He proposes moving the primary elections to warmer months; moving legislation more easily to the floor of the legislature for a vote; creating a greater opportunity for citizens to pressure their legislators; and providing citizens more information through the Freedom of Information Act and the Internet. In short, if citizens are better watchdogs of their government, more active in elections, and better able to influence legislative decision making, there will be fewer opportunities for insiders in government to manipulate the outcomes, accept bribes, and further the culture of corruption.

One specific recommendation from experts on the proposal to provide citizens more information is that "[g]overnment should be encouraged to release public information online in a structured, open, and searchable manner. To the extent that government does not modernize, however, we should hope that private third parties build unofficial databases and make these available in a useful form to the public."[20] More government data is available today, especially through the Internet, than ever before, but it is often not in a form to allow citizens and civic organizations to hold governmental officials accountable. University scholars, civic organizations, and watchdog agencies need to translate this flood of data into a more useful form.

The New Agenda for Political Reform

Cynthia Canary and Kent Redfield pick up on Collins's last point. They maintain that

[p]art of the new agenda for political reform is the old agenda for political reform. Political reform is still about encouraging citizen participation through passing laws facilitating more voter registration, more voting, and greater [ballot] access for candidates and third party candidates and fighting every effort to restrict them. Political reform is still about enhancing the quality of citizen participation by providing access to the processes, decisions and basic policy information of government through Freedom of Information, open meetings, and other [measures]. It is still about . . . requiring disclosure of the economic interests of public officials, and the activities and interests of lobbyists.[21]

Yet, changing the culture of corruption in Illinois requires more than this. Public officials must no longer expect to be bribed, and citizens must no longer expect to bribe them to get legitimate government services or a government job or contract. There must be limits on the arbitrary authority of public officials and more accountability for their actions.

This transformation requires that we voters elect Illinois officials who pledge to adopt reforms and carry out their promises once in office. These elected officials will need to fire subordinates who engage in corrupt or unethical practices. They must eliminate the remnants of patronage hiring and ghost payrolling. And they must end favoritism in the delivery of government services and in granting government contracts. In short, they must remove the underpinning of machine politics that has produced and institutionalized most of Illinois' corruption.

Second, this change must happen through education. The role and importance of government and law must be taught. Civic education and civic engagement must be facilitated and encouraged in the ways described in the new books by the American Political Science Association and the McCormick Foundation.[22] Ethics, the cost of corruption, and its cure should also be taught explicitly in our schools. The Illinois Task Force on Civic Education in May 2014 recommended that civics should again be a required course in Illinois schools; that social-studies standards be revised to provide civic skills, including news literacy; that students should be required to do service-learning projects in eighth and twelfth grades; that teachers of civics should be licensed and be provided continuing professional development programs; and that efforts should be made in schools to encourage voter registration and voting.[23]

After a generation, as these school children who benefit from these new civic-education programs become adults, they will form a new electorate that, hopefully, will be motivated to take the necessary steps to transform the culture of corruption.

Third, additional laws are necessary to limit the discretion of public officials and to require their accountability. Government documents and financial records must be available in user-friendly databases to allow citizens and watchdog agencies to better hold government officials accountable for their actions.

Fourth, inspectors general and other government watchdogs must be given sufficient power, resources, and authority to ferret out government waste and corruption. Legislators, legislative committees, auditors, inspectors general, news reporters, and civic organizations serve as watchdogs over government waste, abuse, and corruption by investigating and exposing corruption and mobilizing public opinion.[24]

Two examples of changes that would be beneficial are: (1) To increase his effectiveness, the Chicago inspector general must be given easier access to city documents and authority over aldermen and their staff; (2) In the suburbs, a new suburban inspector general is needed not only to investigate hundreds of suburban governments but also to provide a centralized agency to which citizens can meaningfully report corruption. While having the Cook County sheriff play this role for the few suburbs that will allow him to do so is a good first step, a permanent suburban inspector general's office needs to be created by the state legislature.

Fifth, it is time to adopt public financing of Illinois elections. It is also time to adopt term limits for our public officials, from mayors to state legislators to the governor. Finally, a fair remapping of congressional, state legislative, and aldermanic districts under a more equitable remapping process can create legislative bodies more responsive to voters and more willing to limit machine politics and political corruption.

Most of all, we the people must act in large and small ways to reverse the culture of corruption that has been choking Illinois for over a century. The expectations of elected officials and citizens that bribes and crony contracts are normal must be seen as simply unacceptable. The single biggest step is to finally achieve Harold Washington's promise that patronage and machine politics are "dead, dead, dead." For as long as machine politics survives in Illinois, corruption will flourish.

When Dick Simpson was in the city council, he heard Alderman "Fast Eddie" Vrdolyak say in a speech on the floor of the council, "Anyone who would fight the machine had better bring lunch." What Vrdolyak meant is that ending machine politics is a task that requires hard work, day after day, year after year. It is not over with one speech, one election, one report, or one new law. Usually it's not wise to heed advice from Fast Eddie, especially now after his felony conviction, but what he said that day rings true.

Acknowledgments

WE WOULD LIKE PARTICULARLY TO acknowledge the faculty and graduate and undergraduate students at the University of Illinois at Chicago who have helped us research and publish reports on Illinois corruption over the last seven years. The faculty members John Hagadorn and Jim Nowlan were joined by a number of talented graduate students in directing different aspects of our research. The graduate students are: Andris Zimelis, Tom Kelly, Cori Smith, David Sterrett, Douglas Cantor, Esly Sarmineto, and Bart Kmiecik.

Melissa Mouritsen worked with us as a research assistant on the project for four years. She was especially critical in supervising the research for many sections of the book, in helping with the tables and figures, and in checking the endnotes for accuracy.

The undergraduates who assisted in the research included: Kirsten Byers, Chris Olson, David Mulberger, Nirav Sanghani, Kenneth Chow, Alexandra Kathryn Curatolo, Emily Gillot, Marrell Stewart, Erica Adams, Alex Jakubo-wich, Mark Lund, Inna Rubin, Salwa Shameem, Paris Tsongaris, Emily Marr, Mike Ramirez, Nick Yodelis, Ivana Savic, Justin Escamilla, Magdalena Waluszko, Dalibor Jurisic, and Tricia Chebat.

Such a mammoth undertaking, identifying more than seven hundred convicted corrupt individuals and analyzing dozens of different corruption schemes at all levels of government, could not have been accomplished without the dedication of all these researchers.

We also wish to acknowledge the independent political researcher Don Wiener for his advice and encouragement, and the election attorney Richard

Means for his input. We are grateful for the more than four decades of research and reports by the Better Government Association and for assistance provided over the years by the staff of the Municipal Reference Library at Chicago's Harold Washington Library Center.

Of course, our book depends as well upon scores of researchers, journalists, and book authors who uncovered corruption and recommended reforms. We have tried to acknowledge them in the endnotes.

Production of this book also required the dedicated efforts of many others. We are especially grateful to Willis G. Regier, director of the University of Illinois Press for championing the publishing of our book in the press' new Chicago and Illinois Series. We are grateful to Matthew Mitchell as well, who in copyediting caught many of our errors. We, of course, are responsible for any remaining flaws.

Thomas J. Gradel is indebted to his wife, Corinne D. Peterson, for her understanding and encouragement, and to his late father, Joseph I. Gradel, a librarian at the *Philadelphia Inquirer,* who taught him the great value of archived news reports. Dick Simpson is indebted to Dorothy Storck, who assisted in revising several chapters and in teaching the importance of shorter sentences, stronger verbs, and fewer words.

Highlights in Illinois' History of Corruption, 1833 to 2014

1833

Vote fraud accompanied the incorporation of Chicago. In the initial attempt to elect trustees, two of the thirteen residents who cast votes were ineligible. Later that year, twenty-nine votes were cast to elect trustees, but there were fewer than twenty-nine citizens living in Chicago at the time.

1869

A wooden courthouse that also housed city hall and Cook County offices was painted with white-wash. Aldermen and commissioners were bribed.

1890s

The Gray Wolves was the name given to a group of Chicago aldermen who excelled at leveraging city-council decisions for their own personal profit. They were led by Aldermen "Bathhouse" John Coughlin, Michael "Hinky Dink" Kenna, and Johnny Powers. They made deals for the city's granting of franchises for public services such as electricity, telephones, and mass transit.

1903

The Iroquois Theatre Fire in Chicago kills six hundred people. City inspectors were bribed to approve the new building, even though it lacked a sprinkler system, basic firefighting equipment, and exit signs.

1856

Governor Joel Aldrich Matteson of Will County leaves office owing more than $250,000 he has amassed by selling false script to the state. He is indicted and then not indicted and not tried. He reimburses the state for more than half the amount but claims he didn't steal it.

1871

The Great Chicago Fire destroys all of downtown and much of the North Side. Rapid rebuilding creates new opportunities for politicians and businesses—for those in power and for those who know the angles.

1896–1908

Each year, Aldermen "Bathhouse" John Coughlin and Michael "Hinky Dink" Kenna hold the notorious First Ward Ball, a "lollapalooza" teeming with society thrill-seekers, politicians, prostitutes, police brass, and gamblers. For the final party, more than twenty thousand revelers buy tickets to drink, dance, and misbehave.

1915

William Hale "Big Bill" Thompson is elected mayor of Chicago. He serves for eight years before his reelection bid is torpedoed when his campaign

1920

Prohibition enforcement begins. The Eighteenth Amendment of the U.S. Constitution, prohibiting the manufacturing, transportation, and sale of beer and liquor, takes effect.

1933

Prohibition is repealed. Congress passes the Twenty-first Amendment, which repeals the Eighteenth Amendment that banned the selling and drinking of alcohol.

1955

Richard J. Daley is elected Chicago's mayor two years after becoming chairman of the Cook County Democratic party.

1960–61

Summerdale police scandal: eight Chicago cops are convicted of conspiring with a burglar who broke into businesses in Chicago's Edgewater neighborhood. While on duty, the cops provided cover for the burglar and received stolen goods.

1970

Illinois Secretary of State Paul Powell dies with eight hundred thousand dollars in cash hidden in shoeboxes in his hotel room. Powell, whose annual salary never topped thirty thousand dollars, also had three million dollars in banks and sixty-one thousand shares of racetrack stock.

1972–74

Chicago Avenue Police District Commander Clarence Braasch and eighteen police officers are convicted for shaking down taverns and nightclubs on Rush St., in Old Town, and on Michigan Ave. In the Austin District, Commander Mark Thanasouras and fifteen officers are also convicted for tavern shakedowns. After getting out of prison, Thanasouras is gunned down by a mob hitman.

manager is accused of shaking down school-supply vendors for bribes.

1923

The gangster Al Capone moves his headquarters to Cicero, Illinois, to avoid Mayor William Dever's crackdown on brothels, bootlegging, and speakeasies.

1927

"Big Bill" Thompson, out of office for four years, is again elected mayor. Al Capone, who raised money for Thompson and provided election-day workers, returns to Chicago and sets up headquarters at the Metropole Hotel. Thompson promises to let people drink their beer, and he appoints Capone's agent to be the city sealer.

1956

Illinois Auditor Orville Hodge, from downstate Granite City, pleads guilty to stealing $1.5 million from the State of Illinois.

1968

Out-of-control Chicago police beat protestors in Grant Park while the Democratic National Convention meets across Michigan Ave. in the Hilton Hotel.

1969

Police officers assigned to Cook County State's Attorney Edward Hanrahan raid the West Side apartment of the Black Panther leaders Fred Hampton and Mark Clark, who are shot dead. A grand jury investigates, but no charges are brought against the police.

1972

James R. Thompson is named U.S. Attorney for the Northern District of Illinois by President Richard Nixon. Thompson serves until July 1975.

1972

Shakman consent decree: Democratic and Republican party leaders agree to a federal court order banning the firing or punishment of government employees for not participating in political activities.

1973

Governor Otto Kerner is convicted, after leaving office, of fraud and other crimes for obtaining bargain racetrack stock from an owner who benefited from Kerner-administration decisions.

1974

Earl Bush, Mayor Daley's press secretary, is found guilty of mail fraud after hiding his ownership of an advertising firm that received a $202,000 city contract for display advertising at O'Hare airport.

1974

Cook County Circuit Court Clerk Matthew Danaher is found dead in his room at the Ambassador West Hotel. Danaher, a former key aide to Mayor Richard J. Daley and former Eleventh Ward alderman, was scheduled to go on trial in a month for accepting four hundred thousand dollars in bribes from South Side builders.

1977

State Representative Robert McPartlin is convicted for accepting a bribe in the Metropolitan Sanitary District sludge-hauling scandal.

1979

Federal Judge Nicholas Bua rules that patronage hiring in Cook County is unconstitutional. His ruling reinforces the legal basis of the Shakman decree.

1980

Illinois Attorney General William Scott is found guilty of income-tax fraud for underreporting his income. Evidence suggests that Scott converted campaign donations for personal use.

1984–89

Operation Incubator uncovers bribery to obtain a parking-fine-collection contract and other crimes. In a Lake Point Tower apartment, the FBI records a mole dispensing eighty-two thousand dollars in bribes. Four Chicago aldermen, a friend of Mayor Washington's, the Circuit Court clerk, and ten others are convicted.

1973

Fred Hubbard, alderman of Chicago's Second Ward, is convicted of embezzling ninety-eight thousand dollars from a job-training program he ran.

1974

Chicago Alderman Tom Keane (Thirty-first Ward) is found guilty of mail fraud for using insider knowledge to buy property cheaply and sell it to government agencies for huge profits.

1976

Richard J. Daley dies. Michael A. Bilandic is named acting mayor by the Chicago city council. A few months later, he is elected mayor by the voters.

1977–78

The *Chicago Sun-Times* and the BGA open a typical neighborhood bar, the Mirage tavern. Soon it attracts a parade of health, fire, building, and electrical inspectors seeking bribes, who are photographed and videotaped. Hundreds of indictments follow, and initially eighteen inspectors are convicted.

1980–91

Operation Greylord: federal investigators use moles, hidden microphones, and cooperating witnesses to win conviction of fifteen Cook County judges and sixty-nine other court denizens, including lawyers, clerks, police officers, and sheriff's deputies.

1983

Harold Washington is elected mayor of Chicago.

1985

A federal court in Chicago orders an end to the Chicago Police Department's Red Squad and its surveillance of radicals, minority organizations, and political opponents of the Daley administration. The city settles lawsuits and pays $335,000 to

1986–97

Operation Gambat: a mob lawyer turned FBI mole exposes the fixing of court cases by the mob and First Ward Democratic pols. Two judges, a state senator, an alderman, the mob's political liaison, and a hitman are convicted.

1987

Governor Dan Walker is convicted of bank fraud, perjury, and misallocation of funds at a Savings and Loan bank he owned and operated after he left office.

1989

A hidden FBI camera is discovered by a busboy at the Counselor's Row restaurant across the street from Chicago's city hall. The camera and a bugged telephone spied on deals between aldermen, city officials, police, and mob-connected politicians.

1992–2001

Operation Silver Shovel starts when Southwest Side residents complain to federal investigators about a huge high pile of construction debris. Then an FBI mole records bribes to aldermen and others. Six aldermen and twelve others are convicted.

1993–2006

Operation Safe Roads, or Licenses for Bribes, starts when a whistleblower reports that examiners have been issuing licenses for bribes and funneling money to Secretary of State George Ryan's campaign fund. The probe is accelerated after a truck accident kills six children and the driver had allegedly obtained his license illegally. A total of seventy-five persons are convicted, mostly workers at state driver's-licensing facilities but including the governor's chief of staff and the Secretary of State inspector general. Convictions lead to an investigation of Governor Ryan's income, campaign fund, and spending.

2001

Chicago Chief of Detectives William Hanhardt pleads guilty to operating a nationwide jewelry-theft ring, often using information from Chicago Police Department databases.

individuals and groups who were spied on by the police.

1987–89

Operation Phocus: a sweeping federal crackdown on bribery of Chicago's licensing officials and code enforcers, resulting in convictions of fifty-six inspectors, the director of the Consumer Services Department, the Park District's marine director, an alderman, a state senator, and a judge.

1990

In the case of *Cynthia Rutan et al. v. the Republican Party of Illinois,* the U.S. Supreme Court reaffirms that patronage hiring and firing is unconstitutional throughout Illinois.

1993–99

Operation Haunted Hall: Cook County Treasurer Edward Rosewell, four Chicago aldermen, a state senator, and Undersheriff James Dvorak are among thirty-five officials and employees convicted for ghost payrolling at county and city offices.

1994

U.S. Representative Dan Rostenkowski, chairman of the powerful House Ways and Means Committee, is indicted for converting government stamps for cash, ghost payrolling, and using campaign funds for personal benefit. In 1996, Rosty pleads guilty to felony mail fraud. He also admits using government funds to provide gifts to friends and to using federal employees to perform personal services.

2001

Peter J. Fitzgerald is appointed U.S. Attorney for the Northern District of Illinois by President George W. Bush.

2003–9

Operation Board Games: shortly after Governor Blagojevich was elected, he, fund-raisers Chris Kelly and Tony Rezko, and several close advisors planned to use the governor's decisions and appointing authority to raise campaign funds and to enrich themselves. Rezko, Kelly, Stuart Levine, William Cellini, Edward Vrdolyak, and numerous others are convicted.

2004–9

The Hired Truck Scandal: the *Chicago Sun-Times'* "Clout on Wheels" series exposes a Chicago program for hiring trucks and paying for them even when they aren't needed, which costs taxpayers ten to fifteen million dollars per year. Many of the truck owners are related to city workers and others have mob connections. More than forty-five persons are convicted, including city clerk James Laski. Following the series, one hundred trucking companies are dropped from the program.

2006

Governor George Ryan is found guilty of racketeering, conspiracy, mail fraud, perjury, obstructing the IRS, and filing false tax returns.

2007–9

Operation Family Secrets: four members of the Chicago Outfit are found guilty of racketeering conspiracy and are held accountable for ten murders. A Chicago cop is convicted for passing information to an imprisoned mob killer. A U.S. marshal is found guilty of leaking secrets about an informant to a mob associate.

2008

Governor Blagojevich appoints former Illinois Attorney Roland Burris to fill the vacant Senate seat until the next election.

2009

Recently appointed U.S. Senator Roland Burris is admonished by the Senate after its Ethics Panel claims that he provided incorrect, misleading, and incomplete information about his contacts with Governor Blagojevich and his team before Burris was appointed to fill the vacant U.S. Senate seat.

2006

Robert Sorich, Mayor Richard M. Daley's patronage chief, is found guilty of fraud for rigging and concealing City of Chicago patronage that had been outlawed by earlier Shakman court rulings. Several other city employees are also convicted. Sorich maintained a Clout List of more than five thousand names of city and county job holders and their political sponsors, which is presented as evidence at the trial.

2006–10

Operation Crooked Code: an investigation by the city inspector general, U.S. postal inspectors, and the FBI results in the conviction of twenty-one persons, including fifteen building and zoning inspectors, mostly for paying or accepting bribes for permits.

2007

Two days after being questioned by the FBI, Orlando Jones, John Stroger's godson and former chief of staff, is found dead on a Michigan beach with a gunshot wound to his head. Police determine that it was a suicide.

2008

Governor Rod Blagojevich is arrested by the FBI. The feds say he allegedly conspired to leverage his sole authority to appoint a U.S. senator and that he threatened to withhold substantial state assistance from the *Chicago Tribune.*

2009

Chris Kelly, a confidant and key fund-raiser for Governor Blagojevich, commits suicide after pleading guilty to mail fraud as part of a scheme to rig bids for roofing work at O'Hare Airport. He was scheduled to go to prison in a few days.

2009

Governor Blagojevich becomes the first governor in Illinois history to be impeached, convicted, and removed from office.

2010

Second District Commander Jon Burge is found guilty of obstructing justice and perjury for lying about the torture when he was Commander of the Second District on the city's far South Side. Burge and his officers are implicated in more than one hundred cases of forcing confessions by torturing African American suspects. By the end of 2013, the city had paid out ninety-six million dollars to settle Burge-related wrongful-conviction cases.

2012

U.S. Representative Jesse Jackson Jr. resigns his congressional seat while under investigation for possibly sending an emissary to bribe Governor Blagojevich to appoint him to President Barack Obama's vacated Senate seat.

2013

Congressman Jackson and his wife, Alderman Sandi Jackson, plead guilty to misusing $750,000 in campaign funds to renovate their home and to buy fur coats, luxury items, and celebrity memorabilia.

2013

Cook County Commissioner William Beavers, a former Chicago alderman, is found guilty of failing to pay taxes on campaign funds he spent on gambling and other personal purposes.

2013

Cook County Commissioner Joseph Mario Moreno pleads guilty to extortion conspiracy for forcing a minority contractor to lend him one hundred thousand dollars. He also admits to agreeing to a kickback in a Stroger Hospital bandage-contract deal.

2011

Former Governor Rod Blagojevich is found guilty on seventeen of twenty counts, including fraud, extortion, bribery, and conspiring to sell Barack Obama's Senate seat.

2012

Rita Crundwell pleads guilty to embezzling fifty-three million dollars from the city of Dixon, Illinois, where she was treasurer. She used the money to purchase a home, dozens of vehicles, and more than four hundred expensive horses.

2013

Former Alderman Ambrosio Medrano pleads guilty to wire fraud for his role in a scheme with Commissioner Moreno to take bribes and kickbacks for arranging the sale of bandages to public hospitals. Medrano is the first Illinois politician to be convicted for three separate and unrelated crimes.

2013

Zachary Fardon is appointed U.S. Attorney for the Northern District of Illinois by President Barack Obama.

APPENDIX II

Illinois Governors, 1961–2014

Name	Party	Years Served	Record
Otto Kerner	D	1/9/1961–1/11/1968	Before running for governor, Otto Kerner was the U.S. Attorney for the Northern District of Illinois and then a Cook County Judge. As governor, he won passage of a sales-tax increase and a new tax on hotel and motel rooms. With the legislature he created the Department of Public Aid. His executive order prohibited discrimination in the sale and rental of real estate. He chaired the National Advisory Commission on Civil Disorders. In 1968, Kerner resigned as governor to become a judge on the U.S. Circuit Court of Appeals. Scandal: In 1973, he was convicted of conspiracy, income-tax evasion, and mail fraud for receiving and concealing ownership in racetrack stock for providing favorable treatment to a racetrack owner.
Samuel H. Shapiro	D	5/21/1968–1/13/1969	As governor, Shapiro mobilized the Illinois National Guard to assist the Chicago police during the 1968 Democratic Convention in Chicago. Like other Illinois governors, he had to deal with fiscal problems. He was successful in getting the legislature to borrow sixty million dollars from the gasoline-tax fund to keep the state government operating.

Name	Party	Years Served	Record
Richard B. Ogilvie	R	1/13/1969–1/8/1973	Served as Cook County sheriff and then president of the Cook County Board before becoming governor. He was the only Illinois governor to have a lieutenant governor of a different party. Ogilvie modernized state government, supported the adoption of the new (1970) state constitution, and pushed for and signed into law the state's first income tax. He created the Illinois Department of Transportation and appointed William Cellini as director.
Daniel Walker	D	1/8/1974–1/10/1977	Defeated the Daley-machine candidate for governor in the Democratic primary, and after the general election he often backed anti-Daley candidates. He supported and signed legislation requiring disclosure of campaign contributions. By executive order Walker prohibited corrupt practices by state workers and allowed state employees to form unions and to bargain collectively for wages and working conditions. Scandal: After leaving office, Walker was convicted of federal bank fraud in 1987.
James R. Thompson	R	1/10/1977–1/14/1991	Thompson was the U.S. Attorney for the Northern District of Illinois before becoming governor. He and his prosecutors convicted Otto Kerner, Alderman Tom Keane, Cook County Clerk Matt Danaher, and Republican County Commissioner Floyd Fulle. Thompson, who held the post for fourteen years, was the longest serving Illinois governor ever. He supported and achieved significant tax increases then made budget cuts. He backed legislation giving government workers and teachers collective-bargaining rights. He worked to pass a public subsidy for the new White Sox ballpark. He tried but failed to bring the 1993 World's Fair to Chicago's lakefront.
Jim Edgar	R	1/14/1991–1/11/1999	Governor Edgar presided over the last Illinois General Assembly to have Republican majorities in both houses. He cut

Name	Party	Years Served	Record
			spending, reduced a backlog in state payments, shrunk the size of government, and created a surplus. With the legislature, Edgar gave Richard M. Daley authority over the Chicago Public Schools and improved the level of funding for schools while raising taxes on cigarettes, telephones, and riverboats.
George H. Ryan	R	1/11/1999–1/13/2003	Issued moratorium on executions and commuted 160 death sentences to life sentences. He increased funding for education and infrastructure and created a state health plan for poor kids. He was the first sitting U.S. governor to meet with Fidel Castro. Scandal: There were seventy-six convictions in connection with the Licenses for Bribes investigation, which started when he was Secretary of State. Ryan, his chief of staff, and his inspector general were all convicted.
Rod R. Blagojevich	D	1/13/2003–1/29/2009	Created All Kids, state-subsidized health care for all Illinois children. Withheld state business from Bank of America to pressure it to make loans to small businesses. He appointed Roland Burris to the U.S. Senate. Scandal: Impeached and removed from office January 29, 2009. Convicted and sentenced to fourteen years in prison for corruption.
Patrick J. Quinn	D	1/29/2009-present	Succeeded Rod R. Blagojevich, then elected to a full term on November 2, 2010. Presides over the worst fiscal crisis in state history. Attempted to withhold pay from members of the General Assembly to force them to solve pension crisis. Created Ethics Reform Commission but implemented only a few of its findings.

Sources: *Chicago Tribune*; *Chicago Sun-Times*; *Illinois Blue Book 2001–2002*, published by the Secretary of State of Illinois; and *Illinois Blue Book 2012–2013* (http://www.cyberdriveillinois.com/publications/illinois_bluebook/home.html)

APPENDIX III

Chicago Mayors, 1955–2014

Name	Years Served	Record
Richard J. Daley	4/21/1955–12/20/1976	Presided over building of Sears Tower, McCormick Place, O'Hare Airport, University of Illinois at Chicago campus. Saw the decline of the manufacturing economy and transition to service economy. Also was the chairman of the Cook County Democratic party. Said to be the last of the big-city bosses. Died of a heart attack in office.
Michael Bilandic	1/20/1976–4/16/1979	Chosen by city council after the death of Mayor Richard J. Daley to serve as acting mayor; won by popular election in 1977. Lost 1979 election due to slow response to major snowstorm.
Jane Byrne	4/16/1979–4/29/1983	First female mayor of Chicago. Began as a reformer but then reached an accommodation with the machine's ward bosses.
Harold Washington	4/29/1983–11/25/1987	First African American mayor of Chicago. Presided over "Council Wars" but gained a city-council majority near the end of his first term. Signed Shakman decree. Declared the Chicago machine dead. Increased spending in the neighborhoods. Hired many African Americans and com-

Name	Years Served	Record
		munity activists in key positions. Died of a heart attack in office.
David Orr	11/25/1987–12/2/1987	Served as mayor for a week after the sudden death of Harold Washington until a new mayor was selected.
Eugene Sawyer	12/2/1987–4/24/1989	Chosen by city council to fulfill Harold Washington's term.
Richard M. Daley	4/24/1989–5/16/2011	Longest-serving mayor (twenty-two years), took over Chicago Public Schools, demolished Meigs Field, built Millennium Park, privatized parking garages and meters. Presided over transition to global economy. Failed to bring the 2016 Olympics to Chicago.
Rahm Emanuel	5/16/2011–present	First Jewish mayor. Strongly encouraged charter schools; fought the teachers union, resulting in a strike. Closed fifty public neighborhood schools. Established the Infrastructure Trust and a bike-sharing program.

APPENDIX IV

U.S. Attorneys for the Northern District of Illinois, 1964–2014

Time in Office	U.S. Attorney	President		U.S. Senators from Illinois	
March 1964 to March 1968	Edward V. Hanrahan	Lyndon B. Johnson	(D)	Paul Douglas Everett Dirksen	(D) (R)
March 1968 to July 1970	Thomas A. Foran	Lyndon B. Johnson	(D)	Everett Dirksen Charles Percy	(R) (R)
July 1970 to Nov. 1971	William J. Bauer	Richard M. Nixon	(R)	Ralph Smith Charles Percy	(R) (R)
Nov. 1971 to June 1975	James R. Thompson	Richard M. Nixon	(R)	Charles Percy Adlai Stevenson III	(R) (D)
June 1975 to July 1977	Samuel K. Skinner	Gerald Ford	(R)	Charles Percy Adlai Stevenson III	(R) (D)
July 1977 to May 1981	Thomas P. Sullivan	James E. Carter	(D)	Adlai Stevenson III Charles Percy	(D) (R)
April 1981 to Feb. 1985	Dan K. Webb	Ronald Reagan	(R)	Charles Percy Alan Dixon	(R) (D)
Feb. 1985 to Dec. 1989	Anton Valukas*	Ronald Reagan	(R)	Alan Dixon Paul Simon	(D) (D)
Aug. 1990 to Feb. 1993	Fred Foreman	George H. W. Bush	(R)	Alan Dixon Paul Simon	(D) (D)
Nov. 1993 to Aug. 1997	James Burns	William Clinton	(D)	Paul Simon Carol Moseley-Braun	(D) (D)
Aug. 1997 to Sept. 2001	Scott R. Lassar	William Clinton	(D)	Carol Moseley-Braun Richard J. Durbin	(D) (D)

Time in Office	U.S. Attorney	President		U.S. Senators from Illinois	
Sept. 2001 to June 2012	Patrick J. Fitzgerald	George W. Bush	(R)	Peter G. Fitzgerald	(R)
				Richard J. Durbin	(D)
Oct. 2013 to present	Zachary Fardon	Barack H. Obama	(D)	Richard J. Durbin	(D)
				Mark Kirk	(R)

* Recommended by U. S. Representative Robert Michel
Sources: *Chicago Tribune* and *Chicago Sun-Times*

Notes

Chapter 1. Corrupt Illinois

1. William Stead, *If Christ Came to Chicago!* (1894; reprint, Chicago: Chicago Historical Bookworks, 1990), 182.

2. Ibid., 183; Lincoln Steffens, *The Shame of the Cities* (New York: McClure, Phillips, 1904), 169. Steffens estimated that fifty-seven of the sixty-eight aldermen were crooked based upon studies done by the Municipal Voter League.

3. Stead, *If Christ Came to Chicago!* 183. At the time there were two aldermen for each of the thirty-four and later thirty-five wards in Chicago.

4. Dick Simpson et al., *Chicago and Illinois, Leading the Pack in Corruption: Anti-Corruption Report No. 5* (Chicago: Department of Political Science, University of Illinois at Chicago and Institute for Government and Public Affairs, February 2012), accessed November 15, 2013, http://www.uic.edu/depts/pols/ChicagoPolitics/leadingthepack.pdf.

5. David Sterrett et al., *Green Grass and Graft, Corruption in the Suburbs: Anti-Corruption Report No. 6* (Chicago: Department of Political Science, University of Illinois at Chicago, June 2012), accessed November 15, 2013, http://www.uic.edu/depts/pols/ChicagoPolitics/SuburbanCorruption.pdf.

6. Since our original study, *Chicago and Illinois, Leading the Pact in Corruption,* other studies using different years and methodologies have come up with slightly different rankings. See, for instance, Cheolh Liu and John Mikesell, "The Impact of Public Officials' Corruption on the Size and Allocation of U.S. State Spending," *Public Administration Review* 78.3 (May/June 2014): 346–59. Using ten years of data, they rank Illinois the fourth most-corrupt state after Mississippi, Louisiana, and Tennessee. See also Reid Wilson, "The Most Corrupt State(s) in America," *Washington Post,* January 22, 2014, accessed July 8, 2014, http://www.washingtonpost.com/blogs/govbeat/wp/2014/01/22/the-most-corrupt-states-in-america/.

7. Rasma Karklins, *The System Made Me Do It! Corruption in Post-Communist Societies* (Armonk, N.Y.: M. E. Sharpe, 2005), 25.

8. Robert Klitgaard, *Controlling Corruption* (Berkeley: University of California Press, 1988), 75.

9. Transparency International, "National Integrity System Background and Methodology," 2011, accessed May 21, 2014, http://www.transparency.org/files/content/nis/National IntegritySystem_Background_and_Methodology.pdf.

10. Richard F. Winters, "Unique or Typical: Political Corruption in the American States . . . and in Illinois," paper presented at What's in the Water in Illinois: Ethics and Reform Symposium on Illinois Government, Paul Simon Public Policy Institute at Southern Illinois University, Carbondale, September 27–28, 2012.

11. Ibid., 12.

12. Daniel J. Elazar, *Cities of the Prairie* (New York: Basic Books, 1970).

13. James Nowlan, Samuel Gove, and Richard Winkel Jr., *Illinois Politics: A Citizen's Guide* (Urbana: University of Illinois Press, 2010), 2.

14. Elazar, *Cities of the Prairie*, 286.

15. Nowlan, Gove, and Winkel, *Illinois Politics*, 42 and 225.

16. Patrick Fizgerald, "The Costs of Public Corruption—and the Need for the Public to Fight Back," accessed November 15, 2013, http://www.justice.gov/usao/briefing_room/fin/corruption.html.

17. Daniel Egler, "Vote Fraud Started When Chicago Did," *Chicago Tribune,* September 8, 1984, 1–2.

18. Dick Simpson, *Rouges, Rebels, and Rubber Stamps: The Politics of the Chicago City Council from 1863 to the Present* (Boulder, Colo.: Westview, 2001), 48. See also Finis Farr, *Chicago: A Personal History of America's Most American City* (New Rochelle, N.Y.: Arlington House, 1973), 108.

Chapter 2. Machine Politics and Stolen Elections

1. Qtd. in James Nowlan, Samuel K. Gove, and Richard J. Winkel Jr., *Illinois Politics: A Citizen's Guide* (Urbana: University of Illinois Press, 2010), 13.

2. Adam Cohen and Elizabeth Taylor, *American Pharaoh: Mayor Richard J. Daley, His Battle for Chicago and the Nation* (New York: Little Brown, 2000), 273.

3. Richard F. Winters, "Unique or Typical: Political Corruption in the American States . . . and in Illinois," pp. 1–45, paper presented at What's in the Water in Illinois: Ethics and Reform Symposium on Illinois Government, Paul Simon Public Policy Institute at Southern Illinois University, Carbondale, September 27–28, 2012.

4. Milton Rakove, *Don't Make No Waves, Don't Back No Losers* (Bloomington: Indiana University Press, 1975), 4.

5. William Riordan, *Plunkitt of Tammany Hall* (1905; reprint, New York: Signet Classics, 1995), 17–20.

6. Ibid., 3–6.

7. Rasma Karklins, *The System Made Me Do It! Corruption in Post-Communist Societies* (Armonk, N.Y.: M. E. Sharpe, 2005).

8. James Merriner, *Grafters and Goo Goos: Corruption and Reform in Chicago, 1833–2003* (Carbondale: Southern Illinois University Press, 2004), 14.

9. Dick Simpson, *Rogues, Rebels, and Rubber Stamps: The Politics of the Chicago City Council from 1863 to the Present* (Boulder, Colo.: Westview, 2001), chap. 1.

10. Ibid., 41; Merriner, *Grafters and Goo Goos,* 31; Bessie Louise Pierce, *A History of Chicago,* vol. 2 (Chicago: University of Chicago Press, 1940), 297–99.

11. Merriner, *Grafters and Goo Goos,* 31.

12. Richard C. Lindberg, *The Gambler King of Clark Street: Michael C. McDonald and the Rise of Chicago's Democratic Machine* (Carbondale: Southern Illinois University Press, 2009), 23. Most of the details of McDonald's career are taken from this book, although many other historians cover the general story. See Len O'Connor, *Clout: Mayor Daley and His City* (Chicago: Regnery, 1975), 9; and Simpson, *Rogues, Rebels, and Rubber Stamps,* 48.

13. Simpson, *Rogues, Rebels, and Rubber Stamps,* 48.

14. Finis Farr, *Chicago: A Personal History of America's Most American City* (New Rochelle, N.Y.: Arlington House, 1973), 130.

15. Lindberg, *Gambler King of Clark Street,* 104.

16. Merriner, *Grafters and Goo Goos,* 1–9. See his entire book for the struggle between reformers and machine politicians.

17. Cohen and Taylor, *American Pharaoh,* 268.

18. Ibid., 269–70.

19. Ibid., 271 (originally reported in the *Chicago Tribune,* March 23, 1972).

20. Much of this section is taken from Melissa Mouritsen Zmuda, "Patronage from Shakman to Sorich," in *Twenty-First Century Chicago,* rev. ed., ed. Dick Simpson, Constance A. Mixon, and Melissa Mouritsen Zmuda (San Diego: Cognella, 2013), 85–94.

21. *Shakman v. the Democratic Organization of Cook County et al.,* US 69 C 2145.

22. "Court to Hear Case: Kucharski Hails Patronage Suit Action," *Chicago Tribune,* October 25, 1970.

23. "Group to Aid Victims of Political Firings," *Chicago Tribune,* October 29, 1970.

24. Glen Elsasser, "Supreme Court Slaps Machine Politics Here: Top Court Hits City's Patronage," *Chicago Tribune,* April 20, 1971.

25. Robert Enstad, "Patronage Pact Called Hogwash," *Chicago Tribune,* October 21, 1971.

26. Vernon Jarrett, "Last Stand in Salt Mines?" *Chicago Tribune,* January 31, 1975; "City Loses Shakman Appeal," *Chicago Tribune,* April 10, 1976.

27. *Elrod v. Burns,* 427 US 347 (1976); Richard Ciccone, "Democrats Will Tell Court Political Work Leads to Jobs," *Chicago Tribune,* February 25, 1977.

28. Jay Branegan, "U.S. Judge Rules Patronage Jobs in Cook County Illegal," *Chicago Tribune,* September 25, 1979.

29. Judge Nicolas Bua, "Supplemental Findings of Fact," September 24, 1979, from *Michael L. Shakman and Paul M. Lurie et al. v. the Democratic Party of Cook County et al.* Later findings and opinions by Judge Bua are quoted at length in Dick Simpson, ed., *Chicago's Future in a Time of Change* (Champaign, Ill.: Stipes, 1993), 147–54.

30. Christopher Chandler, "Shakman Decrees," *Chicago Tribune,* February 17, 2002.

31. "Illinois, Patronage Battleground," *Chicago Sun-Times,* June 30, 1996.

32. Ray Hanania, "Shakman Covers Orr—Only Hynes, Phelan Out," *Chicago Sun-Times,* October 17, 1991.

33. Lou Ortiz, "County to Limit Patronage Hiring—Board President Accepts Decree," *Chicago Sun-Times,* December 3, 1993; Lou Ortiz, "Hynes OKs Limits on Patronage Positions," *Chicago Sun-Times,* October 20, 1994.

34. Fran Spielman, "Daley Lashes Out at Reformer—Blasts Spending More to Enforce Shakman Ban on Political Hiring," *Chicago Sun-Times,* January 18, 2002.

35. Ibid.

36. Mark Brown, "Shakman Tries to Keep It Civil in City Hall Fight," *Chicago Sun-Times,* July 27, 2005.

37. Fran Spielman, "Council OKs $12 Million Shakman Settlement—Money Goes to Victims of Flawed Process," *Chicago Sun-Times,* April 12, 2007.

38. Ibid.

39. Fran Spielman, "No More Shakman Decree," *Chicago Sun-Times,* June 12, 2014, 8–9. See also Fran Spielman, "Shakman Era Coming to a Close," *Chicago Sun-Times,* May 16, 2014, 8.

40. Fran Spielman, "No More Shakman Decree," *Chicago Sun-Times,* June 12, 2014, 8.

41. Rahm Emanuel and Soo Choi, "City Hiring Now on the Up and Up," *Chicago Sun-Times,* June 17, 2014, 21.

42. Mike Royko, *Boss: Richard J. Daley of Chicago* (New York: Dutton, 1971), 72–73.

43. Simpson, *Rogues, Rebels, and Rubber Stamps,* 1.

44. Qtd. in ibid., 2.

45. Harry Golden Jr., "The Mayor in Crisis: He Can Take the Heat," *Chicago Sun-Times,* March 4, 1973, 3. The conflict is covered in Simpson, *Rogues, Rebels, and Rubber Stamps,* 134–38.

46. "Rutherford over White," editorial, *Springfield State Journal-Register,* October 27, 2006.

47. David Kidwell and John Chase, "Ex-City Official Charged in Red Light Bribery Case," *Chicago Tribune,* May 15, 2014, 1 and 8–9; and Kim Janssen, "Ex-City Hall Official Took Bribes in Red-Light Camera Program: Feds," *Chicago Sun-Times,* May 15, 2014, 8.

48. "In the Clear," *Governing Magazine* (March 2013): 12.

49. Melissa Mouritsen Zmuda and Dick Simpson, "Continuing the Rubber Stamp City Council, Chicago City Council Report No. 6, June 8, 2011-February 13, 2013" (Chicago: University of Illinois at Chicago Department of Political Science, April 8, 2013), 36. See also Steve Rhodes, "Why Chicago's Spineless City Council Just Can't Say No," *Chicago Magazine* (April 2013).

50. David Kidewell, John Chase, and Alex Richards, "Madigan Builds Army One Favor at a Time," *Chicago Tribune,* January 5, 2014, 1 and 10–11. See also Richard Wronski, "Report Finds Madigan 'Prominent' in Hiring," *Chicago Tribune,* April 2, 2014, 4.

51. Jim Suhr and Jan Dinnes, "Corruption in State Knows No Bounds," *Associated Press,* August 29, 2005.

52. Ibid.

53. Jason Meisner, "Ex-Burnham Clerk Admits Stealing $700K, Gambling," *Chicago Tribune,* May 25, 2014, 11 and Kim Janssen, "18 Months for Embezzlement," *Chicago Sun Times,* September 10, 2014, 6.

Chapter 3. The Sorry State of Illinois

1. Jeff Cohen and John Case, *Golden: How Rod Blagojevich Talked Himself out of the Governor's Office and into Prison* (Chicago: Chicago Review Press, 2012), 26.

2. Natashe Korecki, "Kiss Him Goodbye, Ex-Gov Convicted of 17 Charges," *Chicago Sun-Times,* June 28, 2011, 1.

3. Cohen and Case, *Golden,* 51.

4. Elizabeth Brackett, *Pay to Play: How Rod Blagojevich Turned Corruption into a National Sideshow* (Lanham, Md.: Rowman and Littlefield, 2009), 58–64.

5. One article that argues effectively that scandals bring major reforms, including regime change, is Richard Keiser, "Urban Regime Change: A Silver Lining for Scandals," *Urban Affairs Review* (forthcoming, Fall 2014): 1–30.

6. Ninian Wirt Edwards, qtd. in Jim Nowlan, "Corruption in Illinois: An Enduring Tradition," paper presented at What's in the Water in Illinois? Ethics and Reform Symposium on Illinois Government, Paul Simon Public Policy Institute, Southern Illinois University, Carbondale, September 27–28, 2012.

7. Ibid.

8. "Sangamon County Grand Jury, the Great Canal Script Fraud Minutes of Proceeding," 1859, accessed November 15, 2013, http://archive.org/stream/greatcanalscripfoosang#page/n5/mode/2up.

9. *Portrait and Biographical Album of Whiteside County, Illinois* (Chicago: M. A. Leeson and Co., 1887), 147–48.

10. James D. Nolan, *Glory, Darkness, Light: A History of the Union League Club of Chicago* (Evanston, Ill.: Northwestern University Press, 2005), 51.

11. Nowlan, "Corruption in Illinois," 3.

12. Claire Suddath, "A Brief History of Illinois Corruption," *Time,* December 11, 2008, accessed July 8, 2014, http://content.time.com/time/nation/article/0,8599,1865681,00.html.

13. Orville Hodge, "Auditor Who Robbed the State," *Chicago Tribune,* January 1, 1987.

14. "History of the Comptroller's Office," State of Illinois Web site, accessed May 27, 2014, http://www.ioc.state.il.us/index.cfm/about-our-office/history/; and "Illinois: Hodge Dislodged," *Time,* July 30, 1956, accessed July 8, 2014, http://content.time.com/time/magazine/article/0,9171,867023,00.html. The original Orville Hodge exposé won the 1957 Pulitzer Prize for investigative reporting.

15. Earl Aykroid, "Stratton Cleared of Tax Dodge," *Pittsburgh Post-Gazette,* March 12, 1965, 2.

16. Ibid.

17. Stephan Benzkofer, "First Illinois Governor to Do Time Was Known as 'Mr. Clean,'" *Chicago Tribune,* December 11, 2011.

18. Kenneth A. Manaster, *Illinois Justice: The Scandal of 1969 and the Rise of John Paul Stevens* (Chicago: University of Chicago Press, 2001); and Nowlan, "Corruption in Illinois."

19. Ron Grossman, "Bigger than a Shoe Box," *Chicago Tribune,* February 24, 2013, 19.

20. Ibid.

21. "William J. Scott of Illinois Dies: Tax Fraud Halted Political Rise," *Los Angeles Times,* June 25, 1986.

22. Jason Meisner, "Ex-Comptroller to Face the Music," *Chicago Tribune*, February 7, 2013, 6.

23. Walter Pavlo, "Fmr Dixon, IL, Comptroller, Rita Crundwell, Sentenced to 19 ½ Years in Prison," *Forbes*, February 24, 2013, accessed July 8, 2014, http://www.forbes.com/sites/walterpavlo/2013/02/14/fmr-dixon-il-comptroller-rita-crundwell-sentenced-to-19–12-years-in-prison/.

24. Ibid.

25. Jim Suhr and Jan Dennis, "Corruption in State Knows No Bounds," *Associated Press*, August 29, 2005.

26. John Sharp, "Playing around in Peoria," *Peoria Journal Star*, July 24, 2005; and Adriana Colindres, "State's High Court to Hear Appeal of Former Pekin Mayor," *MetroWest Daily News (Framingham, Mass.)*, September 27, 2007.

27. Shur and Dennis, "Corruption in State Knows No Bounds."

28. Becky Malkovich, "Martin Guilty of All Charges," *Carbonale Southern Illinoisan*, September 23, 2010.

29. D. W. Norris, "Sheriff's Ex-Wife Pleads to Reduced Charge," *Carbondale Southern Illinoisan*, September 27, 2012.

30. "Ex-Madison County Treasurer Guilty of Corruption," *Associated Press Illinois State Wire*, February 6, 2013.

31. Steve Horrell, "Bathon Criticized for Office Addition," *Edwardsville Intelligencer*, December 3, 2002.

32. "3 Plead Guilty in Auction Scam," *Edwardsville Intelligencer*, October 18, 2013.

33. "Bedell Pleads Guilty to Embezzlement," *Edwardsville Intelligencer*, April 18, 2013.

34. "Former Chief Gets 18 Months," *Edwardsville Intelligencer*, September 20, 2013.

35. Michael Tarm, "Illinois Lawmaker Gets Community Service in Gun Case," *Associated Press*, April 24, 2013.

36. Meredith Colias, "Legal Charges Loom," *Illinois Issues*, February 2013, 11.

37. Ryan Haggerty, John Chase, and Ray Long, "State Rep. Derrick Smith, of Chicago, Is Charged with Accepting Bribes," *Chicago Tribune*, March 13, 2012.

38. Qtd. in James Dunn, "House Expels Representative Over Bribery Charge," *Illinois Issues*, September 2012, 9.

39. Kim Janssen, "State Rep Smith Convicted in Bribery Trial," *Chicago Sun-Times*, June 11, 2014, 9.

40. Chris Fusco, "Grant-Fraud Tally, 13 Charged, $16 Million Allegedly Embezzled," *Chicago Sun-Times*, September 9, 2013, 4.

41. Perry Case, "Is Yours More Corrupt Than Mine?" *New York Times*, May 18, 2013.

42. Fusco, "Grant-Fraud Tally, 13 Charged, $16 Million Allegedly Embezzled," 4.

43. Dick Simpson et al., *Chicago and Illinois, Leading the Pack in Corruption: Anti-Corruption Report No. 5* (Chicago: University of Illinois at Chicago Department of Political Science and the Institute for Government and Public Affairs, February 2012), accessed May 27, 2014, http://www.uic.edu/depts/pols/ChicagoPolitics/leadingthepack.pdf.

44. Nowlan, "Corruption in Illinois," 7.

45. Ibid., 8.

46. Juan Perez, Jr. "In Illinois, We of Little Faith in our Politicians," *Chicago Tribune,* April 5, 2014, 1.

47. Nowlan, "Corruption in Illinois," 9.

Chapter 4. Aldermanic Corruption

1. Milton Rakove, *We Don't Want Nobody Nobody Sent: An Oral History of the Daley Years* (Bloomington: Indiana University Press, 1979), 136.

2. Rudolph Unger, "6 Get Jail in S.E. Side Stag Parties," *Chicago Tribune,* March 4, 1971.

3. Pamela Zeckman, "Vrdolyak Faces U.S. Quiz on Favors in Building Home," *Chicago Tribune,* February 9, 1975.

4. "Ed Vrdolyak Timeline," *Chicago Sun-Times,* November 4, 2008.

5. Rakove, *We Don't Want Nobody Nobody Sent,* 136.

6. Paul Kleppner, *Chicago Divided: The Making of a Black Mayor* (Dekalb: Northern Illinois University Press, 1985), 177; Dick Simpson, *Rogues, Rebels, and Rubber Stamps: The Politics of the Chicago City Council from 1863 to the Present* (Boulder, Colo.: Westview, 2001), 208–10.

7. Mark Eissman and Ann Marie Lipinski, "Vrdolyak Hiring Questioned," *Chicago Tribune,* August 14, 1986.

8. Natasha Korecki, "Vrdolyak Tied to Cicero Track Deal: Accused of Working Both Sides in Plan to Revamp Sportsman's," *Chicago Sun-Times,* September 4, 2006.

9. Jeff Coen, "Legal Troubles Trip 'Fast Eddie,'" *Chicago Tribune,* November 3, 2008.

10. U.S. Department of Justice, "Chicago Lawyer Edward R. Vrdolyak Indicted in Alleged Kickback Scheme Involving Gold Coast Real Estate Deal," Press Release, May 10, 2007.

11. Dan Mihalopoulos, Jeff Coen, and Ray Gibson, "Feds Catch up with 'Fast Eddie' Vrdolyak," *Chicago Tribune,* May 11, 2007.

12. Natasha Korecki, "10 Months for Fast Eddie; Also Must Pay $250K in Real Estate Fraud Scheme," *Chicago Sun-Times,* October 16, 2010.

13. Qtd. in Simpson, *Rogues, Rebels, and Rubber Stamps,* 53.

14. Qtd. in *Chicago: Its City Halls and Its City Council,* pamphlet (Chicago: City Council Committee on Finance, the Chicago Historical Society, the *Chicago Sun-Times,* and the *Chicago Tribune,* 1987), 3.

15. Adam Cohen and Elizabeth Taylor, *American Pharaoh: Mayor Richard J. Daley—His Battle for Chicago and the Nation* (New York: Little Brown, 2000), 212.

16. Simpson, *Rogues, Rebels, and Rubber Stamps,* 115–16; Thomas J. Gradel, Dick Simpson, and Andris Zimelis, *Curing Corruption in Illinois: Anti-Corruption Report No. 1,* (Chicago: University of Illinois at Chicago Department of Political Science, February 3, 2009), accessed November 15, 2013, http://www.uic.edu/depts/pols/ChicagoPolitics/ Anti-corruptionReport.pdf.

17. William Griffin, "Keane Era Ends in 31st Ward," *Chicago Tribune,* February 18, 1979, sec. 3.

18. Milton Rakove, *Don't Make No Saves . . . Don't Back No Losers* (Bloomington: Indiana University Press, 1975), 49.

19. Jay McMullen, "Tom Keane—A Man of Power," *Chicago Daily News,* May 14, 1969.

20. Simpson, *Rogues, Rebels, and Rubber Stamps,* 116; Gradel, Simpson, and Zimelis, *Curing Corruption in Illinois,* 27–28.

21. Cohen and Taylor, *American Pharaoh,* 237–38.

22. Qtd. in ibid., 533.

23. Maurice Possley, "Ald. Carothers, Former Aide Indicted," *Chicago Sun-Times,* April 9, 1983; Michael Briggs, "Alderman's Ties to Hospital Probed," *Chicago Sun-Times,* November 29, 1981; William B. Crawford Jr., "Jury Indicts Ald. Carothers and Legislator," *Chicago Tribune,* April 9, 1983.

24. Natasha Korecki and Fran Spielman, "Feds Charge Businessman with Bribing Alderman," *Chicago Sun-Times,* November 6, 2009, 12; Natasha Korecki and Art Golab, "Boender Guilty on All Five Counts," *Chicago Sun-Times,* March 19, 2010, 4.

25. Mary Wisniewski, "Illinois Voters Say 'No' to Candidates Who Were Convicted, Indicted," *Reuters,* March 19, 2014, accessed July 10, 2014, http://www.reuters.com/article/2014/03/19/us-usa-illinois-politics-felon-idUSBREA2I25020140319; and Brian Slodysko, "Felon Loses Bid to Return to Office," *Chicago Tribune,* March 19, 2014.

26. John Seidel, "Ex-Alderman Pleads Guilty in Third Corruption Case," *Chicago Sun-Times,* September 25, 2013, 24; and "Medrano's Three-Peat," editorial, *Chicago Tribune,* September 26, 2013.

27. Kim Janssen, "Ex-Ald. Medrano Sentenced to 10 ½ Years," *Chicago Sun-Times,* January 11, 2014, 6; Jason Meisner, "Ex-Alderman Gets 10 ½-Year Term," *Chicago Tribune,* January 11, 2014, 4; and Kim Janssen, "Medrano Gets More Time Added to Stiff Sentence," *Chicago Sun-Times,* January 14, 2014, 15.

28. George Washington Plunkitt, *Honest Graft and Dishonest Graft: Very Plain Talks on Very Practical Politics,* recorded by William L. Riordon (1905). The current edition of the book is William Riordan, *Plunkitt of Tammany Hall* (1905; reprint, New York: Signet Classics, 1995).

29. Fran Spielman, "No More Shakman Decree," *Chicago Sun-Times,* June 17, 2014, 8–9.

30. Melissa Mouritsen Zmuda and Dick Simpson, "Continuing the Rubber Stamp City Council, Chicago City Council Report No. 6, June 8, 2011-February 13, 2013" (Chicago: University of Illinois at Chicago Department of Political Science, April 8, 2013).

31. Qtd. in Alton Miller, *Harold Washington: The Mayor, The Man* (Chicago: Bonus Books, 1989), 99.

Chapter 5. Chicago City Haul

1. Jim Laski, *My Fall from Grace: City Hall to Prison Walls* (Bloomington, Ind.: Author House, 2008), 81–83.

2. Rasma Karklins, *The System Made Me Do It! Corruption in Post-Communist Societies* (Armonk, N.Y.: M. E. Sharpe, 2005), 25.

3. Robert Klitgaard, *Controlling Corruption* (Berkeley: University of California Press, 1988), 75.

4. Tim Novak and Steve Warmbir, "You Put in Your Eight Hours a Day, but You Just Sit on the Job: City's Hired Truck Program Grants Insiders and Mob-Linked Cronies an Exclusive and Lucrative Side Business," *Chicago Sun-Times,* January 23, 2004.

5. "Reporters Win Third National Award for Hired Truck Series," *Chicago Sun-Times,* April 2, 2005.

6. Steve Warmbir and Tim Novak, "Members of Hispanic Organization Run Program," *Chicago Sun-Times,* February 6, 2004.

7. Fran Spielman, "Clout on Wheels," *Chicago Sun-Times,* February 9, 2004.

8. "Clout Fallout," *Chicago Sun-Times,* February 20, 2004.

9. Matt O'Connor, "Former Hired Truck Boss Gets Two Year Term for Bribes," *Chicago Tribune,* August 3, 2005.

10. Natasha Korecki and Steve Warmbir, "Ex-Daley Patronage Chief Convicted," *Chicago Sun-Times,* July 6, 2006.

11. Patronage: Shakman to Sorich, Supplemental Findings of Fact: *Shakman v. Democratic Organization of Cook County,* September 24, 1979, in *Twenty-First-Century Chicago,* ed. Dick Simpson and Constance A. Mixon (San Diego: Cognella, 2012), 87.

12. *Cynthia Rutan et al. v. The Republican Party of Illinois,* in *Chicago's Future in a Time of Change,* ed. Dick Simpson (Champaign, Ill.: Stipes, 1993), 154.

13. Simpson and Mixon, ed., *Twenty-First-Century Chicago,* 90–93.

14. Qtd. in Harry Golden Jr., "Daley Assails Colleges for 'Agitation and Hate,'" *Chicago Sun-Times,* July 22, 1971, 1 and 4.

15. This text was pieced together from the quotations cited by ibid., 4, and Bill Boyarsky and Nancy Boyarsky, *Backroom Politics* (Los Angeles: J. P. Tarsher, 1974), 21–22. They took their quotations from an audiotape of Daley's speech recorded by the radio station WMAQ.

16. Dan Mihalopoulos, "The Berrios Public Salary Tree," *Chicago Sun-Times,* November 18, 2012, 2A.

17. Royko, *Boss,* 73.

18. "Operation Haunted Hall," *Chicago Sun-Times,* June 26, 1997.

19. James L. Merriner, *Grafters and Goo Goos, Corruption and Reform in Chicago 1833–2003* (Carbondale: Southern Illinois University Press, 2004).

20. Matt O'Connor, "Roswell Makes Deal in Ghost-Job Probe," *Chicago Tribune,* November 26, 1998.

21. Scott Fornek and Cam Simpson, "Probe Still a 35–1 success, Lassar Says," *Chicago Sun-Times,* January 28, 1999.

22. Jim Merriner, "Operation Incubator: Was Probe of Corruption Here Worth the Expense?" *Chicago Sun-Times,* September 17, 1989.

23. "15 Who Were Caught in Influence-Peddling Net," *Chicago Sun-Times,* September 17, 1989.

24. Chuck Neubauer, "Davis 4 Years on Council, 4 Years in Jail," *Chicago Sun-Times,* January 22, 1995.

25. Adrienne Drell, "Teary Plea Fails—Humes Gets 2 Yrs.," *Chicago Sun-Times,* August 1, 1989.

26. Adrienne Drell, "Hutchinson Gets 8 Yrs. in Bribery," *Chicago Sun-Times,* September 30, 1989.

27. William B. Crawford Jr., "Kelley Gets Year, Will Help Probe," *Chicago Tribune,* June 12, 1987.

28. Maurice Possley, Dean Baquet, et al., "9 Indicted in City Payoff Case," *Chicago Tribune,* May 15, 1987.

29. Among the convicted lower-level officials were John Adams, former city deputy revenue director; Herman Mitchell, a precinct captain; Paul Vesper, a gun dealer; Carmen Aiello, a former Water Department supervisor; Melvin DuBrock, a former assistant Streets and Sanitation commissioner; Raymond Akers, former Waste Management Inc. lobbyist; and two officials of an unaccredited South Side law school. See "15 Who Were Caught in Influence-Peddling Net," *Chicago Sun-Times,* September 17, 1989.

30. Zay N. Smith and Pamela Zekman, *The Mirage* (New York: Random House, 1979), 62–65.

31. "City Names 3 Suspended in Tavern Controversy," *Chicago Tribune,* January 11, 1978.

32. Zay N. Smith and Pamela Zekman, *The Mirage* (New York: Random House, 1979), 253.

33. "Santos Indicted on Extortion, Fraud Charges—Treasurer Accused of Squeezing Banks," *Chicago Tribune,* January 27, 1999.

34. "Santos Hit with Extortion Charges," *Chicago Tribune,* January 28, 1999.

35. "Santos Call 'Intimidated' Banker," *Chicago Sun-Times,* April 24, 1999.

36. "Santos Done In by Tape—'Time to Belly Up' Remark Called Key to Guilty Verdict," *Chicago Tribune,* May 4, 1999.

37. Jim Allen, "City Treasurer Accused of Fraud, Extortion," *Arlington Heights (Ill.) Daily Herald,* January 28, 1999.

38. "Santos Done In by Tape—'Time to Belly Up' Remark Called Key to Guilty Verdict," *Chicago Tribune,* May 4, 1999.

39. "Jury Convicts Santos—Found Guilty on 6 of 12 Counts," *Chicago Sun-Times,* May 3, 1999.

40. "Avalanche of Errors Sinks Case," *Chicago Sun-Times,* January 20, 2000.

41. "Santos Pleads Guilty, Quits—City Treasurer Makes Deal to Avoid Retrial on Fraud, Extortion," *Chicago Tribune,* October 10, 2000.

42. "Check-Cashing Scam Smashed at City Hall," *Chicago Sun-Times,* October 12, 1990.

43. Matt O'Connor and Ray Gibson, "Duff Pleads Guilty—for 3 Hours," *Chicago Tribune,* January 11, 2005.

44. Natasha Korecki, "Duff Gets Nearly 10 Years in Prison Minority-Contract Scam Based on 'Pure Greed': Judge," *Chicago Sun-Times,* May 19, 2005.

45. Matt O'Connor, Ray Gibson, and Laurie Cohen, "Duff Told Mom to Lie, U.S. Says," *Chicago Tribune,* November 23, 2004.

46. John William Tuohy, "Cleaning Up with the Duffs," *American Mafia,* September 2001, accessed May 29, 2014, http://www.americanmafia.com/Feature_Articles_157.html.

47. Laurie Cohen and Gary Washburn, "U.S. Alleges Huge Fraud in City Minority Pacts; City Vigilance Again in Doubt; Allegations Reach Back Many Years," *Chicago Tribune,* September 26, 2003.

48. Matt O'Connor and Ray Gibson, "Silver Shovel Corruption Probe Widens—Evans Charged in Latest Round," *Chicago Tribune,* July 17, 1996.

49. Cam Simpson, "Ex-Aide, Consultant Guilty in Bribe Case," *Chicago Sun-Times,* March 7, 1998.

50. Matt O'Connor, "2 Found Guilty in Silver Shovel," *Chicago Tribune*, March 7, 1998.

51. Chuck Neubauer, "FBI Mole Probes Local Politicians; Ex-Con Wired in Feds' Operation Silver Shovel," *Chicago Sun-Times*, January 7, 1996.

52. Fran Spielman, "Dump Cleanup Costs Soar to $21 million for Silver Shovel Site," *Chicago Sun-Times*, April 27, 2001.

53. John Kass, "A Poor Kid's Rise to Outfit Knighthood," *Chicago Tribune*, August 17, 2007.

54. Liam Ford, "Son Says Father 'Schooled' Him to Rise in Mob," *Chicago Tribune*, July 13, 2007.

55. "Restitution Ordered in Outfit Case," *Chicago Tribune*, April 7, 2009.

56. Todd Lighty, "Prosecutors Boast of 'a Hit on the Mob,'" *Chicago Tribune*, April 25, 2005.

57. Emily Ngo, "Streamwood Man Charged in Organized Crime Bust Dies," *Daily Herald*, January 20, 2006.

58. Natasha Korecki and Frank Main, "U.S. Marshal Guilty of Leaking to Mob," *Chicago Sun-Times*, April 29, 2009.

59. Robert Mitchum, "Witnesses' Identities to Be Protected," *Chicago Tribune*, April 9, 2009; and Robert Mitchum, "Marquette 10 Reference Key, FBI Agent Says," *Chicago Tribune*, April 15, 2009.

60. Jeff Coen, "Family Secrets: Mob Turncoat Gets 12 Years," *Chicago Tribune*, March 27, 2009.

61. Steve Warmbir, "1 Less Clown in the Circus—Jury Pins 10 Murders on Outfit Figures," *Chicago Sun-Times*, September 28, 2007.

62. Hal Dardick, "$12.3 Million for Two Burge Victims," *Chicago Tribune*, September 6, 2013.

63. Andrew Schroedtor, "Police Misconduct Bill: 500M," *Chicago Sun-Times*, April 4, 2014, 6.

64. Matt O'Connor, "Ghost Payroller 'Worked' 3 Jobs," *Chicago Tribune*, October 13, 1994; Matt O'Connor, "Ex-deputy Guilty in Job Scheme," *Chicago Tribune*, October 18, 1994; Matt O'Connor, "Laurino Wife Admits Fraud," *Chicago Tribune*, May 12, 1995; Matt O'Connor, "Double-Dipping Ghost in New Haunt," *Chicago Tribune*, February 21, 1996; Matt O'Connor, "Ghost Worker's Job Offer Came over Dinner, She Says," *Chicago Tribune*, April 25, 1996; Matt O'Connor, "Rosewell Makes Deal in Ghost-Jobs Probe," *Chicago Tribune*, November 26, 1998; Daniel J. Lehmann, "Three More Charged with Ghost Payrolling," *Chicago Sun-Times*, August 30, 1995; Mark Brown, "Retired 'Ghost' Admits Guilt," *Chicago Sun-Times*, November 23, 1995.

65. Natasha Korecki, "Witness: Ryan Pal Got Deal on Testing Facility," *Chicago Sun-Times*, November 2, 2005; Natasha Korecki, "Fawell: Ryan's Family, Friends Got Cash," *Chicago Sun-Times*, October 7, 2005; Natasha Korecki, "Appraiser: $900,000 Wasted: Says Ryan Buddies Got Great Deal as State Rented Property," *Chicago Sun-Times*, December 6, 2005; Natasha Korecki, "Ryan Daughter Tells of No-work Job: Former Gov Hired Her Husband for Campaign for $55,000 a Year," *Chicago Sun-Times*, January 19, 2006; Thomas J. Gradel, Dick Simpson, and Andris Zimelis, *The Depth of Corruption in Illinois: Anti-Corruption Report No. 2*, (Chicago: University of Illinois at Chicago Department of

Political Science, May 13, 2009), accessed July 11, 2014, http://www.uic.edu/depts/pols/ChicagoPolitics/Anti-corruptionReportNumber2.pdf.

66. Len O'Connor, *Clout: Mayor Daley and His City* (Chicago: Regnery, 1975), 9.

67. Cheol Liu and John L. Miesell, "The Impact of Public Officials' Corruption on the Size and Allocation of U.S. State Spending," *Public Administration Review* 74.3 (May/June 2014): 346–59.

68. Dana Heupel, ed., *Illinois for Sale: Do Campaign Contributions Buy Influence?* (Springfield: University of Illinois at Springfield, 1997), 7 and 17.

69. Qtd. in ibid., 18–20.

70. Qtd. in ibid., 20.

71. Ibid., 29–30 and 38–39.

72. Ibid., 94.

73. Ibid., 185.

74. Jason Meisner, "Ex-Burnham Clerk Admits Stealing $100 K, Gambling," *Chicago Sun-Times,* May 23, 2014, 11.

75. David McKinney, "Former Suburban Police Chief Gets 5 Years," *Chicago Sun-Times,* May 2, 2014, 13; Becky Schlikerman and Stefano Esposito, "CPS Tech Coordinator Stole $400,000," *Chicago Sun-Times,* January 4, 2014, 4.

Chapter 6. Crook County

1. Len O'Connor, *Clout: Mayor Daley and His City* (Chicago: Henry Regnery Co., 1975), 36. When this book was written, in 2014, there were thirteen Democratic commissioners, or more than three-quarters of the board.

2. Neil Steinberg, "Pol Ruled Cook County for Decades: Scandals Couldn't Dent Charm of Longtime Board President," *Chicago Sun-Times,* May 30, 2006; Gary Washburn, "Powerful, Familiar Faces Celebrate Dunne's Life," *Chicago Tribune,* June 6, 2006.

3. Ronald Koziol, "Dunne Tells Racing Profit," *Chicago Tribune,* September 15, 1971.

4. Ronald Koziol and Thomas Powers, "Report Mrs. Everett Gave Stock Deals for Race Dates," *Chicago Tribune,* September 17, 1971.

5. Michael Sneed, "Exclusive: Pols Get Realty Plum," *Chicago Tribune,* May 13, 1973; Michael Sneed, "Dunne Denies Favors on Investments," *Chicago Tribune,* May 15, 1973.

6. Liam Ford and Joseph Sjostrom, "George Dunne; 1913–2006," *Chicago Tribune,* May 30, 2006.

7. Douglas Frantz, "Dunne Firm Loses McCormick Place Monopoly," *Chicago Tribune,* March 5, 1985.

8. Art Golab, "Lawsuits Reveal Near North's Tactics," *Chicago Sun-Times,* February 13, 2002; Abdon Pallasch and Fran Speilman, "Segal's Courtship of Powerful Friends Gave Firm Plenty of Clout," *Chicago Sun-Times,* January 29, 2002.

9. Ibid.

10. Steve Warmbir, "Insurance Exec Sought Ryan's Aid, Feds Say Segal Allegedly Asked Ex-Gov to Block Action vs. Firm," *Chicago Sun-Times,* February 27, 2004.

11. Matt O'Connor and Ray Gibson, "Exec Who Built Firm on Clout Indicted," *Chicago Tribune,* January 29, 2002.

12. Ibid.

13. Steve Warmbir, Tim Novak, and Natasha Korecki, "Segal Guilty, Could Get 20 Years—Jury Takes Barely Eight Hours to Convict Insurance Czar," *Chicago Sun-Times,* June 22, 2004.

14. Steve Warmbir and Natasha Korecki, "Judge Sends Segal Straight to Jail," *Chicago Sun-Times,* June 23, 2004.

15. "Indictments Charge Kanter with Bribery," *Chicago Tribune,* August 22, 1969; "Kanter Reindicted in Bribe Case," *Chicago Tribune,* November 19, 1969.

16. Henry Wood, "Ex-Deputy Assessor Convicted," *Chicago Tribune,* December 10, 1970.

17. "Borrie Kanter Enters Guilty Plea," *Chicago Tribune,* June 3, 1971.

18. William Jones, "County's Tax Office Probed; 'Fix' Charged," *Chicago Tribune,* March 12, 1970.

19. William Jones, "Former County Tax Aide Indicted," *Chicago Tribune,* March 13, 1970.

20. Robert Davis, "Former Cullerton Aide Indicted," *Chicago Tribune,* October 26, 1972.

21. Thomas Buck, "Probe County Investments: Dunne," *Chicago Tribune,* March 7, 1972.

22. "County Officials' Bank Ties May Bring Conflict Charges," *Chicago Tribune,* March 5, 1972.

23. Michael Sneed, "County Sues to Get Interest on Funds," *Chicago Tribune,* August 19, 1972.

24. Ronald Yates, "Officeholders Hit on Fund Loss," *Chicago Tribune,* August 20, 1972.

25. Adam Cohen and Elizabeth Taylor, *American Pharaoh: Mayor Richard J. Daley, His Battle for Chicago and the Nation* (New York: Little Brown, 2000); "Jury Probing Funds Dismissed," *Chicago Tribune,* December 2, 1972.

26. Ronald Koziol, "U.S. Indicts Barrett for Bribe, Fraud," *Chicago Tribune,* September 29, 1972.

27. Robert Davis, "Barrett Guilty on All Counts," *Chicago Tribune,* March 8, 1973.

28. "Edward Barrett, Longtime Democratic Power, Dies," *Chicago Tribune,* April 5, 1977.

29. "Keane Quits Tax Appeals Board Post," *Chicago Tribune,* December 1, 1972.

30. George Bliss and David Young, "U.S. Investigates Tax-Cut Favors Here," *Chicago Tribune,* March 30, 1973.

31. Ibid.

32. Richard Philbrick, "Keane Banker Pal Indicted for Fraud to Get Tax Breaks," *Chicago Tribune,* May 10, 1973.

33. Richard Phillips, "Find Keane Pal Guilty of Fraud," *Chicago Tribune,* June 28, 1975.

34. Neil Mehler, "Cullerton Bows Out Today; Tully Makes Assessor Bid," *Chicago Tribune,* November 29, 1973.

35. "Ex-Assessor Aide Admits Bribe Guilt," *Chicago Tribune,* January 3, 1974.

36. Neil Mehler and Richard Phillips, "Cullerton Aide Found in Contempt," *Chicago Tribune,* October 31, 1974.

37. "P.J. Cullerton, Former Dem Leader Here, Dies," *Chicago Tribune,* January 27, 1981.

38. "Parky Cullerton left estate of $400,000," *Chicago Tribune,* March 9, 1981.

39. Bureau of Labor Statistics, accessed June 14, 2014, http://www.bls.gov/data/inflation_calculator.htm.

40. Steve Neal, "Cullerton Clan Just Keeps Rolling Along," *Chicago Sun-Times*, February 10, 1991, 46.

41. Chuck Neubauer, "Land Deals Made Tully Rich," *Chicago Tribune*, May 11, 1980.

42. Richard Phillips and David Young, "Indict 2 on County Board," *Chicago Tribune*, February 14, 1975.

43. Richard Phillips, "Daley Cousin Tells $46,500 Bribes to Bonk," *Chicago Tribune*, June 5, 1975.

44. "County Commissioner Charles Bonk Dies at 57," *Chicago Tribune*, April 21, 1976.

45. Richard Phillips, "Council Aide Zima Guilty," *Chicago Tribune*, May 9, 1975.

46. Richard Phillips and David Young, "Indict 2 on County Board," *Chicago Tribune*, February 14, 1975.

47. "B.G.A. Demands Bonk, Fulle Ouster," *Chicago Tribune*, June 4, 1975.

48. Jay Branegan, "Zoning Official Is Guilty in Tax Case," *Chicago Tribune*, October 28, 1978.

49. Rosalind Rossi, "5 Indicted by U.S. in 1st Ward Probe—Roti, Marcy, D'Arco, Shields, DeLeo Named," *Chicago Sun-Times*, December 20, 1990.

50. Tom Seibel, "Pat Marcy Dies—1st Ward Power Linked to Mob," *Chicago Sun-Times*, March 14, 1993.

51. Ed McManus, "Firm Gets Tax Break without Asking," *Chicago Tribune*, July 8, 1979.

52. Ed McManus, "U.S. Indicts 14 in $33-Million Tax Plot," *Chicago Tribune*, September 3, 1980.

53. Ed McManus, "Tax Appeals Case—23 Convictions Later," *Chicago Tribune*, September 11, 1983.

54. Ibid.

55. William Crawford, "Tycoon Tells Court He Bribed County Tax Aide," *Chicago Tribune*, March 23, 1983.

56. William Crawford, "Ex–Tax Aide Is Guilty in Bribery Case," *Chicago Tribune*, April 2, 1983.

57. Mary Mitchell, "How Feds Cracked the Ghost Pay Scam," *Chicago Sun-Times*, December 17, 1995.

58. Dean Baquet, Thomas Burton, and William Gaines, "O'Grady, Aides Flout Patronage Laws," *Chicago Tribune*, November 12, 1989.

59. William Gaines and John O'Brien, "O'Grady's Office Hit with 2d Top-Level Resignations," *Chicago Tribune*, December 1, 1989.

60. Dan Mihalopoulos and Mitch Dudek, "Owner of Firm with O'Hare Contract Has Links to Reputed Mob Figures," *Chicago Sun-Times*, November 29, 2012.

61. Rosalind Rossi, "Payoffs to O'Grady Told by U.S. Witness—Testifies Mob Gave Sheriff $10,000 Monthly," *Chicago Sun-Times*, December 19, 1991.

62. Rosalind Rossi, "Sheriff's Job Screener Pleads Guilty in Bribes," *Chicago Sun-Times*, May 20, 1992; Rosalind Rossi, "Sheriff's Test Rigging Detailed," *Chicago Sun-Times*, August 13, 1992.

63. Matt O'Connor, "Broader Scandal Told in Sheriff Test Results," *Chicago Tribune*, August 13, 1992; and Matt O'Connor, "Guilty Pleas for Dvorak and Hogan," *Chicago Tribune*, October 1, 1995.

64. Rosalind Rossi, "County's Former No. 2 Cop Indicted—Dvorak Bookie Bribes, Feds Charge," *Chicago Sun-Times*, January 20, 1993; and Matt O'Connor, "Sorry 'for Public Trust I Betrayed,' Dvorak Says in an Unusual Apology," *Chicago Tribune*, August 30, 1993.

65. "Dvorak Cleared in Mob Payoffs," *Chicago Tribune*, January 22, 1994.

66. Matt O'Connor, "Guilty Pleas for Dvorak and Hogan," *Chicago Tribune*, October 1, 1995.

67. Bob Sector and Robert Becker, "Courtly Rosewell Facing New Court Tests," *Chicago Tribune*, June 25, 1997.

68. Andrew Fegelman and Ray Gibson, "U.S. Seeks Ghost Payroll Work Records; Lawmakers, Ex-Clerk Among Probe Targets," *Chicago Tribune*, November 9, 1995.

69. Andrew Fegelman, "Top Deputy to Rosewell Resigns Post," *Chicago Tribune*, November 10, 1995.

70. Matt O'Connor, "Rosewell, Top Aide, 2 Others Indicted; U.S. Says Legislators Held 'Ghost' Jobs with County Treasurer," *Chicago Tribune*, June 24, 1997.

71. Michael Gillis, "Rosewell Charged in Ghost Scam—Treasurer, Aide Accused in Payroller Probe," *Chicago Sun-Times*, June 25, 1997.

72. "Cook County Treasurer Pleads Guilty in Ghost Payrolling Case," *Springfield State Journal-Register*, November 26, 1998.

73. Cam Simpson, "Rosewell, Farley Plead Guilty," *Chicago Sun-Times*, November 26, 1998.

74. Cam Simpson, "Santiago Wins Acquittal in Payroll Scheme," *Chicago Sun-Times*, January 27, 1999.

75. Tim Novak, "Ed Rosewell, Ex-Treasurer, Dies at 72," *Chicago Sun-Times*, July 31, 1999.

76. Chuck Neubauer and William B. Crawford Jr., "Rosewell Indicted on 7 Counts of Fraud," *Chicago Tribune*, June 9, 1983.

77. Robert Enstad, "County Treasurer Acquitted of Fraud," *Chicago Tribune*, January 18, 1984; "Ex-County Treasury Aide Pleads Guilty to Fraud," *Chicago Tribune*, June 7, 1984.

78. Tim Novak, "Ed Rosewell, Ex-Treasurer, Dies at 72," *Chicago Sun-Times*, July 31, 1999.

79. Scott Fornek, "First Black County Board President Built Hospital," *Chicago Sun-Times*, January 19, 2008.

80. Lynn Sweet, "Stroger Bond Work Aired; Public Agency Fees Questioned," *Chicago Sun-Times*, December 6, 1990.

81. Ray Hanania, "County Panel Backs Switch to Pol-linked Housing Plan," *Chicago Sun-Times*, April 9, 1991.

82. Mark Brown, "Stroger Will Pay Insurance Agent for Bulls Tickets," *Chicago Sun-Times*, March 6, 1997.

83. Mark Brown, "Stroger Backs Fund-Raisers to Manage County Building," *Chicago Sun-Times*, June 14, 1997.

84. Abdon Pallasch and Steve Patterson, "FBI Investigates County Fraud; Why Did Stroger Hospital Contract Go to Bogus Bidder?" *Chicago Sun-Times*, January 6, 2005.

85. Natasha Korecki, "Business Owner Admits Role in County Fraud," *Chicago Sun-Times*, May 25, 2007; Natasha Korecki, "33 Months for Payoff," *Chicago Sun-Times*, February 29, 2008.

86. Lynn Sweet, "Stroger Bond Work Aired; Public Agency Fees Questioned," *Chicago Sun-Times,* December 6, 1990.

87. Steve Warmbir, Tim Novak, Fran Spielman, and Steve Paterson, "Hired Truck Probe Snags Daley Ally," *Chicago Sun-Times,* January 26, 2005.

88. Tim Novak and Steve Warmbir, "Hired Truck Defendant Pleads Guilty in Tears; His Company Took in $6.8 Million in City Business," *Chicago Sun-Times,* July 22, 2005.

89. Abdon Pallasch and Steve Patterson, "County Workers Push Stroger's Bid," *Chicago Sun-Times,* March 17, 2006.

90. Steve Patterson, "BGA Faults Campaign Contributions to Stroger," *Chicago Sun-Times,* January 12, 2006.

91. Steve Patterson, "Stroger Takes Donations from County Watchdogs," *Chicago Sun-Times,* January 23, 2006.

92. Abdon Pallasch, "Panel OKs High Rates for Pay Phones at Jail—Some Say Contract Benefits Friends of Sheahan, Stroger," *Chicago Sun-Times,* April 10, 2003.

93. Mickey Ciokajlo and Dan Mihalopoulos, "Minority Firm Led by a Dead Woman," *Chicago Tribune,* March 26, 2005.

94. Chris Fusco and Tim Novak, "Finder's Fee Went to Figure in Probe," *Chicago Sun-Times,* August 17, 2005.

95. Mickey Ciokajlo and John Chase, "Stroger Taps Blagojevich Aide," *Chicago Tribune,* April 8, 2005.

96. Dave McKinney, Chris Fusco, and Steve Warmbir, "Gov Fund-Raiser Linked to Man in Indictment," *Chicago Sun-Times,* August 7, 2005.

97. Scott Fornek, "First Black County President Built Hospital—From Arkansas Shack to Dean of Black Politics in Chicago," *Chicago Sun-Times,* January 19, 2008.

98. Steve Patterson and Abdon Pallasch, "Stroger Alert after Stroke: Likely to Spend Rest of the Campaign in the Hospital," *Chicago Sun-Times,* March 15, 2006.

99. Steve Patterson and Stefano Esposito, "Aide Charged in Theft of Job Funds: Hiring of Ex-Con 'Ordered' by Stroger Allies, Authorities Say," *Chicago Sun-Times,* December 16, 2005.

100. Steve Patterson, "Paper Trail; Memos Show John Stroger's Godson Got Job for Ex-Con," *Chicago Sun-Times,* December 25, 2006.

101. Chris Fusco et al., "Suicide Seen in Death of John Stroger's Godson," *Chicago Sun-Times,* September 14, 2007.

102. "4 Years for $100K Theft," *Chicago Sun-Times,* April 18, 2009.

103. Angela Rozas and Gary Washburn, "County Bilked in Scam: 8 Charged; $1.6 Million in Training Funds Gone," *Chicago Tribune,* January 26, 2008.

104. Jason Meisner, "Charges Dropped against Former Cook County Official," *Chicago Tribune,* July 27, 2012.

105. Anne Sweeney, "Ex-county Jobs Official Arrested in Fraud Case," *Chicago Tribune,* July 14, 2012.

106. Kim Janssen, "Job-Training Program Boss Pleads Guilty to Federal Charges," *Chicago Sun-Times,* December 4, 2012.

107. Mickey Ciokajlo, "Aide Gets Big Cook Payday," *Chicago Tribune,* January 8, 2007.

108. Mickey Ciokajlo, "Stroger's Cousin Gets the Nod," *Chicago Tribune,* May 3, 2007.

109. Mark Konkol, "Todd Shoots an Air Ball—Ex-Hoops Player Got Job, but Didn't Reveal Conviction," *Chicago Sun-Times,* April 10, 2009.

110. Mark Konkol, "Paid Vacation in Jail?—Busboy-Turned-County Worker Received Pay for Time He Was Locked Up," *Chicago Sun-Times,* June 15, 2009.

111. Chris Fusco and the Better Government Association, "Workers Give to Stroger, Get Big Raises," *Chicago Sun-Times,* August 24, 2009.

112. Rob Olmsted and the Better Government Association, "In Cook Co., Contracts, Campaign Donations Intertwined," *Daily Herald,* July 6 and 7, 2009.

113. Ibid.

114. Lisa Donnovan and Rosemary Sobol, "Top Stroger Aide Arrested," *Chicago Sun-Times,* October 5, 2010.

115. Hal Dardick and Mathew Walberg, "Stroger Key Aide Arrested," *Chicago Tribune,* October 5, 2010.

116. Rummana Hussain, "Ex-Stroger Aide Guilty of Theft," *Chicago Sun-Times,* August 29, 2013.

117. Annie Sweeney and Hal Dardick, "U.S. Arrests Former Top Stroger Aide," *Chicago Tribune,* August 3, 2012; Lisa Donovan, "Stroger Pal Eugene Mullins Appears in Court on Kickback Charges," *Chicago Sun-Times,* September 5, 2012.

118. Kim Janssen, "Mullins Guilty of Bribery," *Chicago Sun-Times,* September 19, 2013.

119. Kim Janssen and Lisa Donovan, "Guilty on All Counts," *Chicago Sun-Times,* March 22, 2013 and Jon Seidel, "William Beavers Sentenced to 6 Months, Fined $10,000," *Chicago Sun Times,* September 25, 2013.

120. "William Beavers, the 'Hog with the Big Nuts,' Got Caught Hogging," editorial, *Chicago Sun-Times,* March 22, 2013.

121. U.S. Attorney's press release, February 23, 2012.

122. U.S. Attorney's press releases, June 28 and July 26, 2012.

123. Steve Patterson and Abdon Pallasch, "Moreno Denies Clout List," *Chicago Sun-Times,* November 20, 2006.

124. Lolly Bowean, "Former Cook Official Guilty: Ex-Commissioner Accepts Plea Deal, Could Do 17 Years," *Chicago Tribune,* July 2, 2013.

125. Robert Herguth, Patrick Rehkamp, and Dane Placko, "Dorothy's Deed, Done Dirt Cheap," Better Government Association and Fox 32 TV, November 25, 2013.

126. Ibid.

127. Dan Mihalopoulos and Frank Main, "Organizer of Fund-raiser Has Ties to Clerk, Former New Orleans Mayor," *Chicago Sun-Times,* January 21, 2013.

128. Ibid.

129. "Ex-N.O. Mayor's Bribery Trial Postponed until Jan," *Associated Press: Louisiana State Wire,* October 24, 2013.

130. Kathy Finn, "Former New Orleans Mayor Found Guilty," *Chicago Tribune,* February 13, 2014.

131. Andy Shaw and the BGA, "Reform Spotlight Doing Some Good," *Chicago Sun-Times,* February 17, 2013.

132. Robert Herguth, Patrick Rehkamp, and Dane Placko, "Dorothy's Deed, Done Dirt Cheap," Better Government Association and Fox 32 TV, November 25, 2013.

133. Mitch Smith, "Ex-Revenue Inspector Admits to Extortion," *Chicago Tribune,* June 31, 2013; Jason Meisner, "Sheriff's Officer Caught in Bribery Sting, Gets 2 ½ Years," *Chicago Tribune,* November 20, 2013; Kim Janssen, "Prosecutors: Worker Took $10,000 in Bribes," *Chicago Sun-Times,* November 1, 2013; Jason Meisner, "Board of Review Bribery Trial Starts," *Chicago Tribune,* October 22, 2013.

Chapter 7. Suburban Scandals

1. Alex Rodriguez and Andrew Zajac, "Feds Trace Origins of Cicero Plot," *Chicago Tribune,* June 17, 2001.

2. Ibid.

3. Matt O'Connor and Maurice Possley, "For Mob, It's Not Like Bad Old Days," *Chicago Tribune,* August 25, 2002.

4. "New Mob Hierarchy Takes Over Cicero," *Illinois Police and Sheriff's News,* March 26, 1997.

5. William Braden, "Frank Maltese, 63, Former Town Assessor for Cicero," *Chicago Sun-Times,* October 21, 1993.

6. Frank Burgos, "Infelise Guilty on 20 Charges—Jury Split on Murder Conspiracy," *Chicago Sun-Times,* March 11, 1992.

7. Anne Kavanagh, "Trauma Queen," *Chicago,* March 12, 2008, accessed December 20, 2013, http://www.chicagomag.com/Chicago-Magazine/March-2008/Trauma-Queen/.

8. John Fountain, "Town President Is Convicted in Scheme to Steal $12 Million," *New York Times,* August 24, 2002.

9. Randolp Bush and Matt O'Connor, "Loren-Maltese Found Guilty," *Chicago Tribune,* August 24, 2002.

10. Steve Warmbir, Abdon Pallasch, and Annie Sweeney, "Berry Guilty in Cicero Scam," *Chicago Sun-Times,* August 24, 2002.

11. Matt O'Connor, "Northlake's Ex-Cop Chief Admits He Took Payoff," *Chicago Tribune,* February 7, 1997.

12. Matt O'Connor, "Ex-Stone Park Mayor Gets 1 ½ Years," *Chicago Tribune,* January 12, 2002.

13. Matt O'Connor, "Ex-Official Gets Praise, 20 Months," *Chicago Tribune,* July 4, 1991.

14. Matt O'Connor, "Ex-Cop Admits Role in Mob Payoffs," *Chicago Tribune,* February 13, 2002.

15. Rob Olmstead, "Mayor Met with Mob, FBI Says," *Daily Herald,* July 18, 2005.

16. Shamus Toomey, "Gaming Board Memo Links Rosemont to Mob," *Chicago Sun-Times,* May 17, 2004.

17. Ibid.

18. Ray Gibson, "Striking It Rich in Rosemont," *Chicago Tribune,* May 27, 1990.

19. Ibid.

20. Michael Higgins, "Stephens' Wife Gets Rosemont Contracts," *Chicago Tribune,* September 6, 2001; Michael Higgins, "Village to Pay More on Contracts with Firm Run by Stephens' Son," *Chicago Tribune,* February 15, 2001.

21. Jake Griffin, "Family Connections in Rosemont Net $2 Million in Pay," *Daily Herald,* August 31, 2011.

22. Ibid.

23. Linnet Myers, "'Mayor Daley of Waukegan' Back to Show 'em Who's Boss," *Chicago Tribune,* June 9, 1985; Tom Rybarczyk, "Dolton Hires Mayor's Brother to Fight Graft," *Chicago Tribune,* May 5, 2006; Carmen Greco, "Orland Hills Mayor Appoints Son to Village Board," *Southtown Star,* November 5, 2010; and Joseph Ryan, "Lyons Mayor Appoints His Father, a Felon, to Zoning Board," *Chicago Tribune,* July 18, 2011.

24. Steve Warmbir, "Cicero President Admits He Put Nearly Two Dozen Family Members on Town Payroll," *Chicago Sun-Times,* July 7, 2011.

25. Dave McKinney, "Former Suburban Police Chief Gets 5 Years," *Chicago Sun-Times,* May 2, 2014, 13.

26. Mary Sue Penn, "2 Suburb Cops Guilty in Drug Conspiracy," *Chicago Tribune,* August 4, 1992.

27. Ibid.

28. Robert Becker, "Chicago Heights Cop Convicted," *Chicago Tribune,* May 17, 1994.

29. Ibid.

30. John Gorman, "Lyons Cops Plead Guilty to Protecting Strip Joint," *Chicago Tribune,* March 2, 1990.

31. John O'Brien, "Harvey Cops Accused of Forays in Suburbs," *Chicago Tribune,* February 10, 1985.

32. Matthew Walberg, "FBI Raids Harvey Police Headquarters," *Chicago Tribune,* December 6, 2008.

33. Jolie Lee, "Melrose Park's Ex-Chief Guilty," *Chicago Sun-Times,* June 2, 2009; "Former Melrose Park Police Chief Vito Scavo Guilty of Racketeering and Extortion," *Chicago Tribune,* June 2, 2009.

34. Frank Main, "Dolton Badges Tarnished?" *Chicago Sun-Times,* April 26, 2002.

35. Frank Main, "Drug Dealer Testifies Shaw Sold Him Badge—Dolton Mayor Says Testimony in Cops' Trial 'Totally Untrue,'" *Chicago Sun-Times,* April 25, 2002.

36. Frank Main, "Harvey's Armed Marshals Accused of Breaking Law—Lack of Training Puts Them in Violation, State Official Says," *Chicago Sun-Times,* January 15, 2011.

37. Azam Ahmed and Kristen Kridel, "Ex-Niles Mayor Pleads Guilty in Kickback Scheme," *Chicago Tribune,* November 2, 2008.

38. Ibid.

39. Tom Robb, "Perks Aplenty: Niles Records Detail Hand Outs of Cash Bonuses, Vehicles to Ex-Village Employees," *Des Plaines Journal and Topics,* June 15, 2012.

40. Kim Jansen and Lauren Fitzpatrick, "School Officials Allegedly Bribe with Cash, Strip Club Visits," *Chicago Sun-Times,* April 29, 2014, 6.

41. Robert Davis, "4 Former Hoffman Estates Officials Get Prison in Bribes," *Chicago Tribune,* December 19, 1973. Similar schemes in Lyons and Berwyn were also reported. See, for instance, Joseph Ryan, "Lyons Mayor Appoints His Father, a Felon, to Zoning Board," *Chicago Tribune,* July 18, 2011; and Michael Higgins, "Ex-Berwyn Aide Guilty of Bribery," *Chicago Tribune,* May 20, 2006.

42. Gary Wisby, "FBI Seeking Arlington Heights Treasurer in Investment Ploy," *Chicago Sun-Times,* May 8, 1987; Art Petaque, "$5 Million Rip Off? Arlington Hts. Still Toting Up Ex-Aide's Take," *Chicago Sun-Times,* June 7, 1987.

43. Joe Mahr and Joseph Ryan, "Soccer Ball and Chain," *Chicago Tribune,* June 10, 2012, 18.

44. Ibid.

45. Joe Mahr and Joseph Ryan, "Some Firms Faced Little Competition on Contracts," *Chicago Tribune,* June 10, 2012, 19.

46. Joe Mahr and Joseph Ryan, "Soccer Ball and Chain," *Chicago Tribune,* June 10, 2012, 18.

47. Wynn Koebel Foster, "Landek to Resign Lyons Township Post," *The Doings,* May 12, 2011, 18.

48. "Big Stink in Little Burnham," editorial, *Chicago Tribune,* May 14, 2014, 22; Jason Meisner, "Ex-Burnham Clerk Admits Stealing $700K, Gambling," *Chicago Tribune,* May 23, 2014, 11.

49. Terry Wilson, "Ex-Dixmoor Parks Chief Admits Role in Graft," *Chicago Tribune,* June 4, 1998.

50. Ibid.

51. Ibid.

52. Anthony Colarossi, "Settlement Offered in Failed Dixmoor Park District Case," *Chicago Tribune,* September 1, 1999.

53. Matt O'Connor, "2 Plead Guilty in Selling of Park Police Badges," *Chicago Tribune,* July 19, 2001.

54. Patrick Waldron, "Ex-official Admits Stealing," *Daily Herald,* March 13, 2004; Dawn Rhodes, "Posen Official Gets Six Years in Prison for Embezzlement," *Chicago Tribune,* August 3, 2010; Lauren FitzPatrick, "Former Maywood Housing Agency Head Charged with Theft," *Chicago Sun-Times,* July 27, 2011.

55. Thomas Burton, "Guilty Plea in Scheme at Triton," *Chicago Tribune,* May 29, 1985.

56. Kris Brunst, "Former D88 Head to Be Sentenced Dec. 17," *Melrose Park Herald,* December 4, 1996.

57. Becky Schlikermand and Stephano Esposito, "CPS Tech Coordinator Stole $400,000," *Chicago Sun-Times,* January 4, 2014, 4; and Noreen S. Ahmed-Uliah and Steve Mills, "Employee Bilked CPS for $420K, Report Says," *Chicago Tribune,* January 4, 2014, 1–2.

58. Phil Kadner, "Couple Goes from Civic Leaders to Accused Felons," *Chicago Sun-Times,* December 20, 2013, 27; "Couple Charged with Stealing $350,000 in Public Money," CBS Chicago, December 13, 2013, accessed December 20, 2013, http://chicago.cbslocal .com/2013/12/19/couple-charged-with-stealing-350000-in-public-money/.

59. Matthew Walberg and Joseph Ryan, "Sheriff Expands Power in Suburbs," *Chicago Sun-Times,* June 14, 2013, 8.

60. "Gaming Board Picks Right Place for Casino," *Chicago Sun-Times,* December 24, 2008.

61. Chris Fusco, "Feds, Others Scrutinize Des Plaines' Ties to Ex-Undersheriff," *Chicago Sun-Times,* November 17, 2004.

62. Chris Fusco, "Des Plaines Fires Marketing Firm," *Chicago Sun-Times,* August 25, 2004.

63. Chris Fusco, "Feds, Others Scrutinize Des Plaines' Ties to Ex-Undersheriff," *Chicago Sun-Times,* November 17, 2004.

64. Ames Boykin, "Des Plaines Tackles Ethics, Sets Aside Censure Rule Cell-Phone Use by Aldermen, Signs in Council Chambers Both Put Off," *Daily Herald,* April 4, 2007.

65. Ibid.

Chapter 8. Police Abuse and Corruption

1. Rummana Hussain, "Cop Guilty in Bar Beating," *Chicago Sun-Times,* June 3, 2009.

2. Annie Sweeney and Jason Meisner, "Cop Cover-up Found in Bartender Beating," *Chicago Tribune,* November 14, 2012.

3. David Heinzmann and Carlos Sadovi, "City Cop Caught on Video Beating Woman Bartender," *Chicago Tribune,* March 22, 2007.

4. Frank Main, Eric Herman, and Lisa Donovan, "Badge of Dishonor: Cop in Video Attack Allegedly Tried to Bribe, Threaten Woman Following Savage Beating," *Chicago Sun-Times,* March 22, 2007.

5. Annie Sweeney and Jason Meisner, "Cop Cover-up Found in Bartender Beating," *Chicago Tribune,* November 14, 2012.

6. "Camera Catches Officer Beating Bartender," *Associated Press,* March 21, 2007.

7. Frank Main and Eric Herman, "Did 2nd Cop Try to Silence Bartender?" *Chicago Sun-Times,* March 23, 2007.

8. Rummana Hussain, "Cop Guilty in Bar Beating," *Chicago Sun-Times,* June 3, 2009.

9. Rummana Hussain, "Beat Cop Avoids Jail—Bartender Victim Says, 'My World Still Feels Changed Because of This Beating,'" *Chicago Sun-Times,* June 24, 2009.

10. Ibid.

11. Kim Janssen, "$850,000 Verdict for Bartender Beaten by Ex-Cop; We Proved a Code of Silence," *Chicago Sun-Times,* November 14, 2012.

12. Kim Janssen and Fran Spielman, "City to Give Fast Cash for No Judgement," *Chicago Sun-Times,* December 5, 2012; Jason Meisner, "City, Lawyers Clash over Abbate Case," *Chicago Tribune,* December 8, 2012.

13. Art Golab, "Judge Won't Set Aside 'Code of Silence' Ruling," *Chicago Sun-Times,* December 21, 2012.

14. John Hagedorn et al., *Crime, Corruption, and Cover-ups in the Chicago Police Department, Anti-Corruption Report No. 7* (Chicago: University of Illinois at Chicago, Department of Political Science, January 17, 2013, accessed June 23, 2014, http://www.uic.edu/depts/pols/ChicagoPolitics/policecorruption.pdf.

15. Hal Dardick and John Byrne, "Reparations Urged for Burge Victims," *Chicago Tribune,* October 17, 2013.

16. Ibid.

17. Timeline information prepared by Students for Human Rights at the University of Chicago, based on material from the People's Law Office.

18. The People's Law Office is a Chicago law firm known for its civil-rights and police-brutality litigation.

19. John Conroy, "House of Screams; Torture by Electroshock: Could It Happen in a Chicago Police Station? Did It Happen at Area 2?" *Chicago Reader,* January 25, 1990, accessed May 30, 2014, http://www.chicagoreader.com/chicago/house-of-screams/Content?oid=875107.

20. David Jackson, "13 Years of Cop Torture Alleged; Daley, Martin Rip Internal Police Reports," *Chicago Tribune,* February 8, 1992.

21. Qtd. in ibid.

22. Charles Nicodemus, "Burge Fired in Torture Case; Guilty of Abusing '82 Murder Suspect," *Chicago Sun-Times,* February 11, 1993.

23. Jodi Rudoren, "Inquiry Finds Police Abuse, but Says Law Bars Trials," *New York Times,* July 20, 2006.

24. *United States of America v. Jon Burge,* Special February 2008-2 Grand Jury, U.S. District Court, Northern District of Illinois, Eastern Division (print copy obtained from court).

25. United States Attorney for the Northern District of Illinois, "U.S. Indicts Former Chicago Police Cmdr. Jon Burge on Perjury, Obstructing of Justice Charges Related to Alleged Torture and Physical Abuse by Burge and Others," Official News Release, October 21, 2008.

26. Matthew Walberg and William Lee, "Guilty in Torture Trial: Jury Finds Burge Committed Perjury When He Denied Abuse Allegations," *Chicago Tribune,* June 29, 2010.

27. Illinois Coalition Against Torture (ICAT), "Transcript of Judge Joan Lefkow's Sentencing of Jon Burge," January 26, 2011, accessed June 23, 2014, http://illinoiscat.org/2011/01/26/transcript-of-judge-joan-lefkow-at-jon-burge-sentencing/.

28. Hal Dardick and John Byrne, "Mayor: 'Sorry' for Burge Era: Emanuel Offers Apology as City Pays 2 Victims," *Chicago Tribune,* September 12, 2013.

29. Fran Spielman and Tina Sfondeles, "Rahm: 'Sorry' for Burge Torture," *Chicago Sun-Times,* September 12, 2013.

30. Bob Wiedrich, "DiLeonardi Charges Top City Official Fronted for D'Arco," *Chicago Tribune,* April 20, 1980.

31. Steve Mills and Andrew Martin, "Rodriguez's Friendship with Felon Violates Rule," *Chicago Tribune,* November 14, 1997.

32. Andrew Martin and Steve Mills, "Rodriguez Says He'll Retire; Police Superintendent Cites Cumulative Woes," *Chicago Tribune,* November 14, 1997.

33. David Jackson, "Connections Cast Pall over Homicide Probe; Police Integrity Questioned in Exec's Slaying," *Chicago Tribune,* October 23, 2000.

34. Ibid.

35. Ibid.

36. Matt O'Connor, "Hanhardt Guilty Plea Caps Fall from Grace," *Chicago Tribune,* October 26, 2001.

37. Steve Warmbir, "News," *Chicago Sun-Times,* October 25, 2001.

38. "William Hanhardt's Rise and Fall," *Chicago Sun-Times,* October 26, 2001.

39. Abdon M. Pallasch, "One Pleads Guilty in Cop's Alleged Ring of Jewel Theft," *Chicago Sun-Times,* August 25, 2001.

40. Matt O'Connor, "Hanhardt Guilty Plea Caps Fall from Grace," *Chicago Tribune,* October 26, 2001.

41. Tim Novak, "Feds Keep 25 Percent of Crooked Ex-Cop's Pension," *Chicago Sun-Times,* September 22, 2009.

42. John Kass, "Paging 'Doctor' for a Case of Loose Lips," *Chicago Tribune,* August 23, 2007.

43. Jeff Coen, "5 Guilty in Outfit Trial," *Chicago Tribune*, September 11, 2007.

44. Emily Ngo, "Steamwood Man Charged in Organized Crime Bust Dies," *Arlington Heights (Ill.) Daily Herald*, January 20, 2006.

45. Robert Mitchum, "Marquette 10 Reference Key, FBI Agent Says," *Chicago Tribune*, April 15, 2009.

46. John Kass, "Ex-Marshal Goes to Prison, and Corrupt Ex-Cop Vacations," *Chicago Tribune*, October 28, 2009.

47. Chris Fusco and Natasha Korecki, "U.S. Marshal Gets 4 Years," *Chicago Sun-Times*, October 28, 2009.

48. Richard Lindberg, *To Serve and Collect* (Carbondale: Southern Illinois University Press, 2008), 296–305.

49. Ibid.

50. Ibid.

51. Len O'Connor, *Clout: Mayor Daley and His City* (Chicago: Henry Regnery Co., 1975), 170–75.

52. Robert Davis and John O'Brien, "Captain, 23 More Cops Indicted in Shakedowns," *Chicago Tribune*, December 30, 1972.

53. Richard Phillips, "Fired Cop Pleads Guilty to Payoffs," *Chicago Tribune*, February 5, 1974; Richard Phillips, "Ex-Cop Gets 3 ½-Year Term in Austin Tavern Extortion," *Chicago Tribune*, February 12, 1974.

54. Joseph Sjostrom and Jerry Thornton, "Ex-cop Commander Killed; Tavern Shakedown Figure," *Chicago Tribune*, July 23, 1977.

55. Richard Lindberg, *Return to the Scene of the Crime* (Nashville: Cumberland House, 1999), 215.

56. Joseph Sjostrom and Jerry Thornton, "Ex-cop Commander Killed; Tavern Shakedown Figure," *Chicago Tribune*, July 23, 1977.

57. Ibid.

58. Hagedorn et al., *Crime, Corruption, and Cover-ups in the Chicago Police Department*.

59. William Crawford, "City Cop Scandal; 10 Charged with Accepting Pushers' Bribes," *Chicago Tribune*, November 13, 1981.

60. Ibid.

61. Philip Wattley, "Tip by a Fellow Officer Led to Cop Drug Probe," *Chicago Tribune*, June 13, 1982.

62. Rudolph Unger, "3 City Cops, Wife of One Indicted on Drug Charges," *Chicago Tribune*, July 14, 1982.

63. Robert Blau and John Gorman, "A District Betrayed; 12 Cops Indicted," *Chicago Tribune*, October 14, 1988.

64. Adrienne Drell and Art Petacque, "'Bag Lady' Plays Key Role in Exposing Cop Bribe Ring," *Chicago Sun-Times*, October 14, 1988.

65. Ibid.

66. Adrienne Drell, "Cop Kept Her Cool Undercover; Even as Mate Suspected Her of Infidelity," *Chicago Sun-Times*, January 14, 1990.

67. Frank Main and Carol Marin, "4 Elite Chicago Cops Arrested: Each Could Face Terms of up to 30 Years," *Chicago Sun-Times*, September 8, 2006.

68. Frank Main and Eric Herman, "Corruption Probe Nets 3 More Cops: Join 4 Others Charged from Elite Unit," *Chicago Sun-Times,* December 5, 2006.

69. U.S. Attorney for the Northern District of Illinois, "Suspended Chicago Police Officers Arrested on Federal Charge of Planning Murder-for-Hire of Fellow Officer," official news release, September 26, 2007.

70. Rummana Hussain, "4 Ex-SOS Cops Get 6 Months Apiece in Shakedown Scheme— Officers Agree to Cooperate as Probe Targets Others," *Chicago Sun-Times,* September 19, 2009.

71. Matthew Walberg, "1st Guilty Pleas in Cop Scandal," *Chicago Tribune,* September 20, 2009.

72. Annie Sweeney, "Rogue Officer Gets 12 Years," *Chicago Tribune,* September 9, 2011.

73. Cam Simpson, "Cop Faces More Charges; Allegedly Betrayed Undercover Police," *Chicago Sun-Times,* April 9, 1999.

74. Todd Lightly, "U.S. Indicts Cop as Drug Kingpin; Prosecutors Say 22-Year Police Vet Not Only Gave Protection to a Drug Ring, He Took It Over," *Chicago Tribune,* April 9, 1999.

75. Todd Lightly and Matt O'Connor, "'Most Corrupt' Cop Guilty; Veteran Officer Ran Cocaine Ring," *Chicago Tribune,* April 24, 2001.

76. Ibid.

77. Todd Lightly, "Former Cop Crossed the Line, Destroyed It; He Vacationed with Drug Dealers, Sold Them Arms, Talked Too Much," *Chicago Tribune,* January 19, 2003.

78. Todd Lightly and Matt O'Connor, "Rogue Cop Gets Life; Drug Ring Leader Called Betrayer of Society, Honest Police," *Chicago Tribune,* January 25, 2003; Steve Warmbir, "Mistress of Convicted Cop Gets 30 Years in Cocaine Ring," *Chicago Sun-Times,* February 8, 2003.

79. Todd Lightly, "Former Cop Crossed the Line, Destroyed It; He Vacationed with Drug Dealers, Sold Them Arms, Talked Too Much," *Chicago Tribune,* January 19, 2003.

80. Michele Campbell and Michael Gillis, "7 W. Side Officers Held in Drug Sting; Charged with Conspiracy to Commit Robbery, Extortion," *Chicago Sun-Times,* December 21, 1996.

81. Michael Gillis, "New Counts Leveled vs. Austin Cop," *Chicago Sun-Times,* May 16, 1997.

82. Matt O'Connor, "4 Austin Officers Convicted, Face Stiff Prison Sentences," *Chicago Tribune,* May 22, 1998.

83. Ibid.

84. U.S. Attorney for the Northern District of Illinois, official news release, November 29, 2012.

85. Frank Main and Dan Mihalopoulos, "Cop-Turned-Snitch Charged in Tow-Truck Scam," *Chicago Sun-Times,* January 29, 2013.

86. Ibid.

87. Jason Meisner, "Ex-Hendon Aide Gets Probation," *Chicago Tribune,* January 25, 2014.

88. Diana Novak, "Former Cop Pleads Guilty to Extortion in Towing Scam, Selling Weapons to Felon," *Chicago Sun-Times,* April 22, 2013.

89. Naomi Nix, "Veteran Cop Pleads Guilty to Tow Scam," *Chicago Tribune,* July 27, 2012.

90. Jeff Danna, "Towing Scam Gets Ex-Cop 2 Years," *Chicago Tribune,* June 19, 2012.

91. Steve Warmbir and Tim Novak, "Ex-Criminals behind the Wheel of City's Police Tow Trucks," *Chicago Sun-Times,* November 11, 2004.

92. Ibid.

93. Fran Spielman, "City Awards Clout-Heavy Firm Towing Contract, Again—Company Linked to Daley Pal Has Held Job for 20 Years," *Chicago Sun-Times,* February 2, 2010.

94. Jay Branegan, "Ald. Roti's Son Pleads Guilty in Motor Pool Fraud," *Chicago Tribune,* January 20, 1981.

95. Joseph Sjostrom, "7 Guilty in Police Motor Pool Fraud," *Chicago Tribune,* February 27, 1981.

96. Andy Knott, "Relatives of Key Byrne Aides Go on City Payroll," *Chicago Tribune,* April 29, 1983.

97. United Press International, "Chicago Chooses a Criminologist to Head and Clean Up the Police," *New York Times,* February 23, 1960, accessed June 24, 2014, http://query .nytimes.com/mem/archive-free/pdf?res=9502EFD91F39EF32A25750C2A9649C946191 D6CF.

98. "Chicago Names Police Panel but Refuses a Review Board," *New York Times,* July 26, 1966, accessed June 24, 2014, http://query.nytimes.com/mem/archive-free/pdf?res= 9E02EFDA1030EF30A25755C2A9619C946791D6CF.

99. "Conlisk Warns on Corruption," *Chicago Tribune,* December 6, 1967.

100. Ralph Knoohuizen, *Public Access to Police Information Chicago Law Enforcement Study Group Report* (Chicago: Chicago Law Enforcement Study Group, 1974).

101. Human Rights Watch, "Shielded from Justice, Police Brutality and Accountability in the United States," June 1998, accessed January 27, 2014, www.columbia.edu/itc/journalism/ cases/katrina/Human%20Rights%20Watch/uspohtml/usp055.htm#TopOfPage.

102. John Conroy, "Town without Pity," *Chicago Reader,* January 11, 1996.

103. Craig H. Futterman, Melissa Mather, and Melanie Miles, "The Use of Statistical Evidence to Address Police Supervisory and Disciplinary Practices: The Chicago Police Department's Broken System," *DePaul Journal for Social Justice* 1.2 (2008): 251–91.

104. Independent Police Review Authority, *Annual Report 2007–2008* (Chicago: City of Chicago, 2008).

105. Tracy Siska and Sherie Arriazola, "Chicago Police Board: A Ten-Year Analysis," Chicago Justice Project, December 14, 2009, accessed June 2, 2014, http://www.chicagojustice .org/research/long-form-reports/chicago-police-board-a-ten-year-analysis.

106. Mick Dumke, "Chicago Forks over More Money in Lawsuits—Especially Lawsuits against Police," *Chicago Reader,* November 27, 2008.

107. Ibid.

108. People's Law Office, "Summary of Documented City and County Expenditures in Burge Torture Scandal," March 25, 2013, accessed June 24, 2014, http://peopleslawoffice .com/wp-content/uploads/2014/01/1.6.14.Latest-SUMMARY-OF-DOCUMENTED-CITY -COUNTY-AND-STATE-EXPENDITURES-IN-BURGE-TORTURE-SCANDAL.pdf.

109. Don Babwin, "Chicago Police Misconduct Settlements Surge as the City Pays Out Millions in Taxpayer Dollars," *Associated Press,* March 14, 2013.

110. Annie Sweeney and Jason Meisner, "Jury Finds in Favor of Bartender in Cop Bar Beating Case, Justice Was Served," *Chicago Tribune,* November 14, 2012.

111. Fran Spielman, "Council Approves Settlement for Unarmed Man Shot by Cop," *Chicago Sun-Times,* February 14, 2013.

112. Fran Spielman, "3 More Settlements in Cop Cases," *Chicago Sun-Times,* March 12, 2013.

113. Adrienne Drell, "City Ordered to Pay $51,000 to Victims of Red Squad Spying," *Chicago Sun-Times,* January 1, 1986.

Chapter 9. Jailbird Judges and Crooked Courts

1. Maurice Possley, "Lack of Tip-off Riled Judge, Jury Told," *Chicago Tribune,* May 24, 1985.

2. George Estep and Maurice Possley, "LeFevour: Innovative, Funny—and Now in Trouble," *Chicago Tribune,* November 15, 1984.

3. James Tuohy and Rob Warden, *Greylord: Justice Chicago Style* (New York: G. P. Putnam's Sons, 1989), 26.

4. Ibid., 26–27.

5. Ibid., 28–30.

6. Ibid., 171.

7. Maurice Possley and William B. Crawford Jr., "Judge LeFevour, 7 Others Indicted," *Chicago Tribune,* November 15, 1984.

8. Ibid.

9. Maurice Possley, "LeFevour Billed as a Big Spender," *Chicago Tribune,* May 31, 1985.

10. Webb had earlier resigned his position as U.S. Attorney to go into private practice but came back to lead the prosecution team for LeFevour's trial.

11. Maurice Possley, "Webb Tears into LeFevour; Judge 'Peddled Justice,' Prosecutor Charges," *Chicago Tribune,* July 13, 1985.

12. Maurice Possley, "LeFevour Convicted in Greylord," *Chicago Tribune,* July 14, 1985.

13. Maurice Possley, "LeFevour Gets 12-Year Term," *Chicago Tribune,* August 28, 1985.

14. Tuohy and Warden, *Greylord,* 252.

15. Irv Kupcinet, "Kup's Column," *Chicago Sun-Times,* January 15, 1997.

16. Ibid.

17. Tuohy and Warden, *Greylord,* 31.

18. William Crawford Jr. and Marianne Taylor, "Greylord Ax Falls on 9," *Chicago Tribune,* December 15, 1983.

19. Maurice Possley, "Greylord Judge Pleads Guilty; Olson Took Bribes from Attorney," *Chicago Tribune,* July 19, 1985.

20. Ibid.

21. Tuohy and Warden, *Greylord,* 209.

22. Ibid., 209.

23. Ibid., 210.

24. Ibid., 211.

25. Ibid. 213.

26. Maurice Possley, "Judge Indicted in Bribery Scheme," *Chicago Tribune,* May 2, 1985.

27. William B. Crawford Jr., "Greylord Jury Convicts Holzer," *Chicago Tribune,* February 19, 1986.

28. Ibid.

29. William B. Crawford Jr., "Holzer Gets a Bit of a Lift on Appeal," *Chicago Tribune,* February 20, 1988.

30. Touhy and Warden, *Greylord,* 259.

31. Pleading guilty were Martin Hogan, John Laurie, Francis Maher, John McCollom, Joseph McDermott, John McDonnell, Michael McNulty, John Murphy, John Reynolds, Frank Salerno, Roger Seaman, and Raymond Sodini.

32. Anne Keegan, "Inside Greylord," *Chicago Tribune,* December 17, 1989.

33. John R. Waltz, Rev. of *Operation Greylord: Brocton Lockwood's Story,* by Brocton Lockwood, Harlan Mendenhall, and Peter Manikas, *Chicago Tribune,* January 7, 1990.

34. "FBI Finds 'Justice' Is a Bargain," *Chicago Tribune,* August 11, 1983.

35. William Recktenwald, "Downstate Judges Lend Hand in Chicago," *Chicago Tribune,* August 22, 1983.

36. Adrienne Drell, "Rep. DeLeo Indicted in Greylord," *Chicago Sun-Times,* July 20, 1989.

37. William B. Crawford Jr. and Marianne Taylor, "Greylord Ax Falls on 9," *Chicago Tribune,* December 15, 1983.

38. Robert Cooley and Hillel Levin, *When Corruption Was King* (New York: Carroll and Graf, 2004), 5.

39. Maurice Possley and Ray Gibson, "Informant Says Life as Fixer Got to Him," *Chicago Tribune,* August 17, 1997.

40. Cooley and Levin, *When Corruption Was King,* 174–77.

41. Ibid., 177.

42. Rosalind Rossi, "Guilt Made Me a Mole, Lawyer Says," *Chicago Sun-Times,* August 24, 1991.

43. James Strong and John O'Brien, "FBI Camera Found at Politicians' Hangout," *Chicago Tribune,* July 13, 1989.

44. Ibid.

45. Cooley and Levin, *When Corruption Was King,* 117.

46. Harlan Draeger and William Braden, "U.S. Indicts Roti, Marcy, and D'Arco; Shields, DeLeo Also Accused in 1st Ward Probe," *Chicago Sun-Times,* December 19, 1990.

47. Rosalind Rossi, "5 Indicted by U.S. in 1st Ward Probe," *Chicago Sun-Times,* December 20, 1990.

48. Lee Strobel, "Aleman Gets 30-Yr. Term," *Chicago Tribune,* January 17, 1978.

49. Draeger and Braden, "U.S. Indicts Roti, Marcy, and D'Arco; Shields, DeLeo Also Accused in 1st Ward Probe," *Chicago Sun-Times,* December 19, 1990.

50. Rosalind Rossi, "Ex-judge Shields Guilty of Bribery; Jurors Also Convict Lawyer Pat De Leo," *Chicago Sun-Times,* September 24, 1991.

51. Rosalind Rossi, "D'Arco Guilty in Bribe Case," *Chicago Sun-Times,* December 7, 1991.

52. Matt O'Connor, "Roti Joins Aldermen's Hall of Shame," *Chicago Tribune,* January 16, 1993.

53. Rosalind Rossi, "Fred Roti Guilty on 11 Counts," *Chicago Sun-Times,* January 15, 1993.

54. Gary Washburn, "Fred Roti: 1920–1999," *Chicago Tribune,* September 21, 1999.

55. Tom Seibel, "Pat Marcy Dies; 1st Ward Power Linked to Mob," *Chicago Sun-Times,* March 14, 1993.

56. Matt O'Connor, "Judge Maloney Found Guilty in Corruption Case," *Chicago Tribune,* April 17, 1993.

57. Ibid.

58. Trevor Jensen, "Thomas J. Maloney: 1925–2008," *Chicago Tribune,* October 22, 2008.

59. Maurice Possley and Ray Gibson, "Informant Says Life as Fixer Got to Him," *Chicago Tribune,* August 17, 1997.

60. Lorraine Forte, "Hit Man Convicted—Aleman's '77 Trial Ended in Acquittal," *Chicago Sun-Times,* October 1, 1997; Lorraine Forte, "100-Year Sentence for Aleman; No Mercy for Hit Man in '72 Murder," *Chicago Sun-Times,* November 26, 1997.

61. Robert Herguth, "Mob Hit Man Harry Aleman Dies in Downstate Prison," *Chicago Sun-Times,* May 16, 2010.

62. Qtd. in David Jackson, "'A Death Wish'; Because of an Ex-Corrupt Attorney with a Near-Photographic Memory, We Live in a Different City. But His Life, He Says, 'Is Over,'" *Chicago Tribune,* August 20, 2004.

63. Abdon M. Pallasch, "Lawyers Aspiring to be Cook County Judges Lay It on Thick," *Chicago Sun-Times,* November 5, 2011; and Dick Simpson, "Judicial Elections," *Chicago Journal,* January 20, 2011.

64. Steve Mills, "Judicial Hopefuls Hire Pros for Votes," *Chicago Tribune,* May 22, 2003.

65. Jeff Coen and Todd Lightly, "Defeated Judges Find Way Back to Bench," *Chicago Tribune,* December 23, 2012.

66. Jeff Coen and Todd Lightly, "How Law Clerk Became a Judge," *Chicago Tribune,* March 7, 2013.

67. Jeff Coen and Todd Lightly, "Madigan's List: The Selection of Cook County Associate Judges Is Supposed to be Based on Merit. That Doesn't Stop House Speaker Michael Madigan and Others from Having Their Say-So," *Chicago Tribune,* April 17, 2011.

68. Abdon M. Pallasch, "Illinois Court Asked to Review Alleged Bias by Justice," *Chicago Sun-Times,* September 15, 2011.

69. "Ethics? Ethics? Now Where Did We Put Those," editorial, *St. Louis Post-Dispatch,* March 11, 2006.

70. Matt O'Connor and Robert Becker, "Judge Indicted on Federal Charges," *Chicago Tribune,* May 5, 2000.

71. "Judge Pleads Guilty to Tax Evasion, Currency Violation," *Joliet Herald News,* March 6, 2002.

72. Tim Novak and Chris Fusco, "Questions over R.J.'s Judge," *Chicago Sun-Times,* December 11, 2012.

73. Ibid.

74. Chris Fusco and Tim Novak, "Chief Judge: Case Needs Outsider," *Chicago Sun-Times,* December 18, 2012.

75. Chris Fusco and Tim Novak, "New Vanecko Judge: 'I Do Not Know Anyone Involved,'" *Chicago Sun-Times*, January 19, 2013.

76. Mark Brown, "Judge Should Step Down—or Explain Why Not," *Chicago Sun-Times*, May 15, 2013.

77. Tim Novak and Chris Fusco, "Daley Nephew Charged in Koschman Killing; Vanecko Judge Has Link to Old Daley Machine," *Chicago Sun-Times*, March 11, 2013.

78. Ibid.

79. Ibid.

80. "Judge Should Step Aside," editiorial, *Chicago Sun-Times*, May 20, 2013.

81. "Step Aside, Judge," editorial, *Chicago Sun-Times*, March 12, 2013.

Chapter 10. Congressional Corruption

1. Richard E. Cohen, *Rostenkowski: The Pursuit of Power and the End of the Old Politics* (Chicago: Ivan R. Dee, 1999), 249; James L. Merriner, *Mr. Chairman: Power in Dan Rostenkowski's America* (Carbondale: Southern Illinois University Press, 1999), 259–60.

2. Merriner, *Mr. Chairman*, 259.

3. "Indictment: United States of America v. Daniel D. Rostenkowski," U.S. District Court, District of Columbia, May 31, 1994.

4. Kenneth J. Cooper and Michael York, "Rostenkowski Subpoenaed; Postal Probers Summon 3 Lawmakers, 2 Aides," *Washington Post*, May 15, 1992.

5. David Johnston, "House Post Office Inquiry Examines Cash Outlays," *New York Times*, May 29, 1992.

6. Basil Talbot and Michael Briggs, "Rosty Stamp Spree Probed—$17,500 in Postal Charges to Office," *Chicago Sun-Times*, May 16, 1992.

7. Elaine S. Povich and Christopher Drew, "U.S. Subpoenas Rostenkowski's Records," *Chicago Tribune*, May 15, 1992.

8. Basil Talbot and Michael Briggs, "Rosty in Clear, Prober Suggests—Sees No Wrongdoing in Post Office Case," *Chicago Sun-Times*, May 22, 1992.

9. Michael Briggs, "Top Rosty Aides Subpoenaed in Post Office Probe," *Chicago Sun-Times*, December 24, 1992.

10. Chuck Neubauer, "Rosty's Phantom Office; Campaign Fund Pays Him Rent," *Chicago Sun-Times*, December 13, 1992.

11. Chuck Neubauer and Mark Brown, "Rosty's Car Trouble; Vehicle Records Raise Questions," *Chicago Sun-Times*, January 24, 1993.

12. Associated Press, "Reno Urges Full Probe of Rostenkowski; 'Full Steam Ahead' Investigators Are Told," *Washington Post*, April 14, 1993.

13. Paul M. Rodriquez, "Rostenkowski Records Sought—Subpoena Includes Files of Friend of Congressman's," *Washington Times*, April 30, 1993.

14. Kenneth J. Cooper, "Former Postmaster for House Pleads Guilty in Scandal; Admission of Embezzling Scheme Appears to Threaten Rostenkowski," *Washington Post*, July 20, 1993.

15. Hanke Gratteau and Ellen Warren, "Netsch, Rostenkowski Win; Congressional Stalwart Rolls over Cullerton," *Chicago Tribune*, March 16, 1994.

16. Michael Briggs, "Rosty Indicted; Corruption Charges Involve $685,000," *Chicago Sun-Times*, May 31, 1994.

17. U.S. Department of Justice, U.S. Attorney for the District of Columbia's news release, May 31, 1994.

18. Michael Briggs, "Rosty Hires a New Attorney; Chicagoan Webb Takes Case; Both Vow to Fight All Charges," *Chicago Sun-Times,* June 5, 1994.

19. Ibid.

20. Jan Crawford Greenberg, "Rostenkowski: Case Unconstitutional," *Chicago Tribune,* October 6, 1994.

21. "Tough Call in the 5th: We Endorse Rosty," editorial, *Chicago Sun-Times,* October 16, 1994.

22. "What to Do with Rosty and Reynolds?" editorial, *Chicago Tribune,* October 25, 1994.

23. Michael Briggs, "Ghost Found Guilty in Rosty Pay Case," *Chicago Sun-Times,* November 9, 1995.

24. Lynn Sweet and Basil Talbot, "Rosty Pleads Guilty, Admits to 2 Counts of Fraud, Agrees to 17 Months in Prison," *Chicago Sun-Times,* April 10, 1996.

25. Donald L. Barlett and James B. Steele, "Disguising Those Who Get Tax Breaks," *Philadelphia Inquirer,* April 13, 1988. Rostenkowski also wrote into the law a provision that let North Pier Terminal in Chicago get a twelve-million-dollar tax break benefiting Daniel Crow Searle and two dozen members of the Searle family.

26. *Congressional Record,* September 27, 1986, p. S13870–71, 13907, and 13916; *Congressional Quarterly,* October 18, 1986, p. 2621.

27. Steve Neal, "The Congressman Who Cries Wolf," *Chicago Sun-Times,* March 3, 1993; Lee Bey and Maureen O'Donnell, "A Quiet Mystery Surrounds Marisol," *Chicago Sun-Times,* August 27, 1995.

28. Michael Barone and Grant Ujifusa, *The Almanac of American Politics 1996* (New York: Random House, 1996), 422.

29. Maureen O'Donnell and Lee Bey, "Guilty: Jury Convicts Congressman on All Counts," *Chicago Sun-Times,* August 23, 1995.

30. Michael Sneed and Michael Gillis, "U.S. Rejects Deal with Reynolds," *Chicago Sun-Times,* November 8, 1996.

31. Michael Sneed and Brenda Warner Rotzoll, "Reynolds Beat Me, Wife Says," *Chicago Sun-Times,* November 24, 1996.

32. Matt O'Connor, "Reynolds Found Guilty on 15 of 16 Fraud Counts," *Chicago Tribune,* April 17, 1997.

33. Kate N. Grossman, "Reynolds Sprung, Thanks to Clinton," *Chicago Sun-Times,* January 21, 2001.

34. Curtis Lawrence, "It's Jackson with 88 Percent, vs. 6 Percent for Reynolds," *Chicago Sun-Times,* March 17, 2004.

35. Katherine Skiba, "Reynolds Soon May Depart Zimbabwe," *Chicago Tribune,* February 22, 2014.

36. Kim Geiger and Katherine Skiba, "Reynolds Detained in Africa," *Chicago Tribune,* February 19, 2014. See also "Reynolds Pleads Not Guilty to Porn Charges," *Chicago Tribune,* February 20, 2014.

37. "Libonati, Roland Victor," *Biographical Directory of the U.S. Congress,* accessed June 4, 2014, http://bioguide.congress.gov/scripts/biodisplay.pl?index=L000299.

38. Art Petacque, "Big Al's Pal Unmoved by 'Untouchables,'" *Chicago Sun-Times,* June 7, 1987.

39. Ibid.

40. "Libonati Wins in Congress Race by 8 to 1," *Chicago Daily Tribune,* January 1, 1958.

41. "Libonati, Roland Victor," Ibid.

42. "Libonati Wins in Congress Race by 8 to 1," *Chicago Daily Tribune,* January 1, 1958.

43. Gus Russo, *The Outfit: The Role of Chicago's Underworld in the Shaping of Modern America* (New York: Bloomsbury, 2001), 441.

44. Ibid.

45. Sandy Smith, "4,000 Mobsters under Thumb of Cosa Nostra," *Chicago Sun-Times,* October 6, 1963.

46. The reporter Fred Bayles quoting secretly recorded tapes of Kennedy's phone calls, *Associated Press,* July 5, 1984.

47. Qtd. in Steve Neal, "Reeves' Book on JFK Takes Full Measure of a President," *Chicago Sun-Times,* November 29, 1993.

48. Steve Neal, "Annunzio Reluctantly Coming Home," *Chicago Sun-Times,* December 30, 1991.

49. "Libonati Wins in Congress Race by 8 to 1," *Chicago Daily Tribune,* January 1, 1958.

50. Mark Brown and Chuck Neubauer, "3 on State Board Unaware of Payout," *Chicago Sun-Times,* May 19, 1986.

51. Libonati obituary, *Chicago Sun-Times,* May 28, 1991.

52. "Hint Governor Orders Labor Chief to Quit," *Chicago Daily Tribune,* February 27, 1952.

53. Johnson Kanady, "Annunzio Fired from Labor Job by Stevenson," *Chicago Daily Tribune,* March 8, 1952; Robert Cooley, *When Corruption Was King* (New York: Carroll and Graf, 1971), 108.

54. "Disbarment Action Urged against Tisci," *Chicago Tribune,* June 30, 1965.

55. "Clearing Corp. Fined $100,000," *Chicago Tribune,* October 20, 1984.

56. Timothy Curry and Lynn Shibut, "The Cost of the Savings and Loan Crisis: Truth and Consequences," *FDIC Banking Review* 13.2 (December 2000): 26–35.

57. Steve Neal, "S&L Sleuth Annunzio Should Use Mirror," *Chicago Sun-Times,* September 17, 1990.

58. Raymond R. Coffey, "Some Pols Still Can't Kick the S&L Habit," *Chicago Sun-Times,* July 22, 1990.

59. Greg Hinz and Donal Quinlan, "Cash, Kin Tie Rep. to S&Ls," *Harlem Foster Times,* August 29, 1990.

60. "S&Ls versus Tax Payers," editorial, *Washington Post,* June 7, 1989.

61. Although the Hyde Amendment over the years has been modified to allow some federal funding of some abortions, it is essentially still in effect in 2014.

62. Lynn Sweet, "Nothing to Hyde; 30-Year-Old Affair Revealed; Lawmaker Not Intimidated," *Chicago Sun-Times,* September 17, 1998.

63. "A Lobbyist's Tale—No Charges in the Parkinson Case," *Washington Post,* August 29, 1981.

64. "Railsback Denies Lobbyist Influence," *Chicago Tribune,* March 7, 1981.

65. Rudy Maxa, "The Paula Parkinson Story," *Washington Post,* March 29, 1981.

66. Douglas Frantz and James Worsham, "Report Bares Dan Crane Sex Scandal," *Chicago Tribune,* July 15, 1983.

67. James Worsham, "Rep. Crane Is Censured," *Chicago Tribune,* July 21, 1983.

68. Jim McGee, "Peace Corps Worker Alleges Rep. Savage Assaulted Her," *Washington Post,* July 19, 1989.

69. Basil Talbot, "Savage Ethics Probe OK'd; Sex Related Inquiries Also Hit Two Others," *Chicago Sun-Times,* August 5, 1989.

70. Michael Briggs and Basil Talbot, "House Panel Drops Savage Ethics Probe," *Chicago Sun-Times,* February 2, 1990.

71. Saundra Torry, "U.S. Drops Probe of Fauntroy in Hiring of Gus Savage's Son," *Chicago Sun-Times,* April 25, 1990; Michael Briggs, "Probe of Savage Son Pushed; Agency Calls for Special Prosecutor," *Chicago Sun-Times,* March 11, 1989; Linda P. Campbell, "Rep. Savage's Son Won't Be Prosecuted," *Chicago Tribune,* May 9, 1990.

72. Statement released by U.S. Attorney Peter J. Fitzgerald, December 9, 2008.

73. Natasha Korecki, Chris Fusco, Lynn Sweet, and Abdon M. Pallasch, "Fund-raiser: Jackson behind $6M Scheme," *Chicago Sun-Times,* September 21, 2010; Natasha Korecki, Abdon M. Pallasch, and Fran Spielman, "The Fallout; Jackson Denies Allegation about Senate Seat; 'Deeply Sorry' about Relationship," *Chicago Sun-Times,* September 22, 2010.

74. Natasha Korecki, "'Suspicious Activity' Related to House Seat; FBI Probes Jackson Finances," *Chicago Sun-Times,* October 13, 2012.

75. Katherine Skiba and Rick Pearson, "Jackson Resigns House; Congressional Career Ends amid Health Questions, Federal Probe," *Chicago Tribune,* November 22, 2012.

76. Katherine Skiba and David Heinzmann, "Jackson, Wife Face Federal Charges," *Chicago Tribune,* February 16, 2013.

77. Natasha Korecki, Lynn Sweet, and Maudlyne Ihejirika, "'Not a Proud Day,'" *Chicago Sun-Times,* February 21, 2013.

78. Katherine Skiba, "Jacksons Guilty in Tale of Excess," *Chicago Tribune,* February 21, 2013.

79. Ibid.

80. Katherine Skiba, "Both Jacksons Going to Prison," *Chicago Tribune,* August 15, 2013.

81. Ibid.

82. Rick Pearson and Ray Long, "A Defiant Pick: Gov. Blagojevich Appoints Former Illinois Atty. Gen. Roland Burris to Fill Obama's Senate Seat. But Will the Appointment Stick?" *Chicago Tribune,* December 31, 2008.

83. Dave McKinney and Jordan Wilson, "Change in Burris' Story?" *Chicago Sun-Times,* January 9, 2009.

84. Natasha Korecki and Dave McKinney, "Blago Hit up Burris for Cash," *Chicago Sun-Times,* February 15, 2009.

85. Katherine Skiba, "Senate Ethics Panel Admonishes Burris," *Chicago Tribune,* November 21, 2009.

86. "Sen. Burris Lied about Lying," editorial, *Chicago Sun-Times,* November 22, 2009.

87. Matthew DeFour, "Hastert's $2M Land Profit," *Aurora (Ill.) Beacon News,* June 15, 2006.

88. Andrew Zajac, Oscar Avila, and Jim Tankersley, "Inside Rep. Weller's Nicaragua Land Deal; Illinois Lawmaker Benefits from Trade Accord, Fails to Report Extent of His Ocean-View Holdings," *Chicago Tribune,* September 7, 2007.

89. John Kass, "Gutierrez's Tax Bill Proves That Miracles Still Do Happen," *Chicago Tribune,* August 2, 1998.

90. John Kass, "Every So Often, a Politician Unseeks Publicity," *Chicago Tribune,* December 2, 1998.

91. Jeff Coen, Todd Lightly, and Dan Mihalopoulos, "Alderman, Builder Indicted," *Chicago Tribune,* March 29, 2009.

92. Todd Lightly, Robert Becker, and Dan Mihalopoulos, "Gutierrez Cashes in with Donors," *Chicago Tribune,* December 8, 2008.

93. John Kass, "Real Estate Fairy Visits Pols Who Believe," *Chicago Tribune,* November 15, 2006.

94. Mark Brown, "Braun to Respond on Ethics Charge; Handling of Mom's Inheritance at Issue," *Chicago Sun-Times,* September 30, 1992.

95. Rob Karwath and Michael Kates, "Braun Reimburses Medicaid: Case Closed; No Criminal Probe, Officials Say," *Chicago Tribune,* October 31, 1992.

96. Basil Talbot, "Moseley-Braun Nearly Alone Opposing Nigerian Sanctions," *Chicago Sun-Times,* May 16, 1996.

97. Mary Jacoby and Mike Dorning, "Furor over Moseley-Braun's Trip," *Chicago Tribune,* August 21, 1996.

98. Lynn Sweet, "Trip Ends in High-Flying Style," *Chicago Sun-Times,* December 31, 1992.

99. Carol Marin, "Talking Some Sense into Moseley-Braun," *Chicago Tribune,* December 13, 2002.

100. Rick Pearson and Graeme Zielinski, "Senator Apologizes for Epithet . . . Used Slur in Calling Columnist Racist," *Chicago Tribune,* September 8, 1998.

101. Sandy Bergo and Chuck Neubauer, "Rush's Tech Center Dream Dead, Where Did $1 Million Go?" *Chicago Sun-Times,* December 13, 2013.

102. Ibid.

103. "We Need Answers to Rush Questions," editorial, *Chicago Sun-Times,* December 26, 2013.

104. Kim Geiger, "Lawmakers' Campaign Accounts Fund Luxuries," *Chicago Tribune,* December 19, 2013.

105. Ibid.

106. Ibid.

Chapter 11. Ending the Culture of Corruption

1. Dick Simpson et al., *Chicago and Illinois: Leading the Pack in Corruption: Anti-Corruption Report No. 5* (Chicago: Department of Political Science, University of Illinois at Chicago and Institute for Government and Public Affairs, February 2012), accessed No-

vember 15, 2013, http://www.uic.edu/depts/pols/ChicagoPolitics/leadingthepack.pdf. See also chapter 1 in this book. The report on our ranking of corruption among cities and states was noted in more than 250 media outlets around the country and nearly every local publication. The news story in the *Chicago Jewish Star* won a Lisagor Award in 2013 from the Headline Club for Political and Governmental Reporting. The report continues to be cited in media stories more than two years after its publication. Since our original report, other studies using different years and methods have come up with slightly different but similar rankings. See, for instance, Cheol Liu and John Mikesell, "The Impact of Public Officials' Corruption on the Size and Allocation of U.S. State Spending," *Public Administration Review* 78.3 (June 2014): 346–59.

2. James L. Merriner, *Grafters and Goo Goos: Corruption and Reform in Chicago, 1833–2003* (Carbondale: Southern Illinois University Press, 2004), 264.

3. Qtd. in ibid.

4. Lenor Vivanco, "2003 Disaster Still Reverberated," *Chicago Tribune,* June 24, 2013, 6.

5. Several versions of this line have been attributed to Dirksen. See *McMillan's Dictionary of Political Quotations* (New York: Macmillan, 1993), 24.

6. Liu and Mikesell, "The Impact of Public Officials' Corruption on the Size and Allocation of U.S. State Spending," 355–56.

7. The entire leased-truck program cost about forty million dollars a year. About ten to fifteen million dollars was found to be wasted on unneeded trucks. Tom Gradel, Dick Simpson, et al., *The Depth of Corruption in Illinois: Anti-Corruption Report No. 2* (Chicago: University of Illinois at Chicago, Department of Political Science, May, 2009), 5–6, accessed July 11, 2014, http://www.uic.edu/depts/pols/ChicagoPolitics/Anti-corruptionReport Number2.pdf.

8. James Nowlan, "Corruption in Illinois: An Enduring Tradition," pp. 9–10, paper presented at What's in the Water in Illinois: Ethics and Reform Symposium on Illinois Government, Paul Simon Public Policy Institute at Southern Illinois University, Carbondale, September 27–28, 2012.

9. Ibid., 10.

10. Juan Perez Jr., "In Illinois, We of Little Faith in Our Politicians," *Chicago Tribune,* April 5, 2014, 1.

11. Roger A. Keats, *Chicago Confidential* (Dipping Springs, Tex.: Heartland Press, 2012), 164–65.

12. Rasma Karklins, *The System Made Me Do It! Corruption in Post-Communist Societies* (Armonk, N.Y.: M. E. Sharpe, 2005).

13. Simpson et al., *Chicago and Illinois.*

14. Lieutenant Governor Sheila Simon, interview with the author, June 26, 2014.

15. Robert Klitgaard, *Controlling Corruption* (Berkeley: University of California Press, 1988).

16. Transparency International, "National Integrity System Background Rationale and Methodology," 2011, accessed June 4, 2014, http://www.transparency.org/files/content/nis/ NationalIntegritySystem_Background_and_Methodology.pdf.

17. Cynthia Canary and Kent Redfield, "Lessons Learned: What the Successes and Failures of Recent Reform Efforts Tell Us about the Prospects for Political Reform in Illinois,"

p. 9, Paper presented at What's in the Water in Illinois: Ethics and Reform Symposium on Illinois Government, Paul Simon Public Policy Institute at Southern Illinois University, Carbondale, September 27–28, 2012.

18. Patrick Collins, *Challenging the Culture of Corruption: Game-Changing Reform for Illinois* (Chicago: ACTA Publications, 2010).

19. Canary and Redfield, "Lessons Learned," 66.

20. Jerry Brito, "Hack, Mash, and Peer: Crowd Sourcing Government Transparency," *Columbia Science and Technology Law Review* 9 (2008): 148–57.

21. Canary and Redfield, "Lessons Learned," 67.

22. For specifics on teaching civic engagement, see Alison Rios, Millett McCartney, Elizabeth A. Bennion, and Dick Simpson, *Teaching Civic Engagement: From Student to Active Citizen* (Washington, D.C.: American Political Science Association, 2013). Also see Shawn Healy, *Illinois Civic Blueprint,* 2d ed. (Chicago: McCormick Foundation, 2013).

23. Members of the Illinois Task Force, "Illinois Task Force on Civic Education Report," May 2014.

24. For the fullest treatment of best practices for government watchdogs, see Daniel Feldman and David Eichenthal, *The Art of the Watchdog: Fighting Fraud, Waste, Abuse, and Corruption in Government* (Albany: State University of New York Press, 2014).

Index

Abachi, Sani, 189
Abbate, Anthony, 131–32, 148
Abolt, Bill, 75
Accardo, Tony "Big Tuna," 119
accountability, lack of, 113–14
Acoustic Development Corporation, 97
Adamowski, Ben, 23, 61, 98, 139
aldermen, Chicago, 3, 5–6, 12, 197; convicted,
   60–61; Council of the Gray Wolves, 3, 23,
   53, 57–58; Eddie "Fast Eddie" Vrdolyak, 38,
   52, 53–56, 61, 65, 66, 120, 208; lessons from
   corruption of, 66–68; Operation Gambat
   and, 13, 87, 157–60; pattern of corruption
   among, 61–66; Rubber Stamp Council,
   58–61; Thomas E. Keane, 29–30, 58–61, 65,
   66. See also Chicago, Illinois
Aleman, Harry, 159, 160
Allen, Tom, 100
Allstate Arena, 122
Altgeld, John Peter, 22
Altobello, Guy, 138
Alvarez, Anita, 164
Amalgamated Trust and Savings Bank, 98
Ambrose, John, 87, 138
Ambrose, Thomas, 138, 141
American Civil Liberties Union, 146
American Political Science Association, 207
Amoco Oil Company, 136–37
Andersen, Wayne, 27
Annunzio, Frank, 158, 179–81, 183, 200
appointments, judicial, 162

Arthur Rubloff and Company, 29
Ata, Ali, 38
"Austin Seven," 143–44

Barrett, Edward, 99–101
Bathon, Fred, 47
Beaver, Darcel, 108
Beavers, William, 50, 92, 108, 111–12, 158
Bedell, James, 47
Benjamin, Gerald, 49
Bennett, Robert, 173
Berger, Robert, 102
Bergo, Sandy, 190
Berrios, Joe, 30, 80
Berrios, Joey, 80
Berrios, Vanessa, 80
Better Government Association (BGA): City
   of Chicago and, 82, 83, 88; congressional
   corruption and, 180, 190–91; Cook County
   and, 95, 97, 98, 107, 110, 112; on cost of cor-
   ruption, 196
Bevers, William, 47
Bilandic, Michael, 54, 154–55
Bills, John, 33
Blagojevich, Rod, 1, 2, 3, 7, 49, 71, 91, 105, 175,
   189, 193, 197, 202; arrest of, 185; campaign
   finance reform after conviction of, 203–4;
   early career of, 38; gubernatorial campaign,
   39; machine politics and, 32–33; Operation
   Board Games and, 13; "pay to play" scheme,
   186–87; state bond rating and, 196; in the

state legislature, 39; trial and conviction of, 37–38; victims of crimes of, 40
Blasé, Nicolas, 124
Blassingame, James, 86
Bloom, Lawrence, 62, 66
Board of Trade Clearing Company, 180
Boehner, John, 185
Boender, Calvin, 188
Bonk, Charles, 98, 101
Borwoski, Samuel, 84
Boscarino, Nick, 121
Boss: Richard J. Daley of Chicago, 29, 80–81
Braasch, Clarence, 140
Brenner, Nathan T., 58
bribery, 65, 159, 201; in Cook County, 99–101; Derrick Smith and, 48; James Laski and, 72; Mirage inspections and, 82–83; Operation Incubator and, 82; Operation Safe Roads and, 13; Redflex Traffic Systems, 33; in suburban Chicago, 124–26; tow scams and, 144–45. *See also* Blagojevich, Rod
Brown, Dorothy, 112–13
Brzeczek, Richard, 136
Bua, Nicholas, 26, 77
bugs, electronic, 153–57
Burge, Jon, *130,* 133–36, 147, 148, 196
burglary ring, Summerdale police, 139–40
Burke, Edward, 23, 54, 55, 66, 96, 161, 162
Burris, Roland, 90, 186–87
Bush, George H. W., 169, 171
Byrne, Jane, 31, 54–55, 58–59, 94, 136

Calabrese, Frank, Sr., 87, 138
Calabrese, Nicholas, 87, 138
campaign finance, 49–50; public, 208; reform, 203–5
Canary, Cynthia, 204
Cannatello, John, 107
Capone, Al, 55, 88, 119, 136, 139, 141, 178, 193, 199
Carey, Bernard, 99
Carothers, Isaac, 62–63, 188
Carothers, William, 62
Cartright, Lenora, 141–42
Cellini, William, 38
Cermak, Anton, 22, 29, 31, 73, 81
CGC Communications, 111
Challenging the Culture of Corruption, 204
Chicago, Illinois: aldermen, 3, 5–6, 12, 53–68; city treasurer's office, 83–85; cost of corruption in, 88–91; early machine politics in, 20–21; hired truck scandal, 12–13, 27, 71–72, 74–76; individualistic political culture in,

10; James Laski of, 71–72; machine politics in, 73; mayors, 1955–2015, 220–21; Mayor's Office of Intergovernmental Affairs (IGA), 27–28, 78; Mirage inspections, 82–83; the mob and city hall of, 86–88; as the most corrupt city in one of the most corrupt states, 4–7; nepotism in, 79–81; Operation Haunted Hall, 81–82; Operation Incubator, 82; patronage at city hall in, 76–78; police (*see* police); procurement contracts, 85; public schools, 126–27; response to police corruption, 145–48; Silver Shovel scandal, 86. *See also* Suburban Chicago
Chicago Bar Association, 146, 180
Chicago Bulls, 106
Chicago Confidential, 198
Chicago Corporation Counsel, 167
Chicago Ethics Ordinance of 1987, 203
Chicago Ethics Reform Task Force, 3
Chicago Fire of 1871, 21, 100
Chicago Heights, Illinois, 121, 123
Chicago Herald, 3
Chicago Justice Project, 147–48
Chicago Law Enforcement Study Group, 146–47
Chicago News, 21
Chicago Park District, 105
Chicago Reader, 134
Chicago Record, 3
Chicago Sun-Times, 75, 81, 106, 107, 109, 110, 145, 159, 165, 175, 180; on congressional corruption, 190–91; on Dan Rostenkowski, 170–71; endorsement of Dan Rostenkowski, 171; investigation of Dan Rostenkowski, 172, 173–74; on Jesse Jackson, Jr., 185; on Roland Burris, 187
Chicago Transit Authority Board, 164
Chicago Tribune, 17–18, 20, 23, 34, 39, 56, 85, 162, 163, 189; on congressional corruption, 191; on Cook County corruption, 95, 98, 99, 101, 102; on Dan Rostenkowski, 171, 174; on judicial corruption, 160; on police corruption, 136; on suburban Chicago corruption, 125
Christopher, John, 86
Cicero, Illinois, 4, 119
Citibank, 84
Citizens for Responsibility and Ethics, 188
Citizens United, 204
city hall, Chicago. *See* Chicago, Illinois
civic education, 207
Civil Rights Act of 1870, 25
Civil Service Reform Act of 1883, 203

Clinton, Bill, 33, 108, 171–72, 173, 177, 182
Clout, 93
Clyde Federal Savings and Loan Association, 181–82
Cocozza, Jean, 162
Cole, Tony, 110
Colella, Michael, 157–58
Colisimo, "Big Jim," 139
college graduates, 9
Collins, George, 180
Collins, Pat, 33, 204–6
conflicts of interest, 7, 40; congressmen with mob ties and, 178–81
congressional corruption: campaign finance and, 49–50, 203–5; Dan Rostenkowski and, 2, 7, 29, 38, 71, 81, 95, 96, *166,* 167–76, 199–200; Henry Hyde and, 181–82; Jesse Jackson, Jr., 44, 48, 49, 50, 177, 184–86; Mel Reynolds and, 98, 176–78; mob ties and conflicts of interest in, 178–81, 200; other scandals, 187–91; Roland Burris and, 186–87; scandals fade, 191; sexual indiscretions and, 182–84
Conlisk, James, Jr., 146
Conroy, John, 134
Controlling Corruption, 8, 202
Cook, Benton, III, 112
Cook County, 9, 13, 63–64, 93–97; bribes and kickbacks in, 99–101; Democratic machine control over, 93–94; favoritism in, 101–2; ghost payrolling in, 103–5; lack of accountability in, 113–14; other scandals in, 109–13; President's Office of Employment Training (POET), 109–10; sheriff's office, 102–3; Stroger era, 105–9; tradition of corruption, 97–99. *See also* Chicago, Illinois
Cooley, Robert, 157–59, 160
corruption: among aldermen, 3, 5–6, 12, 53–68; among congressmen, 2, 44, 48, 49, 50; among governors, 1–2, 42–45; among law enforcement, 102–3, 122–24, 127; congressional (*see* congressional corruption); culture of, 10–11, 193–94; downstate, 46–47; favoritism and, 101–2; financial costs of, 14, 40, 50–51, 81–82, 88–91, 148–49, 195–96; future studies of, 200–201; ghost payrolling, 65, 74, 103–5, 198, 199, 200; history of Illinois', 11–14, 41–46, 211–16; human costs of, 14, 194–95; nepotism, 29–30, 79–81, 107, 121–22; patronage, 24–27, 76–78, 89, 107, 197–98; patterns of, 49–50, 196–200; police (*see* police); ratings by Transparency International, 8; in the Rubber Stamp Council,

58–61; in state legislature, 47–49; at the state level in Illinois, 4–7; theories of, 7–9, 41
Costello, James, 154
Coughlin, John "Bathhouse," 12, 22, 53, 57, 65, 66, 193
Council of the Gray Wolves, 3, 23, 53, 57–58, 65
court cases, phony, 153–57. *See also* Judges
Crane, Daniel, 183
Cronson, Robert, 90
crony contracting, 106
crony hiring, 107
Crowell, Grace Nowell, 79
Crundwell, Rita, 2–3, 46, 49, *192,* 193
Cullerton, Bill, 100
Cullerton, P. J., 97–98, 100, 113, 199
Cullerton, Patricia, 100, 107
Cullerton, Tom, 100
culture of corruption, 10–11, 193–94; history of Illinois', 11–14
Currie, Barbara Flynn, 48
Cynthia Rutan et al. v. The Republican Party of Illinois et al., 77–78

Daily Herald, 110
Daley, John, 101, 161
Daley, Richard J., 2, 14, 22, 54, 62, 66, 73, 197; Cook County and, 93, 94, 99, 101, 104, 105, 113; Dan Rostenkowski and, 168–69; judges and, 151; Keane appointment, 30, 79; machine politics and, 18, *19,* 31; patronage and, 25, 28; police and, 139–40, 146; Roland Libonati and, 178–80; stolen elections and, 23; Thomas Keane and, 61
Daley, Richard M., 12, *16,* 54, 62, 67, 73–74, 84, 96, 108, 164, 181, 188, 197; Duff family and, 85; endorsement of Dan Rostenkowski, 171; Jesse Jackson, Jr. and, 185; judges and, 151; machine politics and, 31–32; Mel Reynolds and, 176; patronage and, 26–27, 28; police and, 133–34, 136, 147; tow scam and, 145
Damato, Frank, 158
D'Amico, Marco, 158
D'Amico, Marie, 81
D'Arco, John, Jr., 136, 157, 159
D'Arco, John, Sr., 157–58, 179
Dart, Tom, 127
Davis, Wallace, Jr., 82
Dawson, Hanley, Jr., 152
De Leo, Pat, 159
Democratic party, 17, 22, 23, 30, 34, 55, 62, 66; control over Cook County, 93–94; slating, 161
Des Plaines, Illinois, 128–29

Despres, Leon, 39–40, 59
DeStefano, Sam, 138
Devers, William, 22
Devine, Richard, 164
DiLeonardi, Joseph, 136, 140
Dirksen, Everett, 44, 91, 196
Dixmoor Park District, 126
Dixon, Alan, 189
Dixon, Illinois, 2–3
Dobrowski, Nancy, 35, 126
Dominick, Larry, 122
Don't Make No Waves, Don't Back No Losers, 19
Douglas, Paul, 39–40
Doyle, Anthony "Twan," 87, 138
Dragnet, 4
Drake, Bernice, 47
drugs: gangs and, 141, 195; officers selling,
    141–42; rings, police, 143–44, 199
Duff, James M., 85
Duff, Patricia Green, 85
Duffy, William, 136
Duke, David, 4
DuMont, Bruce, 85
Duncan, Joseph, 12, 42
Dunne, Edward, 22
Dunne, George, 93–97, 101, 105, 113, 199
Dunnings, Donna, 110
Dvorak, James, 81, 102–3, 114, 128

East Lake Management and Development
    Corporation, 106
Edgar, Jim, 90
education, civic, 207
Edwards, Edwin, 4
Edwards, Ninian, 41, 42
Egyptian Trotting Association, 175
Ekl, Terry, 132
Elazar, Daniel J., 10
el Rukn gang, 159–60
Emanuel, Rahm, 28–29, 67, 88, 91, 132, 197,
    203; machine politics and, 33–34; police
    abuse and, 136
Emerald Casino, 121
Environmental Auto Removal (EAR), 145
"Era of the Gray Wolves," 22
Errera, Patricia, 84
Ethics Reform Task Force, 203
Eto, Ken, 138
Evans, Regina, 122–23

fake warrants, 49
False Claim Act, 89
Farley, Bruce, 81, 104

Fauntroy, Walter E., 184
Faustech Industries, 106
favoritism, 101–2
Fecarotta, John, 138
Federal Bureau of Investigation (FBI), 12, 64,
    82, 111, 178–79; corruption investigation in
    Illinois, 12–13; judge investigations, 153–57;
    police investigations, 123, 138, 144–45. *See
    also* individual operations
Federal Election Commission, 177, 190
Federal Home Loan Bank Board, 180
Federal Judicial District of Northern Illinois,
    4, 5, 135; U.S. attorneys for, 222–23
Federal Strike Force Chicago, 157
Feinberg, Bernard, 99–100
Fifielski, Edwin, 99–100
financial cost of corruption, 14, 40, 50–51,
    81–82, 88–91, 148–49, 195–96
Finley, Morgan, 82
Finnigan, Jerome, 142–43
Fitzgerald, Patrick, 11, 38, 135, 190
Flanagan, Michael, 174
Fleming, John, 132
Fletcher, Virginia, 170
Flores, Manuel, 189
Forbes, 46
Ford, LaShawn, 47, 48
Forest Preserve District, 107
Fox News Chicago, 110, 112
Frais, Rafael "Ray," 64
Freedom of Information Act, 206
Freeman, Aaron, 55
Freeman, Charles, 162, 163–64
Fuglsang, James, 104
Fuji Securities, 84
Fulle, Floyd, 98, 101
Fuller, Thomas, 86
Futterman, Craig B., 147
future studies of corruption, 200–201

Gabinski, Terry, 96, 172
gangs, 141, 195, 199
Gardner, Joseph, 86
ghost payrollers, 65, 74, 103–5, 198, 199, 200
Giancana, Momo Salvatore, 179
Giles, Cedric, 109
Glover, Shirley, 109
"Goo Goos," 22
government bureaucracy, 9
governors, Illinois, 1–2, 12, 42–45; Ryan,
    George, 1961–2014, 217–19. *See also* Blago-
    jevich, Rod; Quinn, Pat; Ryan, George
Gradel, Tom, 169

Grafters and Goo Goos: Corruption and Reform in Chicago, 1833–2003, 194
Guide, William, 141
Gutierrez, Luis, 188–89, 191
Gutierrez, Soraida, 191

Haas, William, 141
Hagedorn, John, 141
Hake, Terrence, 154, 156
Haleem, Ali, 144
Hanhardt, William, 137, 158
Hanley Dawson Leasing Company, 152
Hanrahan, Edward, 98
Harris, John, 38
Harrison, Carter, 21–22, 57
Hart-Glover, Brendolyn, 109
Harvey Police Department, 123
Hastert, Dennis, 187
Hatch Act of 1939, 203
Heil and Heil, 30
Hendon, Ricky, 144
Henehan, Raymond, 164–65
Herrera, Keith, 142
Heupel, Dana, 89
Hill, Arthur, 164
Hinz, Greg, 180
Hired Truck investigation, 12–13, 27, 71–72, 74–76, 88, 107, 196
Hispanic Democratic Organization, 28, 74, 75
Hobley v. Jon Burge et al., 135
Hodge, Orville, 43, 49, 197
Hofeld, Al, 189
Hogan, William, Jr., 121
Holder, Eric, Jr., 172
Holzer, Estelle, 155
Holzer, Reginald, 153–57
horse racing, 175
Horseshoe Casino, 111
Howard, Connie, 47, 48
Howard, Lynn, 46–47
Hubbard, Fred, 62
Huels, Pat, 62, 72
Huidobro, Giovana, 185
human costs of corruption, 14, 194–95
Humes, Marian, 82
Humphreys, Curly, 178
Hunter, Mason, 198
Huntington, Samuel J., 194
Hutchinson, Perry, 82
Hyde, Henry, 181–82, 183, 200

Igoe, Mike, 29
Illinois (state): bond rating, 196; downstate corruption in, 46–47; governors, 1961–2014, 217–19; history of corruption in, 11–14, 41–46, 211–16; incorruptible public officials in, 39–40; individualistic political culture of, 10; patterns of corruption, 49–50; scope of corruption in, 4–7, 37, 50–51; state legislature corruption, 47–49
Illinois Ethics Commission, 3, 33, 40, 88, 202, 204
Illinois Racing Board, 175
Illinois State Bar Association, 155
Illinois state legislators, 47–49
Illinois Task Force on Civic Education, 207
Independent Police Review Authority (IPRA), 147
individualistic political culture, 10; machine politics and, 20
Infelise Ernest Rocco, 119–20
inspectors general, 207–8
"Integrity System," 202
Isaacs, Theodore, 44, 95, 175

Jackson, Andrew, 203
Jackson, Bobby, 126
Jackson, Edward Lee, Jr., 143–44
Jackson, Jesse, Jr., 44, 48, 49, 50, 177, 184–86, 200
Jackson, Jesse, Sr., 184
Jackson, Sandi, 177, 184, 185, 186
Jacobson, Buddy, 179
James McHugh Construction Company, 95
J. Donatella and Associates, 186
Jefferson State Bank, 99–100
Johnson, J. Ramsey, 172
Johnson, Mardren, 142
Johnson, Norma Holloway, 174–75
Jones, Mick, 72
Jones, Orlando, 107, 108
Joyce, Jeremiah, 145
Joyce Foundation, 3
judges, 1, *150*; bugs, moles, and phony cases of corrupt, 153–57; curing corrupted courts and, 163–65; depending on money, friends, and clout, 160–63; Operation Gambat and, 13, 87, 157–60, 196; Operation Greylord and, 1, 13, 151, 153–57, 196; Richard LeFevour, 151–53
Judicial Inquiry Board, 164
Jungman, Benjamin, 83

Kankakee County Board, 1
Kanter, Borrie, 97–98
Karbowski, Krzystov, 189

Karklins, Rasma, 7–8, 14, 20, 41, 72, 201–2
Karmeier, Lloyd, 163
Kass, John, 188
Kassam, Kabir, 124
Keane, Adeline, 79
Keane, George, 99
Keane, Thomas, Jr., 29–30, 58–61, 65, 66, 79, 99, 197
Keane, Thomas, Sr., 58, 79
Keats, Roger, 198
Kellogg, Eric, 124
Kelly, Christopher, 38, 39
Kelly, Clifford, 82
Kenna, Michael "Hinky Dink," 12, 22, 53, 57, 193
Kennedy, John F., 23
Kennedy, Robert, 178, 179
Kennelly, Martin H., 58
Kerner, Otto, 1, 2, 29, 44, 81, 95, 175
kickbacks: in Cook County, 99–101; in suburban Chicago, 124–26
Klingbiel, Raymond, 44
Klitgaard, Robert, 8, 14, 41, 72, 113, 202
Klosak, Henry, 119
Kmiecik, Bart, 141
Kolter, Joseph, 171
Kotlarz, Joseph, 96
Kucharski, Edmund J., 25

Lambesis, Michael, 82
Landek, Stephen, 125–26
Lane, Fred, 155
Laski, James, 67, 71–72, 83
Lassar, Scott, 84
Lato, Sal, 180
Laurino, Anthony, 61, 81
law enforcement and corruption. See police
LeFevour, James, 151–53
LeFevour, Richard, 151–53, 156
LeFevour, Virginia, 151, 152
Levar, Patrick, 158
Levine, Stuart, 38, 56
Libonati, Eliador, 178
Libonati, Roland "Libby," 178–80, 200
Lindberg, Richard, 21–22
LoBue, Nick, 121
Lockwood, Brocton, 156
Logan, William, 160
Lombardo, Joey "the Clown," 87
Loren-Maltese, Betty, 116, 119–20
Lorimer, William J., 3, 42–43, 49, 194, 197, 203

machine politics, 17, 200, 201; aura of invincibility, 19–20; challenge of controlling, 35;
in Chicago city hall, 73; defined, 19; early, 20–22; end of Chicago hiring monitor and, 28–29; evolution of, 31–34; nepotism and, 29–30; patronage and, 24–27; police and, 139; under Richard J. Daley, 18, 19; Robert Sorich and, 27–28; stolen elections and, 22–24; vote rigging and, 17–18
Madigan, Lisa, 163
Madigan, Michael, 34, 162–63
Madrzyk, John, 64–65, 81, 158
mafia. See organized crime
mail fraud, 170–75
Mallul, John, 121
Maloney, Thomas, 150, 159–60
Maltese, Frank, 13, 119
Mangialardi, Sam, 123
Marcello, Jimmy, 87
Marcello, Michael, 87
Marcy, Pat, 101, 157–58, 159, 179
Marin, Carol, 190
Marovitz, Abraham, 25
Marquette District Police, 141
Martin, Kristina, 47
Martin, Raymond, 47
Martinez, Joseph, 64, 81
Marzullo, Vito, 29
Mason, Billy, 57
Mason, Roswell, 20–21
Matteson, Joel, 1, 12, 42, 43, 44, 49, 197
Matthews, Kgosie, 189–90
Mayor's Office of Intergovernmental Affairs (IGA), 27–28, 78
Maze, Louis, 35
McCain, Clarence, 82
McCarthy, Timothy, 27–28, 76
McCauley, James, 20
McCauley's Nineteen, 12, 20
McCormick Foundation, 207
McDonald, Michael Cassius, 21–22, 31, 73, 139
McGovern, James, 142
McHugh, James, 95
McIntyre, Maureen P., 164, 165
McManus, Ed, 102
McMullen, Jay, 59
Medrano, Ambrosio, 61, 63, 70, 81, 112
Mell, Dick, 32, 38–39, 158
Mell, Patti, 38
Mendeloff, Scott, 160
Merriam, Robert, 136–37
Merriner, James, 20, 194
Metcalfe, Ralph, 105, 198
Metropolitan Bank and Trust Company, 98

Metropolitan Water Reclamation District (MWRD), 86, 184
Meyers, Bill, 46
Miedzianowski, Joseph, 143
Mikva, Abner, 17
Milito, Frank, 136–37
Milito, Nicolina, 137
Minority-Owned Businesses (MBE), 85
Mirage inspections, 82–83
moles, 153–57
Monk, Lon, 38, 187
Montt, Efrain Rios, 188
Moore, Otis, Jr., 123
moralistic political culture, 10
Moran, Robert, 100
Moreno, Alex, 110
Moreno, Joseph Mario, 63, 110, 112
Morrison, Richard, 139–40
Moseley-Braun, Carol, 189–90
Mullins, Eugene, 111
Myerscough, Sue, 122–23

Nagin, Ray, 113
Natale, Robert, 121
Natarus, Burton, 24, 158
National Integrity System, 8
Nayak, Raghuveer, 185
Neal, Steve, 180
Near North Insurance Agency, 96, 106
Neistein, Bernie, 154–55
nepotism, 29–30, 79–81, 107
Netsch, Dawn Clark, 43, 203
Neubauer, Chuck, 171, 190
New Deal, 139
New Orleans, Louisiana, 113
New York state legislators, 48–49
Nichols, Gerald, 109
Nicosia, George, 137
Nigeria, 189, 190
Nitti, Frank "the Enforcer," 119, 139
Northside Towing, 145
Novelli, James, 103
Nowlan, Jim, 10, 17, 50, 51, 90, 196

Oak Trust Savings Bank, 98
Obama, Barack, 2, 33, 37, 186
O'Brien, Jessica, 161
Obrycka, Karolina, 131–32, 148
O'Connor, Len, 93
O'Connor, Pat, 33
O'Connor, Tim, 140, 146
Ogilvie, Richard B., 25, 101
Oglesby, Carla, 111

O'Grady, James, 81, 102–3, 114
O'Hare Airport, 59–60, 96, 103, 105, 121
Olson, Wayne, 153–57
Operation Board Games, 13
Operation Family Secrets, 86–88
Operation Gambat, 13, 87, 157–60, 196
Operation Greylord, 1, 13, 151, 153–57, 173, 196
Operation Haunted Hall, 81–82, 89
Operation Incubator, 82, 88
Operation Safebet, 13
Operation Safe Roads, 13, 45
Operation Tow Scam, 144–45
organized crime, 86–88, 119–21; congressmen with ties to, 178–81, 200; police and, 136–38
Orr, David, 114

Packwood, Bob, 176
palm cards, 161
Palos Township Regular Township Democratic Organization, 107
Pappas, Harry, 122
Pappas, Sharon, 122
Parkinson, Paula, 182
Patel, Naren, 112
patronage, 24–27, 89, 107, 197–98; at city hall, 76–78
"Patronage Pact," 25–26
patterns in state corruption, 49–50, 196–200
"pay to play," 49, 65, 186–87
Peace Corps, 183, 184, 200
Peoria County Historical Society, 47
Petrucelli, Joseph, 46
Philadelphia Inquirer, 176
phony court cases, 153–57
phony repairs and police, 144–45
Placko, Dane, 110
Playboy, 182
Plunkitt, George Washington, 20, 66
Poder, Lee, 125
police: abuse of citizens, 131–33, 198; abuse under Jon Burge, *130*, 133–36; burglary ring, Summerdale, 139–40; Chicago's response to corruption of, 145–48; corruption in suburban Chicago, 122–24; drug rings, 143–44; gangs, drugs, and, 141, 199; high cost of corruption of, 148–49, 195; Independent Police Review Authority, 147; machine politics and, 139; Marquette Ten payoffs for protection, 141; officers selling drugs, 141–42; Red Squad, 149; substance abuse by, 131; tavern shakedowns, 140; towing and phony repairs, 144–45
political culture, 10; machine politics and, 20

Postal Service, U.S., 170–75
Powell, Charles, Jr., 35
Powell, Paul, 1, 2, 18, 31, 45, 49, 76, 95
Power, Joseph A., 99
Powers, Johnny "Da Pow," 12, 53, 193
Prado, Juan, 145
Preckwinkle, Toni, 114
Presumed Innocent, 155
procurement contracts, 85
Prohibition, 139
property taxes, 188
prostitution, 21, 123, 124
protection payoffs, 141
Public Building Commission, 106

Quinn, Kenneth, 145
Quinn, Pat, 33, 34, 40, 91, 204
Quinn, Robert J., 83

Railsback, Thomas, 182, 200
Rakove, Milton, 17, 19, 53
Raymond, Michael, 82
Reagan, Ronald, 2, 169
Rebirth of Englewood Community Development, 190
Recktenwald, Bill, 17–18, 23
Redfield, Kent, 204
Redflex Traffic Systems, 33
Red Squad, 149
reform, 22, 33, 201–2; attempts at, 203–6; new agenda for political, 206–8
Remedial Environment Manpower, 85
Reno, Janet, 172
Republican party, 22, 23, 26, 55, 66
Retention elections, judicial, 162
Reynolds, John, 153
Reynolds, Marisol, 176, 177
Reynolds, Mel, 98, 176–78, 183–84, 200
Rezko, Antoin, 189
Rezko, Rita, 108
Rezko, Tony, 38, 39, 105, 107
Ricci, Michael, 87, 138
Richard House Hotel, 21
Rochford, James, 147
Rodriquez, Matt, 136–37
Roemer, William F., Jr., 159
Ronan, Al, 39
Rosemont, Illinois, 4
Rosemont Exposition Center, 122
Rosewell, Edward, 81, 104, 113
Rostenkowski, Dan, 2, 7, 29, 38, 71, 81, 95–96, *166,* 167–76, 199–200; ascension in Congress, 168–69; conviction of, 174–75; early

career, 167–68; indictment of, 172–73; mail fraud and, 170–75; special tax breaks approved by, 175–76
Rostenkowski, Gale, 172
Rostenkowski, Joe, 29, 81
Rostenkowski, Joseph, 167
Rostenkowski, Priscilla, 167
Rostenkowski, Stacy, 172
Rota, Robert, 170, 172
Roth, Bruce, 154
Roti, Bruno, 29, 145
Roti, Fred, 29, 59, 145, 158, 159
"rotten apple" theory, 200–201
Royko, Mike, 10, 29, 58, 80–81
Rubber Stamp Council, 58–61
Rush, Bobby, 190
Russo, Gus, 178
Russo, Robert, 174
Rutan v. Republican Party of Illinois, 26
Ryan, Dan, 81, 83, 91, 96
Ryan, George, 1, 2, 31, *36,* 38, 39, 40, 49, 197; conviction of, 45; costs of corruption of, 195, 196; Operation Safe Roads and, 13, 45; pardoning of death-row inmates by, 135
Ryan, George, Jr., 96

Sanchez, Al, 28, 31, 78
Santiago, Miguel, 104
Santos, Miriam, 83–84
Sapoznik, Seymour, 120
Savage, Gus, 176, 183–84
Savage, Thomas J., 184
savings-and-loan industry, 181–82, 200
Schenkier, Sidney, 28
Schiro, Paul "the Indian," 87, 137–38
Schneider, William, 128
Schock, Aaron, 191
Scholl, Edward, 66
schools, suburban, 126–27
Scott, William, 45, 50, 179
Secretaries of State, Illinois, 1–2
Segal, Michael, 96, 106
Semrow, Harry, 102
Senderowitz, Stephen, 164
sexual indiscretions by congressmen, 182–84
Shakman, Michael L., 25, 26–27, 76
Shakman v. Democratic Organization of Cook County, 76–77
Shapiro, Gary, 138
Shaw, Andy, 110, 196
Shaw, Bill, 177
Shaw, Robert, 158
Sheriff, Cook County, 102–3

Sherry, Thomas, 142
Shields, David, 159
Shoup Company, 99
Siemens Medical Systems, 106
Silver Shovel scandal, 86
Simon, Richard, 103
Simon, Sheila, 33
Simone, Sam, 107
Simpson, Dick, 24, 29–30, 169–70, 208
Singer, William, 80
Sintic, George, 123
Skinner, Samuel, 140
slating, 161–62
Slattery, Patrick, 27–28, 76
Small, Len, 1, 43, 44
Smith, Derrick, 47, 48
Smith, George, 163–64
Smith, James, 170
Solfisbug, Roy, 44
Sopko, Charles, 127
Sopko, Michele, 127
Sorich, Robert, 12, 27–28, 31, 74, 76, 78, 89
Sosa, Zury Rios, 188
Soultanali, Jowhar, 124
Spano, Michael, Sr., 120
special-purpose districts, suburban, 126–27
Springfield State Journal-Register, 30, 89–90
Stead, William, 3
Steele, Bobbie, 108–9
Steele, Robert, 109
Stephens, Bradley, 122
Stephens, Donald, 121
Stephens, Jay, 170, 171
Stephens, Mark, 121
St. Eve, Amy, 133
Stevens, John, 24
Stevenson, Adlai, 179
stolen elections and machine politics, 22–24
Stone, Bernard, 158
Stone Park, Illinois, 120–21
St. Pierre, Mark, 112–13
Stratton, William, 1, 43–44, 197
Stroger, John, 93, 105–9, 110, 113, 199
Stroger, Todd, 105, 108–11, 199
suburban Chicago, 117–19; bribery and
    kickbacks in, 124–26; bribes from big eco-
    nomic developments in, 125–26; ending
    corruption in, 127–29; links to organized
    crime, 119–21; nepotism in, 121–22; police
    corruption in, 122–24; schools and special-
    purpose districts in, 126–27. *See also* Chi-
    cago, Illinois
Suchocki, Carl, 142

Sullivan, John, 27, 76
Summerdale police burglary ring, 139–40
super PACs, 205
System Made Me Do It!, The, 72

Tadin, Michael, 75
Tammany Hall, 20
tavern shakedowns, 140
tax-law changes, 175–76
Thanasouras, Mark, 140
theories of corruption, 7–9, 41
Thompson, James, 140
Thompson, William "Big Bill," 88, 136, 139, 193
Tirado, Roberto, 126–27
Tisci, Anthony, 179, 180
Tocco, Albert, 121
Tomczak, Donald, 75–76
Torres, Angelo, 75
towing, police, 144–45
traditionalistic political culture, 10
Transparency International, 8, 14, 202
Trotter, Donne, 47–48
trucking contracts, 12–13, 27, 71–72, 74–76, 88,
    107, 196
Tuchow, Martin, 111
Tucker, Oscar, 100
Tully, Thomas, 100–101
Turow, Scott, 155
Tynan, Kevin, 180

University of Chicago Law School, 147
Urbinati, Robert, 121
U.S. Equities, 106
U.S. Public Interest Research Group, 33
U.S. Savings and Loan League, 180
*U.S. v. Robert Sorich, Timothy McCarthy, John
    Sullivan, and Patrick Slattery*, 78

Vanecko, Richard, 164
Vaughn, Charles, 144
vote rigging, 17–18
Vrdolyak, Eddie "Fast Eddie," 38, 52, 61, 65, 66,
    71, 94, 160, 208; Betty Loren-Maltese and,
    120; Cicero, Illinois and, 55–56; "Council
    Wars" and, 55; early career of, 53–54

Wade, Deloris, 107
Walker, Dan, 1, 45
Ward, Daniel, 23
Washington, Harold, 31, 54–55, 66–68, 77, 82,
    85, 105, 203, 208
Washington Post, 172, 181, 183
Washington Times, 170, 172

Water Reclamation District, 105
Webb, Dan K., 141, 153, 156, 164, 173
Weisberg, Bernie, 76
Weller, Jerry, 188
Wentworth District Police, 142–43
Werner, George, 123
When Corruption Was King, 160
White, Cynthia, 142
White, Jesse, 30
Wigoda, Paul, 165
Williamson, Rich, 189
Wilmington News Journal, 182
Wilson, Andrew, 134
Wilson, O. W., 140, 146, 158–59, 160
Windy City Maintenance, 85

Winters, Richard, 8–9, 18, 41
Women-Owned Businesses (WBE), 85
Woods, Joseph, 97–98
Worsek, Earnest, 155
Wyma, John, 38

Yerkes, Charles T., 42, 57
YouTube, 132

Zagel, James, 87
Zenkich, Elias, 171
Zima, Stanley, 101
Zimbabwe, 177–78
Zobjeck, Rodney, 104
Zydlo, Stanley, 64

THOMAS J. GRADEL spent 35 years as a media consultant and served on the staff of Governor Dan Walker. He is a freelance writer and political researcher.

DICK SIMPSON is a professor, former head of the Department of Political Science at the University of Illinois at Chicago, former Chicago alderman and congressional candidate. His books include *Rogues, Rebels, and Rubber Stamps: The Politics of the Chicago City Council from 1863 to the Present* and *Teaching Civic Engagement*.

The University of Illinois Press
is a founding member of the
Association of American University Presses.

Designed by Jim Proefrock
Composed in 10.75/14 Minion Pro
with Univers Condensed display
at the University of Illinois Press
Manufactured by Cushing-Malloy, Inc.

University of Illinois Press
1325 South Oak Street
Champaign, IL 61820-6903
www.press.uillinois.edu